T0315455

PgMP® Exam

Practice Test & Study Guide

Fourth Edition

ESI International Project Management Series

Series Editor

J. LeRoy Ward, Executive Vice President

ESI International, Arlington, Virginia

PgMP® Exam: Practice Test and Study Guide, Fourth Edition
Ginger Levin and J. LeRoy Ward • 978-1-4822-0135-2 • 2013

PgMP® Exam Challenge!
Ginger Levin and J. LeRoy Ward • 978-1-4822-0208-3 • 2013

PMP® Exam: Practice Test and Study Guide, Ninth Edition
Ginger Levin • 978-1-4822-0224-3 • 2013

PMP® Exam Challenge! Sixth Edition
J. LeRoy Ward and Ginger Levin • 978-1-4665-9982-6 • 2013

Determining Project Requirements, Second Edition: Mastering the BABOK® and the CBAP® Exam
Hans Jonasson • 978-1-4398-9651-8 • 2012

Team Planning for Project Managers and Business Analysts
Gail Levitt • 978-1-4398-5543-0 • 2012

Practical Project Management for Building and Construction
Hans Ottosson • 978-1-4398-9655-6 • 2012

Project Management Concepts, Methods, and Techniques
Claude H. Maley • 978-1-4665-0288-8 • 2012

Program Management Complexity: A Competency Model
Ginger Levin and J. LeRoy Ward
978-1-4398-5111-1 • 2011

Project Management for Healthcare
David Shirley • 978-1-4398-1953-1 • 2011

Managing Web Projects
Edward B. Farkas • 978-1-4398-0495-7 • 2009

Project Management Recipes for Success
Guy L. De Furia • 978-1-4200-7824-4 • 2008

Building a Project Work Breakdown Structure: Visualizing Objectives, Deliverables, Activities, and Schedules
Dennis P. Miller • 978-1-4200-6969-3 • 2008

A Standard for Enterprise Project Management
Michael S. Zambruski • 978-1-4200-7245-7 • 2008

The Complete Project Management Office Handbook, Second Edition
Gerard M. Hill • 978-1-4200-4680-9 • 2007

PgMP® Exam

Practice Test & Study Guide

Fourth Edition

Ginger Levin, PMP, PgMP
J. LeRoy Ward, PMP, PgMP

CRC Press is an imprint of the
Taylor & Francis Group, an **informa** business
AN AUERBACH BOOK

Parts of A Guide to the Project Management Body of Knowledge, 2013, are reprinted with permission of the Project Management Institute, Inc., Four Campus Boulevard, Newtown Square, Pennsylvania 19073-3299 U.S.A., a worldwide organization advancing the state of the art in project management.

Parts of The Standard for Program Management, 2013, are reprinted with permission of the Project Management Institute, Inc., Four Campus Boulevard, Newtown Square, Pennsylvania 19073-3299 U.S.A., a worldwide organization advancing the state of the art in project management.

"OPM3" is a trademark of the Project Management Institute, Inc., which is registered in the United States and other nations.

"PgMP" is a certification mark of the Project Management Institute, Inc., which is registered in the United States and other nations.

"PMBOK" is a trademark of the Project Management Institute, Inc., which is registered in the United States and other nations.

"PMI" is a service and trademark of the Project Management Institute, Inc., which is registered in the United States and other nations.

"PMP" is a certification mark of the Project Management Institute, Inc., which is registered in the United States and other nations.

CRC Press
Taylor & Francis Group
6000 Broken Sound Parkway NW, Suite 300
Boca Raton, FL 33487-2742

First issued in hardback 2018

ISBN 13: 978-1-138-44030-2 (hbk)
ISBN 13: 978-1-4822-0135-2 (pbk)

Visit the Taylor & Francis Web site at
http://www.taylorandfrancis.com

and the CRC Press Web site at
http://www.crcpress.com

Contents

Preface

Based on our experience in helping people to prepare for the PgMP®* Exam, we know that you will have questions, such as "What topics are covered on the exam?" and "What are the questions like?" Not surprisingly, some of the most sought-after study aids are practice tests, which are helpful in two ways. (1) taking practice tests increases your knowledge of the kinds of questions, phrases, terminology, and sentence construction that you will encounter on the real exam; and (2) taking practice tests provides an opportunity for highly concentrated study by exposing you to a breadth of program management content generally not found in a single reference source.

We developed this specialty publication with one simple goal in mind—that is, to help you study for and pass the PgMP® certification exam. Because the Project Management Institute (PMI®) does not sell past exams for prospective certification purposes, the best option is to develop practice test questions that are as representative as possible. And that is exactly what we have done.

This guide contains study hints, a list of exam topics, and multiple-choice questions for each of the five domains covered in the PgMP® exam, according to the *Program Management Professional (PgMP®) Examination Content Outline (April 2011)*. We have prepared 20 practice questions in each of these five domains. For the Program Life Cycle domain, we have prepared 20 questions for each of the five phases in the life cycle. We have also included two 170-question representative practice tests.

As we have done in our *other PgMP® Exam Practice Test & Study Guide books*, we have included a plainly written rationale for each correct answer along with a supporting reference list. References are provided at the end of this study guide for the five domains covered in the exam: Strategic Program Management, Program Life Cycle, Benefits Management, Stakeholder Management, and Governance.

Some of the questions are scenario based, as are some on the PgMP® exam. While some are definition questions, they are worded such that you apply the concepts to your work as a program manager.

* "PgMP" is a certification mark of the Project Management Institute, Inc., which is registered in the United States and other nations. "PMI" is a service trademark of the Project Management Institute, Inc., which is registered in the United States and other nations.

For those who speak English as a second language (ESL), our experience in presenting program and project management courses around the world has shown that most of our ESL clients understand English well enough to pass the PgMP® exam *as long as they know the content.* Nevertheless, in an effort to avoid adding to your frustration before taking the exam, we have painstakingly reviewed each question and answer in the practice tests to ensure that we did not use words, terms, or phrases that could be confusing to people who are not fluent in English. Although the language issue may concern you, and rightfully so, the only difference between you and those who speak English as their first language is the amount of time it takes to complete the exam. If you can grasp the content expressed in this publication, then we believe that a few colloquialisms or ambiguous terms on the real exam ultimately will not determine whether you pass or fail. Your subject matter knowledge will do that.

Earning the PgMP® certification is a prestigious accomplishment, but studying for it should not be difficult if you use the tools available.

Good luck on the exam!

Dr. Ginger Levin, PMP, PgMP
Lighthouse Point, Florida

J. LeRoy Ward, PMP, PgMP
New York, New York

Acknowledgments

We want to acknowledge the efforts of our publisher, CRC Press, and especially that of John Wyzalek, Randy Burling, Jessica Vakili, and the entire CRC team who worked tirelessly to publish this book so it would be available according to the release of the new PgMP® exam from PMI®.

Online Practice Test

An online test is available for download at http://www.ittoday.info/pgmp/examhome.html

To download the test, use the six-character code above the barcode on the book's back cover.

About the Authors

Dr. Ginger Levin is a senior consultant and educator in portfolio, program and project management with more than 40 years' experience in the public and private sectors. Her specialty areas include program management, business development, maturity assessments, metrics, organizational change, knowledge management, and the project management office. She is active in providing training to others as they study for their PgMPs®. She is an Adjunct Professor for the University of Wisconsin-Platteville in its master's degree program in project management and at SKEMA, France and RMIT University in Melbourne, Australia in their doctoral programs in project management. Before her consulting and teaching career, she was President of GLH, Incorporated, a woman-owned small business in the Washington, DC area for 15 years, specializing in project management. Earlier, she had a career in the U.S. Government, working for six agencies in positions of increasing responsibility for 14 years.*

Dr. Levin is the author of *Interpersonal Skills for Portfolio, Program, and Project Managers* and the coauthor of *Program Management Complexity: A Competency Model, Implementing Program Management: Templates and Forms Aligned with The Standard for Program Management*—Third Edition (2013), *Implementing Program Management: Templates and Forms Aligned with The Standard for Program Management*—Second Edition (2008); *Project Portfolio Management*; *Metrics for Project Management*; *Essential People Skills for Project Managers*; *Achieving Project Management Success Using Virtual Teams; The Advanced Project Management Office: A Comprehensive Look at Function and Implementation*; *People Skills for Project Managers; Business Development Capability Maturity Model*; and the *PMP® Exam Challenge!* (now in its Sixth Edition in 2013) and the *PMP® Exam Practice Test and Study Guide* (now in its Ninth Edition in 2013). She is the editor of *Program Management: A Life Cycle Approach,* published in 2012. Along with Mr. Ward, she is the co-author of the *PgMP® Exam Challenge!* and this *PgMP® Exam Practice Test and Study Guide* (now in its Fourth Edition), published in 2013.

* "*OPM3®*" is a trademark of the Project Management Institute, Inc., which is registered in the United States and other nations.

Dr. Levin is a member of the Project Management Institute (PMI®) and a frequent speaker at PMI® Congresses and Chapters and the International Project Management Association. She is certified by PMI® as a Project Management Professional (PMP®), and a Program Management Professional (PgMP®), and she was the second person in the world to earn the PgMP® designation. She is also certified as an Organizational Project Management Maturity Model (*OPM3*®) Professional.

Dr. Levin holds a doctorate in public administration from The George Washington University, where she also received the Outstanding Dissertation Award for her research on large organizations. She also holds a master of science in business administration from The George Washington University and a bachelor of business administration from Wake Forest University.

J. LeRoy Ward, is the Executive Vice President of ESI International, where he is the principal executive responsible for R&D, Product Strategy, Consulting, and Corporate Marketing ESI International is the world's largest project-focused training company with curriculums addressing project and program management, business analysis, contract management, sourcing management, and business skills. His 17-year career with four U.S. federal agencies has served to complement Mr. Ward's delivery of project management programs to clients around the world.

Mr. Ward has authored numerous articles and publications, including *Project Management Terms: A Working Glossary*; with Ginger Levin, *Program Management Complexity: A Competency Model*, *PgMP® Exam Practice Test and Study Guide* (now in its Fourth Edition), *PMP® Exam Practice Test and Exam Challenge!* (now in its Sixth Edition), *PMP® Study Guide* (now in its Ninth Edition) and, with Carl Pritchard, *The Portable PMP® Prep: Conversations on Passing the PMP® Exam*, a nine-disc audio CD set. He also is the co-author of the *PgMP® Exam Challenge!*, published in 2013.

A dynamic and popular speaker, Mr. Ward frequently presents on program and project management and related topics at professional association meetings and conferences worldwide. Since 1991, he has worked to provide the most comprehensive guidance to project management professionals, helping them to pass the PMP® Exam.

Mr. Ward holds bachelor of science and master of science degrees from Southern Connecticut State University and a master of science degree in technology management, with distinction, from The American University. He is a member of numerous professional associations, including the International Project Management Association, the American Society of Training and Development, and the Project Management Institute (PMI®). He is certified by PMI® as a Project Management Professional (PMP® No. 431) and as a Program Management Professional (PgMP®), and he was one of the first to earn the PgMP® designation. He also is a Certified Scrum Master.

List of Acronyms

AC: actual cost
ANCI: Annual net cash inflows
BAC: budget at completion
CEO: chief executive officer
CFO: chief financial officer
CIO: chief information officer
CMMI: Capability maturity model integration
COBOL: Common Oriented Business Language
CPI: cost performance index
CV: cost variance
EMEA: Europe, Middle East, and Africa
EPMO: enterprise program management office
ESL: English as a second language
ETC: estimate to complete
EV: earned value
HVAC: heating, ventilating, and air conditioning
IP: intellectual property
IRR: internal rate of return
ISO: International Organization for Standardization
IT: information technology
KPI: key performance indicator
M&A: mergers and acquisitions
NPV: net present value
OBS: organizational breakdown structure
***OPM3*®:** Organizational Project Management Maturity Model
PDA: Personal Digital Assistant
PERT: Program Evaluation and Review Technique
PgMP®: Program Management Professional
***PMBOK® Guide*:** *A Guide to the Project Management Body of Knowledge*
PMI®: Project Management Institute
PMIS: program management information system
PMO: program management office
PMP®: Project Management Professional

PPM: project portfolio management
PV: planned value
PWBS: program work breakdown structure
R&D: research and development
R&M: reliability and maintainability
RACI: responsible, accountable, consulted, informed
RFI: Request for Information
RFP: Request for Proposal
RFQ: Request for Quotation
ROI: return on investment
SMART: specific, measurable, actual, reliable and time-based
SME: subject matter expert
SPC: statistical process control
SPI: schedule performance index
SV: schedule variance
SWOT: strengths-weaknesses-opportunities-threats
VOC: Voice of the customer
WBS: work breakdown structure

Introduction

The Program Management Professional (PgMP®) Exam Practice Test & Study Guide includes five sections, each of which corresponds to one of the five domains described in the *Program Management Professional (PgMP®) Examination Content Outline* (April 2011). These domains correspond to those in *The Standard for Program Management*—Third Edition (2013), which are: Program Strategy Alignment, Program Benefits Management, Program Stakeholder Engagement, Program Governance, and Program Life Cycle Management.

Each section contains study hints, a list of major topics that are encountered on the exam, and 20 multiple-choice practice questions complete with an answer sheet, an answer key that includes a rationale for each correct answer, and a bibliographic reference for further study if needed. The Program Management domain is broken into five sections corresponding to the five phases in the program life cycle as described in the *Examination Content Outline*. Given the large number of questions in this domain, we have 20 multiple-choice practice test questions for each of these five sections.

We have also included two complete practice tests, each consisting of 170 questions*, that follow the blueprint of the real PgMP® exam as described in the *Examination Content Outline*. For example:

- 15 percent of the questions relate to strategic program management
- 44 percent relate to the program life cycle as subdivided as follows:
  - 6% of the questions involve initiating
  - 11% of the questions involve planning
  - 14% of the questions involve executing
  - 10% of the questions involve controlling
  - 3% of the questions involve closing

* Of the 170 questions on the real PgMP® certification exam, 20 are pretest questions and do not count for scoring purposes. When taking the real exam, you will not know which 20 are the unscored pretest questions, so you will need to answer each question as if it were one of the 150 to be scored. For the practice test in this publication, we provide all 170 questions as if they were real questions; there are no pretest questions in our practice exams, and the blueprint is applied to all 170 questions.

- 11 percent relate to benefit management
- 16 percent relate to stakeholder management
- 14 percent relate to governance

To use this study guide effectively, work on one section at a time. It does not matter which section you choose first, but we recommend that you answer the questions in the order presented, because this order reflects the *Examination Content Outline*. Start by reading the study hints, which provide useful background on the content of the PgMP® exam and identify the emphasis placed on various topics. Familiarize yourself with the major topics listed. Then, answer the practice questions that follow, recording your answers on the answer sheet provided. Finally, compare your answers to those in the answer key. The rationales provided should clarify any misconceptions. For further study and clarification, consult the bibliographic reference.

After you have finished answering the questions that follow each section, it is time to take the practice tests. We have developed scenario and other types of questions for each practice test. First take the tests on line and then take them in the book Note your answers on the sheets provided, compare your answers to the answer key, and use your results to determine what areas you need to study further.*

To make the most of this specialty publication, use it regularly. The tips listed below will help you to get the most out of your preparation for the PgMP® exam:

- Take and retake the practice tests on line and in the book. Photocopy the answer sheets so that you have a clean one to use each time you retake the practice tests.
- Consider convening a study group to compare and discuss your answers with those of your colleagues. This method of study is a powerful one. You will learn more from your colleagues than you ever thought possible.
- Make sure that you have a solid understanding of the exam topics provided in each section.
- Consult our bibliography, or other sources that you have found useful, for further independent study.
- Most importantly, create a study plan and stick to it. Your chances of success increase dramatically when you set a goal and dedicate yourself to meeting it.

* PMI® grades the PgMP® exam by assigning each question a degree-of-difficulty factor (which is not know to you) and a certain number of points that will be awarded if it is answered correctly. When you answer a question correctly, the value of that correct answer may, and probably will, be different from the value of other questions because of this "factor." To pass the real PgMP® Certification Exam, a candidate must earn a total score equal to or higher than the "cut score" of 325. We do not have a degree-of-difficulty number for the questions in our practice tests. However, we have written every question as if it had the higher degree of difficulty. We believe that if you can correctly answer at least 90 percent of the questions on these practice tests, then you should be prepared to pass the real PgMP® Certification Exam.

To further enhance your study, the two practice tests are available on-line at http://www.ittoday.info/pgmp/examhome.html. The web-based version of these exams includes a clock so you can see how well you do in the allotted four hours for the exam. One approach to consider is to take one of the web-based exams after you go through the book with the test questions by domain and see how you do. Then see your weak areas and do some additional studying. Follow it and see your progress by taking the exams in the book so you can see the rationale for each answer. Study some more and then try the second exam.

Either in this book or on the web, the practice tests are an essential study tool created with one goal in mind: helping you to pass your exam and become PgMP® certified.

Strategic Program Management

Study Hints

The Strategic Program Management* questions on the PgMP® certification exam constitute 15% of the exam or 25 questions.

These questions relate to the Program Strategy Alignment domain within the *Standard for Program Management—Third Edition (2013).* The emphasis is to ensure that the program initially supports and continues to support the organization's overall strategic goals and objectives.

Before the program is chartered, this area is important to make sure the program should be pursued in the organization. Therefore, time and attention are needed to perform an initial assessment of the program by defining its objectives and requirements to make sure they are in alignment with the organization's goals and objective. A high-level roadmap or timeline for the program also should be part of its business case before the program is officially approved. A mission statement should describe why the program is important. Also, justification for the funds that will be required is needed. Exam questions will emphasize key parts of the program's business case.

Before the program is approved, the sponsor must identify key stakeholders who will be involved in and/or affected by the program and consult with them to make sure the program is one that supports organizational objectives, is feasible, is in line with the organization's priorities as stated in its portfolio, and is aligned with the organization's strategic plan. Exam questions may focus on key stakeholders and how to best ensure their support for the program.

Specific benefits for the program also should be part of the business case and are part of this domain even though benefits management is another domain in the exam. Benefits are the outcomes of the program and in identifying them, a cost-benefit analysis, market analysis, and other research should be conducted. By doing so, a high-level scope statement can be prepared along with a

* Please note that Strategic Program Management is titled Program Strategy Alignment as a domain described in *The Standard for Program Management*—Third Edition (2013); (hereafter referred to as *The Standard*); however, we are using the term Strategic Program Management in this book since it is one of the five domains in the *Examination Content Outline* (2011) that makes up the exam. Nonetheless, a wealth of information from *The Standard* appears in the questions in this part of the exam.

high-level benefits realization plan. It is important to keep in mind that programs are established because through a program greater benefits can be delivered than if the projects, subprograms, and other work in the program were managed in a standalone fashion. A benefit means an improvement to the running of the organization, and benefits can be either tangible ones, which can be quantified, or intangible ones, which are qualitative and more difficult to measure. Both types of benefits should be documented and included in the program's business case. Some benefits will be realized while the program is under way, while others may not be realized until the program has been completed or even after the program has ended.

As well, there are more constraints when managing a program than a project, and these constraints, such as regulations, standards, sustainability, cultural considerations, geographical considerations, politics, and ethical concerns, must be considered before a program is approved. Questions will focus on the impact of the various constraints that will affect the program to help decision makers decide whether or not to approve it.

This domain introduces the program roadmap, which is progressively elaborated during the program, but serves as a graphical, chronological representation of the program's intended direction. The roadmap is helpful to determine whether the program should be approved and also to review it periodically as one way to determine whether or not the program remains aligned with organizational strategies.

Within this domain, environmental assessments often are conducted, including analysis used to assess the business case and the initial program plan. These analyses include comparative advantage analysis; feasibility studies; strength, weakness opportunity, and threat (SWOT) analysis; assumptions analysis; and use of historical information. Enterprise environmental factors require consideration.

Strategic program management also involves evaluating integration opportunities, which means considering resource requirements, facilities, finances, assets, processes, and systems in the various program activities, including the non-project work, so they are aligned and integrated across the organization.

Once the program is approved, then the initiation process begins.

This area covers a substantial volume of material. You should study the contents regarding the Program Strategy Alignment domain in the Standard, but recognize now it contains a far broader treatment.

Following is a list of the major topics in the Strategic Program Management domain. Use this list to focus your study efforts on the areas that are most likely to appear on the exam.

Major Topics

Project, program, and portfolio definitions
Program management definition
Subprogram, component, and program activities
Business value
Relationships between—

- Program management and portfolio management
- Program management and operations management
- Program management and project management

Program factors

- Organizational process assets
- Enterprise environmental factors
- Environmental analyses
  - Comparative advantage
  - Feasibility
  - SWOT
  - Assumptions
  - Historical information
  - Assess validity of the business case and the program plan
- Environmental assessments

Organizational strategy and program alignment
Strategic planning

- Feasibility
  - Readiness
  - Preliminary scope
  - Preliminary benefits realization plan
- Vision
- Mission
- Portfolio management
- Customer-focused programs
- Internal programs

Initial program assessment

- Objectives
- Requirements
- Risks

- Organizational benefits
  - Market analysis
  - Cost/benefit analysis
  - Financial and non-financial
  - Funding requirements

Program business case

- Costs and benefits
- Problems or opportunities
- Business and operation impact
- Alternative solutions
- Financial analysis
- Intrinsic and extrinsic benefits
- Market demand or barriers
- Potential profit
- Social need
- Environmental influence
- Time to market
- Constraints
- Authority, intent, and business need philosophy

Program mandate

- Use with business case for program approval
- High-level charter—costs, milestone schedule, and benefits

High-level program plan

- Vision
- Mission
  - Stakeholder concerns and expectations
  - Establish program direction
- Goals and objectives

Program roadmap—high level

- Intended direction
- Chronological
- Relationship between program activities and expected benefits
- Dependencies
  - Major milestones
  - Link to the business strategy and planned work
  - Decision points

- End point objectives, challenges, and risks
- High-level view of the infrastructure and component plans
- Difference between the schedule
- Preliminary estimates
- Set a baseline for program definition, planning, and executing
- Tool to help in program execution and benefit delivery
- Usefulness for governance
- Validation and approval from the executive sponsor

Program objectives

- Regulatory and legal constraints
- Social impacts
- Sustainability
- Cultural considerations
- Political climate
- Ethical concerns
- Stakeholder alignment
- Program deliverability

Integration opportunities and needs

- Human capital and human resource requirements
- Skill sets
- Facilities
- Assets
- Processes
- Systems
- Align and integrate benefits
- Exploit strategic opportunities for change

Practice Questions

INSTRUCTIONS: Note the most suitable answer for each multiple-choice question in the appropriate space on the answer sheet.

1. Assume you are working for an organization, ABC, which has about 500 people in it. Recently, your executives attended a one-day training program that presented an overview of portfolio, program, and project management. When the CEO, CFO, and CIO returned from this session, you were tasked to provide a list of all of the projects under way in the organization for their review. When you reviewed all the projects before giving the list to the executive team, you recommended to them that some of the multiple projects under way be managed as a program. This is because—

   a. Deliverables are independent
   b. A collective capability is delivered
   c. Resource constraints affect projects
   d. Greater benefits would result

2. You met with the members of the Executive team in your company ABC. They were impressed with your knowledge of program management, and since they had attended the one-day seminar, they told you they wanted to make sure every program they set up supported the organization's strategic goals because—

   a. The organization's strategy is a result of its strategic planning
   b. The organization's strategy affects how its vision will be achieved
   c. Different clients, suppliers, and technologies are included in each program
   d. Benefits and outcomes may affect the entire organization

3. Working to improve the maturity of an organization's work in program management there are a number of items one can do. In the early stage of such an initiative, one recognizes the influence of the program by the needs of the organization's portfolio, an example of which is—

   a. Timelines
   b. Stakeholder expectations
   c. Risk tolerances
   d. Escalated issues

4. Moving into a program environment is a major change for organizations especially in ones in which people are more used to working on projects. Programs have a broader scope, tend to be more complex, and may last for many years. This means it is necessary to—

   a. Focus on benefits management
   b. Exploit strategic opportunities for change
   c. Recognize the vision reveals the organization's truest intent
   d. Focus on market changes

5. You are one of many project managers working on the new plasma screen development program. Your project has not yet started, but the program manager is anxious to have it begin as soon as the program starts. But before you can receive the go-ahead to start, it is necessary to—

   a. Create a schedule and identify risks
   b. Define the expected benefits in the business case
   c. Have a business case and a program mandate
   d. Identify the key stakeholders and determine their level of influence

6. Assume you are the program sponsor for this new program on the new plasma screen development to replace all existing LCD screens and enhance plasma's screens so they can be viewed in 4-D. As you worked to obtain approval for this program, you decided to contribute to the body of knowledge available to the decision makers so you—

   a. Held a focus groups
   b. Consulted with experts for suggestions based on work on previous programs
   c. Conducted a customer acceptance review
   d. Prepared a feasibility study

7. Assume you are working in a Fortune 500 company. Recently, your company hired an outside *OPM3® Certified Professional* to conduct an Organizational Project Management Maturity Assessment of its program management practices in terms of the standardize, measure, control, and continuous improvement areas. Organizational program management relates to program management because it—

   a. Has an approach to foster a sustainable competitive advantage
   b. Has a program management office (PMO)
   c. Has an emphasis to harmonize project and program components
   d. Has a focus on developing and implementing plans toward a common goal

8. As you work to prepare the business case for the new plasma screen program, you recognize it is essential to identify potential benefits that will accrue from establishing this program. You have assembled a team of stakeholders and plan to interview them for their opinions. You want to point out how and when this program's goals will be pursued. It is documented in the—

   a. Program plan
   b. Benefit realization plan
   c. Business case
   d. Program roadmap

9. You are preparing the business case to obtain organizational leadership approval for a new program to implement a company-wide customer relationship management system to better manage sales activities and leads. You have been meeting with many people as you work to prepare this business case, and already you have heard a lot of the more than 600 salespeople in your company object to it. Your business plan therefore should clearly address—

   a. The technical feasibility of the program
   b. Intrinsic benefits
   c. How generally accepted methods of change management will be used
   d. How the return on investment will be calculated to demonstrate success

10. Assume you are working for the Motor Carrier Safety Administration in your government, responsible for the regulation of motor carriers in your country. You are a senior executive in this Administration, and you are getting ready for a meeting with the Administrator of the Agency and the other senior executives to review new programs and projects for the next budget cycle to be part of the overall portfolio. You have suggested that a program be established to consolidate various projects that require overhaul of existing regulations. Such a program is—

    a. One with major resource assumptions
    b. Preceded by the development of a roadmap
    c. A catalyst for change
    d. One with a parent-child relationship with the Agency's portfolio

11. Realizing that before you meet with the Agency Administrator and the other members of the senior staff that funding is limited, especially with your President's mandate to reduce spending at the federal government level by 50%, that you need to estimate the high-level financial benefits of your regulatory overhaul program to ensure it receives approval from your Agency Administrator and the other senior leaders. You need to establish a constant reminder of the objectives and the program's intended benefits so you prepare—

    a. A program vision
    b. A financial framework
    c. An analysis of the net present value
    d. An analysis of the internal rate of return

12. You are a member of your organization's Product Portfolio Committee. The head of your enterprise program management office (EPMO) recommends that a program be undertaken to develop a series of products for the next-generation automobile to be run using helium. In deciding whether or not to approve this program, of the following, which one is the most important for your committee to consider—

    a. Proposed schedule
    b. Benefits
    c. Feasibility studies
    d. Key resources

13. You are a member of your organization's Product Portfolio Committee. The head of your enterprise program management office (EPMO) recommends that a program be undertaken to develop a series of products for the next-generation automobile to be run using helium. An important consideration of your committee is—

    a. Sustainability
    b. Regulatory issues
    c. Market analysis
    d. Key resources

14. You are a functional manager in your organization, the head of the Department of Engineering, and a member of the Selection Committee for new programs. At the committee meetings, you review potential programs. One key factor that you consider as to whether to approve a program is—

    a. Who will be the program manager?
    b. What are the funding requirements?
    c. What is the source of program funding?
    d. What are the next steps to get the program started?

15. As a result of all of your hard work and diligence to get your program started, and based on the business case that you developed, you have received approval form your Portfolio Review Board, which consists of your organization's senior leaders, to proceed to initiate your program. However, you now should—

    a. Define how the program aligns with the strategic plan
    b. Define your program mission statement
    c. Establish a high-level roadmap
    d. Prepare individual plans for components

16. You are on the program planning team to develop a program for the next generation of drugs to combat joint disease. The executive sponsor has asked that you prepare a comparative advantage analysis to—

    a. Show "what-if" analysis
    b. Proceed with benefit analysis and planning
    c. Issue the program mandate
    d. Assess feasibility according to constraints

17. Assume you are a member of your agency's Program Selection Committee, and the Committee has just met to determine which programs and projects it should pursue. Your program to develop the next generation Air Force radar system was approved. Since you now have the authorization to proceed, your committee then has to—

    a. Develop a program budget
    b. Identify and receive the key resources needed for planning
    c. Establish the rules for subcontractor selection
    d. Identify the feasibility studies that need to be conducted

18. As you worked to obtain approval for this Air Force radar program, you realized the necessity of conducting a SWOT analysis. Its analysis then—

    a. Focuses on factors outside of the program
    b. Assists in benefits identification
    c. Helps to develop the program charter
    d. Helps establish meaningful measures to assess program performance

19. You are a member of your insurance company's Program Selection Committee. You are considering a number of programs to pursue. Each has identified benefits that support your company's overall strategic plan, but you need to select the one with the shortest payback period. Program A is estimated to cost $100,000 to implement and have annual net cash inflows of $25,000; Program B is estimated to cost $75,000 with inflows of $20,000; Program C is estimated to cost $225,000 with inflows of $80,000; and Program D is estimated to cost $275,000 with inflows of $90,000. You recommend that your company select—

Program A NPV at	*Program B NPV at*	*Program C NPV at*	*Program D NPV at*
5% = $2,399	5% = $2,105	5% = $6,400	5% = $4,065
10% = $3,112	10% = $1,254	10% = $3,275	10% = $1,852
15% = $1,402	15% = $1,001	15% = $1,679	15% = $925

NPV = Net Present Value

a. Program A
b. Program B
c. Program C
d. Program D

20. You are a member of your manufacturing company's Program Selection Committee. You are considering a number of possible programs to pursue. Each one has identified benefits that support your company's overall strategic plan. Data are available on four possible programs, but you can select only one because of resource limitations.

Program A IRR	*Program B IRR*	*Program C IRR*	*Program D IRR*
42%	40%	36%	33%

IRR = Internal Rate of Return

Based on this information, you recommend that your company select—

a. Program A
b. Program B
c. Program C
d. Program D

Answer Sheet

1.	a	b	c	d
2.	a	b	c	d
3.	a	b	c	d
4.	a	b	c	d
5.	a	b	c	d
6.	a	b	c	d
7.	a	b	c	d
8.	a	b	c	d
9.	a	b	c	d
10.	a	b	c	d

11.	a	b	c	d
12.	a	b	c	d
13.	a	b	c	d
14.	a	b	c	d
15.	a	b	c	d
16.	a	b	c	d
17.	a	b	c	d
18.	a	b	c	d
19.	a	b	c	d
20.	a	b	c	d

Answer Key

1. d. Greater benefits would result

   The purpose of managing projects, subprograms, and program activities as a program is to realize more benefits than if they were managed individually.

   PMI®, *The Standard for Program Management*, 2013, 4

2. d. Benefits and outcomes may affect the entire organization

   Organizations initiate programs to deliver benefits and accomplish agreed-upon outcomes that may affect the entire organization.

   PMI®, *The Standard for Program Management*, 2013, 26

3. a. Timelines

   As an organization manages its portfolio, programs are influenced by portfolio needs, one of which is timelines. Others include organizational strategy and objectives, benefits, funding allocations, requirements and constraints.

   PMI®, *The Standard for Program Management*, 2013, 10–11

4. b. Exploit strategic opportunities for change

   To maximize the program's realization of benefits for the organization, it is necessary to exploit strategic opportunities for change.

   PMI®. *Program Management Professional* (PgMP)® *Examination Content Outline*, April 2011, 7

5. c. Have a business case and a program mandate

   Before a program can be chartered, the business case and program mandate must be approved by organizational leadership.

   PMI®, *The Standard for Program Management*, 2013, 28

6. d. Prepared a feasibility study

   The feasibility study builds on the business case, organizational goals, and existing initiatives to assess the organization's finance, sourcing, complexity, and constraint profile; therefore, it contributes to the information available to decision makers in program selection.

   PMI®, *The Standard for Program Management*, 2013, 31

7. c. Has an emphasis to harmonize project and program components

   Organizational Project Management is a strategy executing framework that uses project, program, and portfolio management and organizational enablers to predictably and consistently deliver organizational strategy. In program management, the emphasis is to harmonize project and program components and control interdependencies to realize benefits.

   PMI®, *The Standard for Program Management*, 2013, 7–8

8. a. Program plan

   A program plan is prepared in Program Strategy Alignment. Among other things, it defines how and when the goals of the program will be pursued in each program component.

   PMI®, *The Standard for Program Management*, 2013, 29

9. b. Intrinsic benefits

   This scenario is an example of an internal program. The business case contains a number of items, one of which is intrinsic and extrinsic benefits. As an internal program, intrinsic benefits should be part of the business case.

   PMI®, *The Standard for Program Management*, 2013, 28

10. c. A catalyst for change

   Internal programs, such as the one in this question, are enterprise-wide process improvement programs and are undertaken by the organization as a catalyst for change.

   PMI®, *The Standard for Program Management*, 2013, 27

11. a. A program vision

   The vision describes the future state of the program. It also acts as a constant reminder of the objectives of the program and its intended benefits.

   PMI®, *The Standard for Program Management*, 2013, 28

12. b. Benefits

Program selection criteria and materials may range from vague and informal to detailed, specific, and formal. Programs are established to deliver more benefits than if the projects, subprograms, and other work were managed as standalone activities.

PMI®, *The Standard for Program Management*, 2013, 4

PMI®. *Program Management Professional* (PgMP)® *Examination Content Outline*, April 2011, 6

13. b. Regulatory issues

In considering whether to select or approve a program, in this situation, regulatory approval would be required; therefore, the objectives must be evaluated relative to regulatory and legal constraints.

PMI®, *The Standard for Program Management*, 2013, 31

PMI®. *Program Management Professional* (PgMP)® *Examination Content Outline*, April 2011, 6

14. b. What are the funding requirements?

Enterprise environmental factors influence the selection decision even if they are outside of the program; funding is a key example.

PMI®, *The Standard for Program Management*, 2013, 30

PMI®. *Program Management Professional* (PgMP)® *Examination Content Outline*, April 2011, 6

15. b. Define your program mission statement

The mission statement describes the purpose of the program and states the reason the program exists.

PMI®, *The Standard for Program Management*, 2013, 28

PMI®. *Program Management Professional* (PgMP)® *Examination Content Outline*, April 2011, 6

16. a. Show "what-if" analysis

Comparative advantage analysis is used to assess the validity of the business case. The business case includes analysis and comparison against real or hypothetical efforts, including "what-if" analysis to show how the program's objectives and intended benefits may be achieved by other means.

PMI®, *The Standard for Program Management*, 2013, 31

17. b. Identify and receive commitment of key resources needed for planning

Once the organizational leadership has approved the program, it then is necessary to identify and evaluate integration opportunities and needs. This identification includes human capital and human resource requirements as resources will be needed in initiating the program and for planning it. The people who will plan the program will not necessarily end up on the core program team.

PMI®. *Program Management Professional* (PgMP)® *Examination Content Outline*, April 2011, 6

18. c. Helps to develop the program charter

SWOT analysis is a type of environmental analysis that can be conducted. It provides information useful in developing the program charter and program plan.

PMI®, *The Standard for Program Management*, 2013, 31

19. c. Program C

In using net present value (NPV) as a selection criterion, a dollar one year from now is worth less than a dollar today. The more the future is discounted (higher discount rate), the less the NPV of the program. If the NPV is high, then the program is rated high. In this situation, you would select Program C.

PMI®. *Program Management Professional* (PgMP)® *Examination Content Outline*, April 2011, 6

Milosevic, Dragan Z. 2003. *Project Management ToolBox: Tools and Techniques for the Practicing Project Manager*. Hoboken, NJ: John Wiley & Sons, Inc., 42–44

20. a. Program A

The Internal Rate of Return (IRR) is the discount rate where the NPV for the cash flow is zero. There is no closed-form formula for it. IRR is computed iteratively and "hone's in" on the exact discount rate that produces a NPV of zero. Most spreadsheet software can calculate it. Given the data in this question, Program A is superior to the others. While the IRR discounts future values, it does not consider the size of a program.

PMI®. *Program Management Professional* (PgMP)® *Examination Content Outline*, April 2011, 6

Milosevic, 2003, 44–45

Initiating the Program

Study Hints

PMI® in the *PgMP® Examination Content Outline* has established a Program Life Cycle consisting of:

- Initiating
- Planning
- Executing
- Controlling
- Closing

In this life cycle, Initiating represents 6% of the questions or 10 questions on the exam.

We have elected to provide 20 questions for you for practice in this book, even though the sample 170-question exams will contain 10 questions.

The questions on the exam concentrate on additional methods to gain greater support and approval for the program. They focus on the need to ensure that the program's values and objectives are aligned with those of the organization as documented in the program mandate.

In *The Standard for Program Management*—Third Edition (2013), initiating is covered in the "Program Management Supporting Processes" in the program definition phase in its program management life cycle. It focuses on further definition of the program's purpose, securing financing, and showing how the program will deliver its desired benefits. A program manager is assigned, a program charter is prepared, the financial framework is prepared, and the program roadmap is defined in greater detail. Once the charter is approved, its authorization leads to program commencement.

Questions may address the roles and responsibilities of the program manager and the core team as well as possible program organizational structures. Other questions may address the contents and purpose of the charter, when the business case should be updated, and a high-level program scope statement that then sets the stage for a more detailed scope statement in the planning phase of the life cycle. As well, questions may involve developing a high-level milestone plan by using the goals and objectives of the program to ensure the program is aligned with stakeholder expectations, especially those of the sponsor. A program resource accountability matrix is another potential area for questions during this phase as roles and responsibilities are identified for the program's core team. The importance of a program kickoff meeting with stakeholders is another area of emphasis.

Following is a list of the major topics covered in Initiating the Program. Use this list to focus your study efforts on the areas that are most likely to appear on the exam.

Major Topics

Program Initiation

- Purpose
- Scope, resource, and cost estimates
- Initial risk assessment
- Updating the business case

Key Roles

- Assignment of program sponsor
- Assignment of program manager
- Identification of key decision makers/stakeholders

Program charter

- Purpose
- Initiate and design the program and benefits
- Justification
- Vision
- Strategic fit
- Outcomes
- Scope
- Benefit strategy
- Assumptions and constraints
- Risks and issues
- Timeline
- Resources needed
- Stakeholder considerations
- Measurement criteria for component success
- Program governance

Program roadmap elaboration

- High-level scope statements
- High-level milestone plan

Program cost estimates
Program financial framework

- Purpose
- Funding structure
- Funding source

- Funding goals
- Payment schedules
- Funding methods
- Updates to the business case

Resource accountability matrix

- Core team
- Differentiate between program and project resources

Program kickoff meeting with stakeholders

Practice Questions

INSTRUCTIONS: Note the most suitable answer for each multiple-choice question in the appropriate space on the answer sheet.

1. Although your program is part of a portfolio with four other programs and 14 separate projects, it has no direct relationship or interdependencies with any of these other initiatives. However, the success of your program will depend on which two areas for which all these other initiatives are competing?

    a. Physical space and technology assets for team members
    b. Funding and executive sponsorship
    c. Funding and available resources
    d. Available resources and technology assets

2. You have recently joined a corporation that is a leader in the development of products for the automotive industry. You are pleased to be selected as a program manager, because you know that this company has established a culture of management by programs. The company operates within a program management structure, and each program manager is responsible for products in certain years. To best align your program with your stakeholders' expectations, this means that—

    a. You should develop a high-level milestone plan
    b. In performing a stakeholder analysis, you need to consider the other program managers
    c. The way the organization is structured means that there is no need to compete for resources
    d. The roadmap is essential

3. Assume that in your automotive company, you will be appointed as the program manager for the 2016 new line of hybrid cars that only will use gasoline if the vehicle has traveled more than 300 miles. This program is a major change for your company as it has not entered the hybrid market until this past year, and the new line of vehicles is to have an average of 75 miles per gallon. The current hybrid gets 30 miles per gallon. You are going to produce at a minimum five different vehicles: a coupe, a sedan, a luxury SUV, a minivan, and an inexpensive SUV. Finally, your program charter was approved, and you were officially named as the program manager. You were fortunate to work with your sponsor in developing the charter, and you also—

   a. Used input from all stakeholders
   b. Relied extensively on historical information
   c. Convened a panel to assist in its preparation using the Delphi technique
   d. Sent a draft of the charter to the proposed members of the Governance Board for their input

4. Assume you are working for a dry foods company. For the past five years, all of your projects in this company have met their goals of being on schedule, within budget, and meeting specifications. You are a successful project manager, and you have identified a potential new line of business for your company, which you feel will enhance its sales. You met with your Portfolio Review Board and presented a business case for this new line of work, which would move your firm into the chocolate market building on research that shows that a small amount of dark chocolate can be extremely healthful. You now have a business mandate to proceed into more in depth work to determine whether or not the program should proceed to the planning phase. You now are considering questions such as: "is the program financially smart?", "do the program's benefits align with those of the organization?", and "can the company afford the program?". Answers to these questions basically serve to translate strategic objectives into:

   a. The program management plan
   b. The program's roadmap
   c. A high-level program scope statement
   d. An accountability matrix

5. You are responsible for a program to develop the next-generation cellular phone. The program includes a number of key products and is set up according to the "father-son" model. Because programs are responsible for delivering benefits, you want to ensure that the targeted benefits are measurable. You now are working in the Program Initiation phase; one purpose is to—

   a. Establish and staff the infrastructure that the program will use
   b. Set up the program control framework for planning, monitoring, and controlling the program
   c. Expand on the roadmap that provides a chronological representation of the program's direction
   d. Complete the program team staffing

6. You have recently been assigned as the program manager on a global drug development project. You have read and thoroughly understand the program's business case and overall objectives. However, you are curious as to the key program outcomes that are required to achieve the program vision. These outcomes are stated in the—

   a. Program mandate
   b. Preliminary project scope statement
   c. Technical and economic feasibility study
   d. Program charter

7. Assume you now have obtained approval of your charter for your program in your automotive company for the development of the new line of hybrid vehicles. This program will be extremely complex given its development of the five vehicles and also the goals and objectives to be met. You realize as well that you are going to have a number of issues and risks to resolve. However, you are pleased you are the program manager and that the charter has been issued. Your next step is to—

   a. Perform a more detailed analysis of the identified risks in the charter to help in deciding how best to respond to them should they occur
   b. Determine the key benefits to be realized by the program
   c. Describe the program outcomes required to achieve the program's vision
   d. Conduct a program kickoff meeting with key stakeholders

8. You are the program manager responsible for building a dam that will provide flood control and generate electricity for millions of residents. The dam will have five turbines generating electricity. The program sponsor, the local provincial government, has only enough money to install three turbines. The income generated from those three turbines will then be used to fund the remaining two turbines. As part of your planning, you estimate that in month 26, Turbine No. 4 will be fully operational, and in month 38, Turbine No. 5 will come on line. You and the team document this in the—

   a. Benefits realization plan
   b. Roadmap
   c. Benefits analysis phase
   d. Constraints and assumptions

9. You are a program manager working for a conference planning company. Your program has been launched as a component of your company's portfolio. Your organization has been in existence for 10 years; therefore, as you prepare your program charter and roadmap, you should consider the—

   a. How the program will deliver the desired benefits
   b. How program components will be unified
   c. Authority tolerance levels
   d. Program budget baseline

10. Your company, a major dairy cooperative, has embraced portfolio management. Previously, some projects continued indefinitely, even after their sponsors had left the company, and no one could remember why they had been initiated. Now all programs and projects are part of the portfolio, which is where investment decisions are made. In response to a growing consumer demand for organic foods, the company is attempting to capitalize on this demand by entering the organic foods market. You are appointed as program manager. Your program is the result of—

   a. Business intelligence
   b. The need to remain competitive with others in the field
   c. A program mandate
   d. A recommendation from your major customer

11. You have been appointed program manager for a Motor Carrier Safety Administration program to develop new regulations that avoid the need for highway weigh stations yet ensure that weight restrictions are followed. You must complete the program in two years, and the administration must approve the regulations in one year. You have not started the planning process. At this time, your first step is to—

    a. Secure program funding
    b. Assign project managers to each project in the program
    c. Plan the program's TO-BE state
    d. Manage each of your stakeholders

12. You work for a company that produces and distributes catalogs focused on luxury items such as jewelry, home furnishings, clothing, and accessories. In addition to the major undertaking of catalog production, several projects are under way to make the catalogs available online; ease of ordering and faster delivery time are key objectives. Many people in the company support the catalog production initiatives as well as some of the Web-based initiatives. The company should—

    a. Aggressively pursue the Web and discontinue its print production of the catalogs
    b. Assign a program sponsor for these initiatives
    c. Appoint a project manager to report directly to the CEO to coordinate activities
    d. Implement critical chain scheduling to avoid potential bottlenecks in resource allocation

13. Your city is in the early stages of determining whether or not it should construct a new shopping mall. Already, there is a major shopping mall at the northern part of the city, but its location is inconvenient for many residents of the city given the extensive traffic. In the southern part of the city, there is a small mall that lacks large department stores. The city is considering a program to develop a mall in the center of the city, and if it is approved, you will be the program manager. You believe approval is basically guaranteed, and you are looking forward to this challenge. Your funding will largely come from—

    a. The parent organization
    b. Bonds
    c. Equity partners
    d. Payment from future lease income

14. As the portfolio manager for an aerospace and defense contractor, you recommend that programs be initiated when your company decides to bid on contracts. Given the business development process and the need to focus on capture management, the pre-proposal phase may last several years, especially on major government defense projects. As you work to initiate the program, which of the following is critical—
    a. Statement of Work
    b. Contract program work breakdown structure (PWBS)
    c. Program financial framework
    d. Program outcomes

15. You are working in your city to have a new shopping mall that is centrally located. Your charter is under development, and if it is approved, you will be the program manager. You have not managed a program as complex as this one as in the past; instead, you worked on smaller programs or projects. This program is to have at least seven different projects, and they have been identified so far in the charter. You believe you should prepare—
    a. A description of the other projects you believe you should add
    b. A business case for a Program Management Office to support this program
    c. A description of the methods you plan to use to procure external resources
    d. A high-level milestone plan

16. Assume you are working for an international training company. It has decided to add several new lines of courses because it tracks its courses now to the Project Management Institute's publications and standards. You will be the program manager for these new courses, and you plan to have a team of people located in different countries to support you as you will want to translate each course into at least four other languages and pilot test them in other parts of the world. After your program is initiated, you then will work to authorize the various projects within it. Furthermore, it is important to have a high-level plan for the program's components. This plan is—
    a. Used to start initiating the program
    b. Part of program authorization
    c. Stated as part of the program charter
    d. Set forth in the preliminary program scope statement

17. While fax machines are basically considered to be outdated, a number of people still use them to send and receive information. Your company is considering a new line of fax machines as it has specialized in them and wants to make sure fax remains as a way to distribute information. This new line of fax machines would make it easy to send information from one's computer or a tablet to the fax machine and not have to rely on printed documents. It also would enable transmission of printed materials at a far faster speed with immediate confirmation that the recipient received it. As you determine funding methods for your program, you should first consider—

    a. Performing a program financial analysis
    b. Various funding methods
    c. Payment schedules
    d. Program funding source

18. As you prepare your program charter for your new program for your international training company, you have a vision of continuing as the industry leader. However, this is an internal initiative, and funding is a key concern, especially given the economic downturn, and many people do not sign up for the existing courses until the last minute. You are working to initiate the program. This means which of the following people should be identified by this time?

    a. Program manager and program sponsor
    b. Program manager and core program team members
    c. Program manager and program management office (PMO) director
    d. Program manager and program control officer

19. Your government agency has been considering adding a new program to its existing portfolio of the development of national parks in your country. You have heard about this possible program through a friend, who is on the agency's Portfolio Review Board. Once you learned about this possible program, you went to others on the Review Board and requested to be the program manager for it and were pleased to be assigned to manage it. One reason you were selected early is so you can—

    a. Authorize the program
    b. Provide expert judgment
    c. Prepare the strategic directive
    d. Guide the initiation process

20. You are one of the core team members developing the program charter for the next generation of medical imaging technology. There is significant market opportunity, but the competition is strong, and the wrong technical approach could set the company back several years. To ensure that the program charter is viable, a best practice is to—
    a. Conduct a SWOT analysis
    b. Conduct an assumptions analysis
    c. Use the nominal group technique
    d. Use an influence diagram

Answer Sheet

1.	a	b	c	d	11.	a	b	c	d
2.	a	b	c	d	12.	a	b	c	d
3.	a	b	c	d	13.	a	b	c	d
4.	a	b	c	d	14.	a	b	c	d
5.	a	b	c	d	15.	a	b	c	d
6.	a	b	c	d	16.	a	b	c	d
7.	a	b	c	d	17.	a	b	c	d
8.	a	b	c	d	18.	a	b	c	d
9.	a	b	c	d	19.	a	b	c	d
10.	a	b	c	d	20.	a	b	c	d

Answer Key

1. c. Funding and available resources

   Programs are often unrelated to other initiatives within a common portfolio; however, all initiatives typically compete for funding and other resources, both of which are finite in most organizations.

   PMI®, *The Standard for Program Management*, 2013, 10

2. a. You should develop a high-level milestone plan

   Such a plan uses the goals and objectives of the program, any applicable historical information, and other available resources. It is useful to align the program with the expectations of stakeholders including sponsors.

   PMI®. *Program Management Professional* (PgMP)® *Examination Content Outline*, April 2011, 8

3. a. Used input from all stakeholders

   Stakeholder involvement in the development of the charter helps to gain their support for it and their commitment to the program.

   PMI®. *Program Management Professional* (PgMP)® *Examination Content Outline*, April 2011, 8

4. c. A high-level program scope statement

   Building on the program mandate and the strategic goals and objectives of the program, a high-level scope statement should be prepared by negotiating with stakeholders.

   Miller, L. Trae. "Program Initiation" in Levin, Ginger. 2012. *Program Management A Life Cycle Approach*. Boca Raton, FL: CRC Press, 68–69

   PMI®. *Program Management Professional* (PgMP)® *Examination Content Outline*, April 2011, 8

5. c. Expand on the roadmap that provides a chronological representation of the program's direction

   In program initiation, the roadmap along with the program charter is used to communicate overall program direction.

   PMI®, *The Standard for Program Management*, 2013, 84

6. d. Program charter

   The program charter provides the basis to commence the program. Among other things, the charter defines the vision (or the end state) of the program, describes how the program will benefit the organization, and describes the key program outcomes that are required to achieve the vision.

   PMI®, *The Standard for Program Management*, 2013, 84–85

7. d. Conduct a program kickoff meeting with key stakeholders

   A kickoff meeting with the program team is a recommended best practice once the team has been established. However, one is also recommended with the key stakeholders in the initiating phase and is especially important after the charter has been approved to familiarize the organization with the program and continue to obtain stakeholder buy in to it.

   PMI®. *Program Management Professional* (PgMP)® *Examination Content Outline*, April 2011, 8

8. b. Roadmap

   Among other things, the roadmap shows the various milestones, details, descriptions, and the benefits to be delivered. It establishes the relationship between the program activities and expected benefits.

   PMI®, *The Standard for Program Management*, 2013, 29, 84

9. a. How the program will deliver the desired benefits

   In program initiation, the purpose is to define the program, secure financing, and demonstrate how the program will deliver the desired benefits.

   PMI®, *The Standard for Program Management*, 2013, 83

10. c. A program mandate

   The business case and a program mandate are key inputs for organizational leaders to charter and authorize programs.

   PMI®, *The Standard for Program Management*, 2013, 28

11. a. Secure program funding

   Program costs tend to occur far earlier than related benefits. An objective is to determine the funding source and obtain funds to bridge the gap between paying out monies and obtaining benefits.

   PMI®, *The Standard for Program Management*, 2013, 78

12. b. Assign a program sponsor for these initiatives

    This program could be set up to include project work for the Web initiatives as well as work on the ongoing activities to focus on benefits delivery from this work. A program sponsor should be assigned to oversee the program, secure funding for it, and deliver its intended benefits.

    PMI®, *The Standard for Program Management*, 2013, 83

13. a. The parent organization

    Programs can be funding in different ways. In this situation, the City is the parent organization, and the program will be funded by the City.

    PMI®, *The Standard for Program Management*, 2013, 78

14. c. Program financial framework

    When programs are initiated as a result of a decision to bid on a contract, program costs will occur before benefits are realized. A financial framework for the program will be necessary to dictate the financial environment for the program's duration.

    PMI®, *The Standard for Program Management*, 2013, 78

15. d. A high-level milestone plan

    This plan uses the goals and objectives of the program along with applicable historical information and other available resources such as a work breakdown structure, scope statements, and a benefit realization plan in order to align the program with the stakeholders, including sponsors.

    PMI®. *Program Management Professional* (PgMP)® *Examination Content Outline*, April 2011, 8

16. c. Stated as part of the program charter

    Approval of the charter authorizes program commencement. Among other items, it includes a discussion of program components to describe how the projects and other components are configured to deliver the program's benefits. This often includes a high-level program plan for the components.

    PMI®, *The Standard for Program Management*, 2013, 84

17. d. The program funding source

The program funding source is part of the program's financial framework. Programs have a variety of potential funding sources and can be funded by more than one source, with components funded by different sources.

PMI®, *The Standard for Program Management*, 2013, 78

18. a. Program manager and program sponsor

The program manager and program sponsor are selected and assigned in program initiation.

PMI®, *The Standard for Program Management*, 2013, 83

19. d. Guide the initiation process

The program manager is assigned as the program is initiated as early as possible to guide the initiation activity and facilitate the development of Its outputs.

PMI®, *The Standard for Program Management*, 2013, 83

20 a. Conduct a SWOT analysis

A SWOT (strengths, weaknesses, opportunities, and threats) analysis is a recommended approach to take in developing a viable program charter and project plan.

PMI®, *The Standard for Program Management*, 2013, 31

Planning the Program

Study Hints

The Planning the Program questions on the PgMP® certification exam, which constitute 11 percent of the exam, or 19 questions, focus on many critical areas in program management and emphasize the importance of detailed and comprehensive program planning. In *The Standard for Program Management*, a project plan is mentioned in Program Strategy Alignment, and its Program Definition Phase of its life cycle emphasizes program preparation with a program management plan. In the Standard, its Program Management Supporting processes each have a planning component, most of which will be covered in the questions in this section. According to the Standard, once the program management plan is formally approved, the Program Benefits Delivery Phase begins. Note that Benefits Management; Stakeholder Management, including Communication Management; and Governance are covered in separate sections of this book, and their planning components will not be covered in depth in this section.

Similar to the *PMBOK® Guide*'s work breakdown structure (WBS), which is essential for project planning, the PgMP® includes the preparation of a program WBS (PWBS). This PWBS does not replace the WBS for each of the projects in the program, but it does provide an overview of the program and shows how the projects and non-project work fit into the overall program structure.

The *Examination Content Outline* has nine tasks on Planning the Program, which also will be covered in the planning questions in this section and in the two practice tests. The emphasis is to ensure that the program's mission, vision, and values support those of the organization. The planning processes are iterative, and because of the length of the program and the multiple projects in it, plans need to be revisited and updated when components are initiated or closed, during the organization's fiscal year and budget planning cycle, and when unplanned events occur.

Following is a list of the major topics covered in Planning the Program. Use this list to focus your study efforts on the areas that are most likely to appear on the exam.

Major Topics

Program Preparation

- Develop Program Management Plan
- Difference from the Program Plan
- Define the Program Organization
- Describe Candidate Components
- Describe Management Plans
- Optimize the Plan
- Obtain Approval to Move to the Program Delivery Phase

Supporting Processes

- Program Financial Management Plan Development
- Program Infrastructure Plan
- Program Infrastructure Development
- Program Procurement Planning
- Program Quality Planning
- Resource Planning
- Program Risk Management Planning
- Program Schedule Planning
- Program Scope Planning

Program Scope Statement

- Program Work Breakdown Structure
- Schedule
- Program Management Information System
- Identifying and Managing Project-Level Issues
- Developing Transition/Integration/Closure Plan

Develop Key Performance Indicators

- Decomposition/Mapping
- Balanced Scorecard
- Implementing a Scope and Quality Management System

Key Human Resources

- Determine Program and Project Roles
- Include Subcontractors
- Team Motivation Opportunities

Practice Questions

INSTRUCTIONS: Note the most suitable answer for each multiple-choice question in the appropriate space on the answer sheet.

1. As you work to develop a new washer and dryer that will not require any electricity and also will decrease your monthly water bill by 50% assuming you use the washer at least once per week, you have a complex program to manage. Thus far, even though you are still in the early phases of your program, you have six separate projects in it. Now, you are developing the schedule for your program. Typically the first step is to—
   a. Use the schedules from the six projects
   b. Determine the component milestones
   c. Determine the interdependencies between the components
   d. Use the scope management plan

2. You are Company A's program manager for the development of an online banking system for your community bank, for which your company will receive $20 million. Because the bank would like to implement this system quickly, it has also contracted with Company B. You must implement your system completely in six months to ensure that you beat Company B's schedule. At this point, you have an expense estimate of $2.5 million. You will lose $10 million if you cannot deliver the product in six months, but if you can complete it sooner, you will earn an additional $25 million, for a total of $45 million. Your risk management officer performs a risk analysis and tells you that there is a 70 percent chance that the program will be completed ahead of schedule. Your company has completed similar programs in the past; judging by these experiences, there is a 30 percent chance that your final expenses will increase by $10 million. What is the expected value of your program if it is completed ahead of schedule?
   a. $29 million
   b. $32 million
   c. $42.5 million
   d. $45 million

3. Working as Company A's program manager for the development of an on line banking system for your community bank, you have been asked to provide a list of deliverables and the success criteria for the program and its products, services, and results that must be included in the procurement documentation that is provided to potential suppliers. This list is derived from an analysis of the—
   a. Benefits realization plan
   b. Project work breakdown structure (WBS)
   c. Contract WBS
   d. Program scope statement

4. You are managing a program to establish a new distribution center. The facility's location was selected because labor costs were low, but it is in a remote area. Now gasoline prices have increased 30 percent and are forecasted to rise another 20 percent in the next six months. In planning for the procurement of transportation services, you need to—
   a. Prepare a competitive analysis of service providers
   b. Recommend to your sponsor that the program be terminated and the distribution center be moved to a more urban area
   c. Prepare a contract management plan
   d. Encourage bidders by providing simplified legal requirements in the form of standard terms and conditions

5. As program manager, you find yourself repeatedly changing and refining the program management plan as a result of a number of factors, such as changing external conditions, market factors, stakeholder requirements, and currency fluctuations. A member of the program Governance Board stops you in the corridor and asks what is wrong with the program. You remind this person that program planning is—
   a. An inexact science, and so long as the program is within acceptable variance levels, everything is fine
   b. An iterative process, and as issues arise and are addressed, the plan will naturally fluctuate
   c. Basically a process of elimination, and as work is accomplished, future work is progressively elaborated
   d. Only done at predefined intervals to reduce administrative expenses

6. You are Company A's program manager for the development of an online banking system for your community bank, for which your company will receive $20 million. However, the bank is so interested in implementing this system quickly that it also contracts with Company B. You must implement your system completely in six months to ensure that you beat Company B's schedule. At this point, you have an expense estimate of $2.5 million. You will lose $10 million if you cannot deliver the product in six months, but if you can complete it sooner, you will earn an additional $25 million. Your risk management officer performs a risk analysis and tells you that there is a 30 percent chance that the bank will change its requirements, and a 70 percent chance that the program will be completed on time or ahead of schedule. Your company has completed similar programs in the past, and on the basis of these experiences, you know that there is a 30 percent chance that your final expenses will increase by $10 million. If no risks occur, the value of your program will be—

   a. $2.5 million
   b. $17.5 million
   c. $29 million
   d. $42.5 million

7. You are conducting a program kickoff meeting for a new accounting system that will affect more than 500 accounting professionals in 10 locations. The preliminary schedule shows that in month 13, the transition of the system to the users will begin. The Director of Accounting is quite concerned about the impact of the new system on the employees. To ensure a smooth transition, you, as program manager, need to ensure that the Director that the program has—

   a. A sufficient number of people to operate the new system
   b. Enough money in the budget to ensure that the employees receive the appropriate training
   c. The necessary lead time to get people ready
   d. An understanding of the steps needed to move from a development state to an operational state

8. Your firm's senior program manager is overwhelmed with stakeholder problems and has asked you to join the team as the program's resource manager. More than 20 people have already joined, and 15 more are expected over the course of the next month. The senior program manager believes that no additional members will be required. However, in casual observation you detect some problems. A handful of people seem to be working extraordinarily hard, whereas others do not seem to have enough to do. As a program resource manager, your first priority must be to—
   a. Identify the compensation package for each team member that will drive the best performance
   b. Determine the people, equipment, materials, and other resources that are needed and obtain them
   c. Identify those competencies that are critical to the program but are not possessed by current team members
   d. Ensure that program resources are allocated across projects to ensure that they are not overcommitted

9. Assume you are working on a program to review and then update as needed all the regulations in your National Highway Transportation Safety Administration especially since people now are using small helicopters for their travel of distances less than 50 miles in your country. Many of the regulations in your Agency were put in place when the Agency was established over 40 years ago, and therefore, a detailed review is needed. You have a major program to manage and are preparing your program work breakdown structure. You believe a bottom-up approach to preparing it is desirable because—
   a. The top two levels of each project's work breakdown structure (WBS) can be included in the PWBS
   b. Project-related artifacts are then part of the PWBS
   c. The management and control responsibilities of the project team are determined
   d. Earned value reporting is simplified

10. You have prepared your program scope statement, your PWBS, and PWBS Dictionary. Now, it is time to develop the schedule for this program. An essential element as you develop it is—
    a. Determining the order and timing of program packages
    b. Estimating required resources for each activity
    c. Focusing on resource leveling across the constituent projects
    d. Adjusting leads and lags

11. You are the program manager on a multiyear, multimillion-dollar transportation program for the provincial government. Funding for your program is allocated on a fiscal year basis, yet your program transcends multiple years. This situation will affect how your costs are—
    a. Estimated
    b. Obligated
    c. Committed
    d. Budgeted

12. You are the program manager on a multiyear, multimillion-dollar transportation program for the provincial government. Funding for your program is allocated on a fiscal year basis, yet your program transcends multiple years. Because of the challenges in cost estimating and the lack of additional funding to support your program, as program manager in preparing the financial management plan, you should—
    a. Ensure infrastructure and operational costs are included
    b. Establish a set amount for the contingency reserve
    c. Derive program estimates by using scenario analysis
    d. Baseline each estimate

13. You are the program manager for a series of new condominium developments in City A. Each of these condo developments is a separate project, as the City has different zoning requirements. Your company has developed similar condos for a neighboring city, City B. The City B program manager tells you that many different sellers can support the various subcontracts. With respect to awarding contracts, a best practice to follow—
    a. Ask each seller to prepare a detailed proposal so that you can evaluate its technical and managerial approaches
    b. Procure the services of a product integrator
    c. Review each potential seller's financial capacity as a key evaluation criterion, along with life-cycle costs
    d. Base your evaluation criteria primarily on an understanding of need and technical capability

14. You are the program manager for a new program in your company that will provide global support services for supply chain integration. This program will support your multi-national corporation, and you have a total of nine countries involved in it; three are in Asia Pacific, one is in Europe, Middle East and Africa (EMEA), two are in Latin America, and three are in the United States. Your corporate headquarters are in London. You plan to outsource a large portion of proprietary development work to a vendor located in Canada. A key evaluation criterion in selecting the vendor is to assess—

    a. Its technical capability
    b. References to see how successful it has been on other contracts of a similar nature
    c. The level of compatibility between your company's culture and processes and the vendors
    d. The provisions the vendor has in place to protect intellectual property

15. As the company's risk expert, you have been requested by the program Governance Board to perform a risk assessment on the Apex program, which includes more than 25 projects. The focus of your assessment should be on—

    a. Analyzing response mechanisms for individual components
    b. Ensuring that each project has a risk mitigation plan
    c. Interproject risks
    d. Stakeholder risk tolerance and thresholds

16. As the organization's troubled program recovery specialist, you have been called in to take over a program that has had difficulties from the start. An initial assessment reveals that the project-level requirements have not been completed. This needs to be accomplished before any work can be initiated. One way to reduce the time needed for the requirements-gathering cycle is to—

    a. Use as many business analysts as you can find in the organization
    b. Require each project manager to function as a business analyst until such time as the requirements have been gathered
    c. Outsource all the requirements activity so each project manager can devote his or her time to the more important parts of the project
    d. Apply the use of normalized templates, forms, and guidelines to make the process consistent across all projects

17. You are the program manager for a new program in your company that will provide global support services for supply chain integration. This program will support your multi-national corporation, and you have a total of nine countries involved in it. You plan to outsource a large portion of proprietary development work to several companies in a province located in Canada. Looking at procurement planning, it is important to—

    a. Adhere to legal and finance obligations
    b. Direct all procurements to be centralized
    c. Prepare complete evaluation criteria
    d. Set standards for the components

18. You are the executive sponsor of a program that provides global support services for supply chain integration. The program is experiencing quality problems in the individual projects. After meeting with the program manager to discuss the issues, you suggest that one way to improve quality is to—

    a. Identify alternatives on scope definition methods through inputs from subject matter experts
    b. Apply a common approach to the creation of the work breakdown structure across projects for consistency in scheduling, resourcing, and cost control
    c. Align acceptance criteria for the deliverables across phases and projects with the program objectives
    d. Set standards that are relevant to the entire program

19. You and your team have prepared the program work breakdown structure (PWBS) shown below in Figure 3.1. Assume that this program involves the development of products, each of which follows the same sequence.

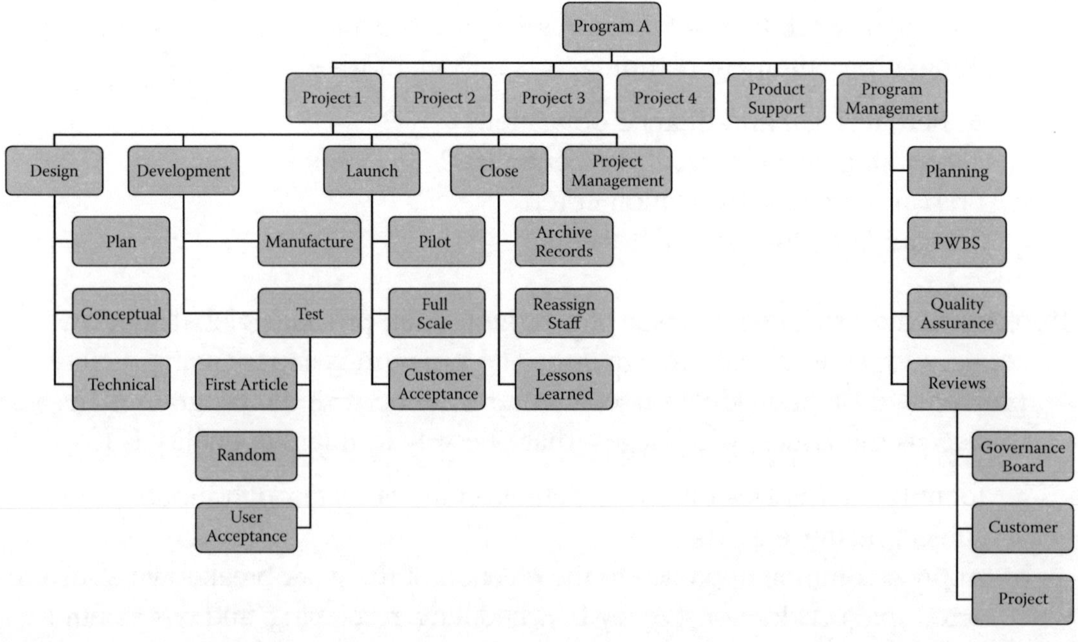

Figure 3.1

In this PWBS, a program package is—

a. Project 1
b. Design
c. Program Management
d. Plan

20. Working for an automotive company and wanting to develop an electric car that can be sold for under $25,000 US and run for 1,000 miles without needing a charge is a major undertaking. Your company is striving to be the first to market. To assess the program regularly, when you became program manager, you were asked to use a strategic performance measurement tool to track execution of the various activities, which means you should develop—

a. Key performance indicators
b. A traffic light system
c. Balanced scorecard
d. Earned value metrics

Answer Sheet

1.	a	b	c	d
2.	a	b	c	d
3.	a	b	c	d
4.	a	b	c	d
5.	a	b	c	d
6.	a	b	c	d
7.	a	b	c	d
8.	a	b	c	d
9.	a	b	c	d
10.	a	b	c	d

11.	a	b	c	d
12.	a	b	c	d
13.	a	b	c	d
14.	a	b	c	d
15.	a	b	c	d
16.	a	b	c	d
17.	a	b	c	d
18.	a	b	c	d
19.	a	b	c	d
20.	a	b	c	d

Answer Key

1. d. Use the scope management plan

   As the program schedule is prepared, it begins with the scope management plan and the PWBS in which the program components that produce the program benefits are identified.

   PMI®, *The Standard for Program Management*, 2013, 101

2. b. $32 million

   You will earn the difference between $20 million plus 70 percent of the additional $25 million and $2.5 million in expenses plus 30 percent of the additional $10 million in expenses, or—

$$[\$20\text{m} + (0.7 \times \$25\text{m})] - [\$2.5\text{m} + (0.3 \times \$10\text{m})] =$$

$$(\$20\text{m} + \$17.5\text{m}) - (\$2.5\text{m} + \$3\text{m}) =$$

$$\$37.5\text{m} - \$5.5\text{m} = \$32\text{m}$$

   NOTE: Remember that expected value is calculated as probability multiplied by the monetary value of the risk.

   Milosevic, Dragan Z. 2003. *Project Management ToolBox Tools and Techniques for the Practicing Project Manager*. Hoboken, New Jersey: John Wiley & Sons, 311–314

   Shimizu, Motoh. *Fundamentals of Program Management Strategic Program Bootstrapping for Business Innovation and Change*. 2012, Newtown Square, PA: Project Management Institute, 146–147

3. d. Program scope statement

   The program scope statement is the basis for future program decisions, and it defines and articulates the scope of the program. It also contains a list of the program's deliverables and success criteria. In program procurement planning a best practice is to evaluate commonalities and differences for the various procurements across the scope of the program.

   PMI®, *The Standard for Program Management*, 2013, 90 and 104

4. a. Prepare a competitive analysis of service providers

   In Program Procurement Planning, the program manager considers all program components and develops a comprehensive plan for procurements to meet goals and objectives. This planning is complemented by considering a program-wide approach to competition.

   PMI®, *The Standard for Program Management*, 2013, 90–91

5. b. An iterative process, and as issues arise and are addressed, the plan will naturally fluctuate

   As competing priorities, assumptions, and constraints are worked and resolved to address critical factors, such as business goals, deliverables, benefits, time, and cost, the plan will change over time.

   PMI®, *The Standard for Program Management*, 2013, 85

6. b. $17.5 million

   Decision-tree analysis is used to show the situation and the implications of each of the available choices. It also provides the expected monetary value for the various alternatives. If no risks occur, the value of your program would be calculated as follows:

   $$\$20m - \$2.5m = \$17.5m$$

   Milosevic, 2003, 311–314

   Shimizu, 2012, 146–147

7. d. An understanding of the steps needed to move from a development state to an operational state

   Transition planning involves identifying all the steps that are necessary to transition the program to an operational state. Transition planning from deliverables to capabilities and benefits to the organization is critical to program success. The transition plan defines the criteria to meet to ensure all administrative, commercial, and contractual obligations are met when the program is complete.

   PMI. *Program Management Professional (PgMP)® Examination Content Outline*, 2011, 9

   Thiry, Michel. *Program Management*. 2010. Surrey, England: Gower Publishing Limited, 139

8. c. Identify those skills that are critical to the program but are not possessed by current team members

Competency is the knowledge, attitudes, and skills, and other personal characteristics that can affect one's job. The first step is to identify the competencies that are critical to the program but are not possessed by existing team members. This ensures that these key resources can be obtained and will be available when required. A competency model can assist in determining the performance and personal competencies deemed necessary in program management.

PMI®, *Project Manager Competency Development Framework*—Second Edition, 2007, Newtown Square, PA: Project Management Institute, 73

Levin, Ginger and Ward, J. LeRoy. 2011. *Program Management Complexity A Competency Model.* Boca Raton, FL: CRC Press.

9. a. The top two levels of each project's work breakdown structure (WBS) can be included in the PWBS

The PWBS typically extends to the first one or two levels of each project's WBS. The bottom-up approach can show these levels as the PWBS is developed.

PMI®, *The Standard for Program Management*, 2013, 105

10. a. Determining the order and timing of program packages

During schedule development at the program level, the order and timing of the program packages and the non-program activities must be determined to produce the program benefits. This enables the scheduler to forecast the completion date of the program and of each milestone within the program and the key deliverables for each project.

PMI®, *The Standard for Program Management*, 2013, 100–101

11. d. Budgeted

Cost budgeting is based, in part, on how any financial constraints impose boundaries on the budget. Fiscal year budgetary planning cycles impose such boundaries, causing the program team to possibly use different techniques over the life cycle. The program's financial management plan should discuss the initial budget as well as funding schedules and milestones. Many organizations as well agree to an overall financial management plan and commit to a budget only for the next phase at each governance milestone.

PMI®, *The Standard for Program Management*, 2013, 78–79

12. b. Ensure infrastructure and operational costs are included

    In developing the program's financial management plan, it expands on the financial framework. While the component costs comprise the majority of the program's budget, operational costs and infrastructure costs are also included.

    PMI®, *The Standard for Program Management*, 2013, 79–80

13. b. Procure the services of a product integrator

    Rather than relying on multiple contractors, on many programs, the program manager and the team may decide to outsource the services of a product integrator to bring together the product outputs of the various projects. The goal of program procurements is to optimize procurements for the components,

    PMI®, *The Standard for Program Management*, 2013, 89

14. d. The provisions the vendor has in place to protect intellectual property

    Protecting intellectual property is of paramount concern for any company when outsourcing, and, in particular, when outsourcing to a company in a foreign nation, especially considering the differences in legal systems and standards of protection. As a performance competency for program managers, it is necessary to ensure intellectual property is properly retained during the program.

    PMI. *Program Management Professional (PgMP)® Examination Content Outline*, 2011, 9

    Levin and Ward, 2011, 60

15. c. Interproject risks

    In Program Risk Analysis, at the program level the emphasis is to integrate relevant component risks and to manage the interdependencies among these risks and the program to provide significant benefits to the program and the projects. A performance competency for program managers is to identify key program risks and issues, which includes identifying interdependencies between component risks.

    PMI®, *The Standard for Program Management*, 2013, 98

    Levin and Ward, 2011, 38

16. d. Apply the use of normalized templates, forms, and guidelines to make the process consistent across all projects

    One function of a program management office is to define the program management processes and procedures to be followed. By having standard processes in place, it can reduce the time involved in requirements gathering because teams can get started right away without first having to design their own methods for gathering requirements. Also, an effective program management information system can include requirements management activities and tools.

    PMI®, *The Standard for Program Management*, 2013, 13, 86

17. a. Adhere to legal and finance obligations

    In procurement planning, a number of activities are performed. Because of the need to optimize program procurement management, and to adhere to legal and financial obligations, the people responsible for procurement at the program level must work together during the planning phase.

    PMI®, *The Standard for Program Management*, 2013, 90

18. c. Set standards that are relevant to the entire program

    A key purpose of program quality planning is to identify the standards that are relevant to the entire program and to specify how to satisfy them. To ensure overall program quality, the different quality assurance and quality control specifications can be coordinated, and others added as needed.

    PMI®, *The Standard for Program Management*, 2013, 92

19. d. Plan

    The PWBS is a deliverable-oriented hierarchical description of the total scope of the program. A program package is the lowest level of the PWBS. Selections a., b., and c. are not at the lowest level of the PWBS.

    PMI®, *The Standard for Program Management*, 2013, 104–105

20. c. Balanced scorecard

The balanced scorecard was developed by Kaplan and Norton to be able to serve as such a strategic performance measurement tool. It tracks the execution of activities of staff members and the impact arising from these actions.

PMI. *Program Management Professional (PgMP)® Examination Content Outline*, 2011, 9

Hibson, Kathleen M., "Change Management The Good, the Bad and the Ugly" in Levin, Ginger. 2012. *Program Management A Life Cycle Approach*. Boca Raton, FL: CRC Press, 45

Executing the Program

Study Hints

The Executing the Program questions on the PgMP® certification exam, which constitute 14 percent of the exam, or 24 questions, focus on the Executing phase in the life cycle from the *Examination Content Outline.* During this phase of the program life cycle, component projects of the program are initiated, component interfaces are managed, and the development of program benefits is managed. The various program management plans are executed, and uniform standards, resources, infrastructure, tools, and processes are used for consistency and informed decision making. The program manager's performance is reviewed to maximize achievement of the program's goals, and the program manager leads the human resource functions. Questions will cover interpersonal skills and competencies to best manage the team and stakeholder expectations. A communications feedback process is set up to capture lessons learned. A continuing activity is to evaluate the program's status and to consolidate program data as well as data from the components. During this process, some components will close.

In *The Standard for Program Management*—Third Edition (2013), executing, along with monitoring and controlling, is in the Program Benefits Delivery phase of the life cycle in this Standard. Therefore emphasis is on information distribution (which is covered in this book in the Stakeholder Management section); program execution management; component cost estimating and program cost budgeting (covered in this book in Planning); program procurement; program quality assurance; resource prioritization (covered in this section); and risk identification, risk analysis, and risk response planning (covered in this book in Planning).

The purpose of Executing is to perform the program's work and produce the program deliverables and intended benefits. Because resources are typically difficult to obtain, questions may cover trade-offs and adaptations in the use of program resources throughout the program life cycle. The emphasis is on the provision of resources at the program level and focusing on selecting suppliers and issuing contracts.

Please recognize that since stakeholder management is a separate domain on the exam, questions involving information distribution and interactions with stakeholders primarily are covered in this domain in this book. Similarly most benefit delivery questions are covered in the benefit management domain in this book, and relevant governance questions are in the governance domain section.

Following is a list of the major topics covered in Executing the Program. Use this list to focus your study efforts on the areas that are most likely to appear in the exam.

Major Topics

Executing Processes in Program Benefits Delivery

- Program Execution Management or Program Delivery Management
- Change requests
- Component initiation and transition

Program Procurement

- Set component standards
- Qualified seller lists
- Pre-negotiated contracts
- Blanket purchase agreements
- Proposal evaluation criteria
- Procurement documents
- Contracts

Program Quality Assurance

- Compliance with policies and standards
- Quality assurance specifications
- Audits
- Standards reports
- Analysis of quality control results
- Change requests

Program Resource Prioritization

- Resource changes
- Resource priorities

Purpose of Program Benefit Delivery

- Component planning
- Component integration
- Component delivery
- Transition requests

Executing program management plans

- Chartering projects
- Assigning project managers
- Establishing uniform standards

- Aditing results
- Evaluating status
- Enabling informed decision making
- Evaluating status

Program manager performance

- Maximize contribution toward achieving goals
- Leading human resource functions
  - Training
  - Coaching
  - Mentoring
- Team engagement

Leading the team

- Training
- Coaching
- Mentoring
- Recognition
- Performance reviews

Capturing lessons learned

Practice Questions

INSTRUCTIONS: Note the most suitable answer for each multiple-choice question in the appropriate space on the answer sheet.

1. As the program manager for the annual construction program for a large government agency, you prepared the program management plan and scope statement that were approved by all stakeholders. Nine months later, a small group of influential stakeholders wants to increase the program's scope by including all maintenance and operations of the buildings. You should—
   a. Demonstrate the return on investment to the organization for increasing the scope of the program
   b. Reject the proposal because maintenance and operations typically are outside of the scope of programs
   c. Respond favorably because programs have a wide scope that may need to change to meet and exceed the organization's benefits expectations
   d. Ask a sponsor to make the business case to approve this new component

2. As program manager for a global payroll application, you have project teams in Bangalore, Singapore, London, and Washington, D.C. Currently, each team is following its own time-reporting process, which seems to be working well. From the perspective of global program management, you should—
   a. Define and apply a mandatory common time-reporting process
   b. Allow each location to use its own process in consideration of its unique cultural norms and local holiday schedule
   c. Define a common time-reporting process that each location has the option to use
   d. Do nothing because the current approach appears to be working well, and there are other more important issues on which to focus

3. An audit of your program has just been completed. The audit report claimed that a new process that had been implemented was receiving strong resistance from the users, thus indicating that a change impact review had not been conducted early enough in the program to detect potential barriers to adoption. Ensuring that such a review is conducted is clearly the responsibility of the—
   a. Program manager
   b. Program sponsor
   c. Program office
   d. Benefits manager

4. You are meeting with the team member who is responsible for the program management information system (PMIS) for your program. Because the data that will be captured are of a scientific and medical nature, the PMIS will generate more than eight terabytes (8,000 gigabytes) of data. Given the critical importance of the PMIS, you and the PMIS team member agree that the first order of business is to—

   a. Consolidate existing data to maximize storage capability
   b. Integrate all financial data
   c. Produce timely and valid inter-project information
   d. Define the program data naming conventions

5. Many organizations that practice portfolio management for programs and projects use enterprise resource planning software. Your large program to implement a culture that focuses first on a standardized approach to portfolio management in which every proposed project or program must be justified with a business case and formally approved by a Portfolio Review Board before it can be initiated is using enterprise resource planning software. It is also beneficial at the individual program and project levels. Since you are using it on your program, your best course of action is to—

   a. Use your program management office (PMO) for support with this software
   b. Handle it through the portfolio management office
   c. Have a core team member work with it throughout the program
   d. Set it up so that a program control framework is also established

6. Your program management plan for your program for new pharmaceutical product to assist people with insomnia without any adverse side effects has been approved. Already, you have three projects in this program, and you have selected the project managers. You also have a core team of four people who report directly to you, and they have been selected and helped in the planning phase. Now, you are ready to assign team members to the various projects in your program. One factor that you should consider in the assignment process is to—

   a. Align pay/compensation to industry norms
   b. Align personnel aspirations to available roles
   c. Assign to the project managers those persons who will be the best performers
   d. Assign team members with similar personalities to the same projects to reduce the risk of team conflict

7. Your company is small and has only 90 people. Its annual sales are about 5 million US and have been at this amount for the last three years. Recently, the CEO and the other two senior executives met and prepared a long-term strategic plan for the next three years. The company provides services primarily in the government market and has a high win rate, but a low capture ratio, which has made it difficult for the company to grow. The executives want to focus on improving the capture ratio. You are the program manager to help lead your organization into one that has annual sales in the 15–20 million range in the next two years. Your program management plan has been approved, and you are now in the executing phase. You must concentrate on—

   a. Managing scope, schedule, and cost
   b. Finding the right fit between the role and the person
   c. Initiating components as planned and indicated on the roadmap
   d. Making make-or-buy decisions

8. With the last Space Shuttle mission completed, you have been selected by the Administrator of the National Aeronautics and Space Administration to plan and execute the next new program at its Cape Canaveral campus. This is a highly classified program, which will take the United States into space throughout the galaxy into the 2030s. It is important to therefore—

   a. Ensure that the architecture is consistent across deliverables
   b. Manage and integrate program components
   c. Produce cumulative benefits
   d. Establish the program's organizational structure with a PMIS that is easy to access and use

9. Your program has seven projects in it. You have a PMO as well, which will support your program, and a core team of five people who also report to you. However, you are working now to manage the resources of your program, and you need to consider as you do so—

   a. Information from status reports
   b. Preparing a human resource plan
   c. The program's communications management plan
   d. Establishing an adequate compensation plan

10. You are managing a program to develop a new source of energy that can be used in the northern and southern hemispheres when solar power is not available. Working with your core program team and your Governance Board, you have identified a number of component projects. However, your company has several key projects under way, and resources will be difficult to acquire for this new program. In determining whether to use internal or external resources, one key consideration is—

    a. The ability to coordinate use of external resources
    b. Your ability to negotiate with functional managers for the needed staff
    c. The availability of external resources
    d. The impact on the morale if external resources are used

11. You are supported on your program by a variety of contractors who need to work closely together to deliver program benefits. Two of the contractors are blaming each other for missed deadlines. It appears that a critical milestone was missed by Contractor A, the output of which was needed by Contractor B. However, Contractor A alleges that Contractor B provided the wrong specifications. In this situation, your first step should be to—

    a. Seek liquidated damages from both contractors because of the missed dates
    b. Alert your attorney to the possibility of litigation and its associated expense
    c. Review the termination clause in each contract to see what your options are
    d. Ensure there are unambiguous contract management procedures

12. You are managing a program to develop a new product to protect all workers from germs in the workplace so everyone is assured that the workplace is clean. They will not have to worry in the future if a co-worker has a transmittable disease. However, you have just learned that there was a failure to adhere to a major element in the work breakdown structure (WBS) of one of the key projects. This problem means that—

    a. Interactions and realignment of this project must be managed
    b. Rebaselining may be required
    c. A change request has been approved
    d. New metrics are required

13. You are working on an emergency response program for your city and have realized that you lack the needed resources to support your program. Over the years, your organization's Procurement and Contracts Department has compiled a qualified seller list. This list will be extremely helpful to you when you—

    a. Prepare your program procurement management plan
    b. Issue requests for proposals (RFPs) or requests for quotations (RFQs)
    c. Plan contract evaluation criteria
    d. Advertise in the local newspaper for your procurement requirements

14. As you work on this emergency response program for your city, you recognize you will need a number of different types of supplies and services to support your program and its component projects. One common approach is to use—

    a. Expert judgment
    b. Formalized proposal evaluation criteria
    c. Screening systems
    d. Weighting systems

15. As a program manager, once your team is in place you need to focus on—

    a. Providing mentoring
    b. Setting up a team-based reward and recognition system
    c. Promoting integrity in all interactions
    d. Striving to be a role model for the team

16. You have identified seven candidate projects to comprise your program. You also have identified seven capable project managers to manage these projects who have the requisite knowledge, skills, and competencies to do the required work against an aggressive schedule and demanding stakeholders. Before each project can officially begin, it is important that—

    a. The program's business case is updated
    b. The scope of work is formalized
    c. A component initiation request is approved
    d. Each project has a defined charter

17. Assume you are the program manager for your pharmaceutical company for a new product designed to cure sleep apnea. As part of your program potential patients will not need to first go to a hospital to diagnose whether they have this condition and stay the night. You of course must get regulatory approval and conduct numerous clinical trials before your new product is ready so your program will last at least five years. You hope to be the first to market with this product even though your business development manager has said that a competitor is also working in this area. Based on your previous work on long programs, you know it is hard to sustain morale among your team, and many often then volunteer to work on projects that may be in trouble just to see results. Therefore, this time, you are—
    a. Setting up a process where your resources are dedicated to your team and cannot be used on other projects
    b. Setting up a master schedule that has some early milestones, which you know you can meet
    c. Asking each team member to sign a commitment statement to your program as they join your team
    d. Having weekly performance reviews with your project managers, who in turn will have similar performance reviews with their team members

18. You have decided to use standard Key Performance Indicators for your program and have adopted the Balanced Scorecard approach as well. You want to do so in order to—
    a. Minimize the information that is to be reported
    b. Make sure that information is available in a format that has a template so a lot of time is not spent on the reporting process
    c. Set up the reports to be provided on a weekly basis to all stakeholders
    d. Evaluate the program status while maintaining current program information

19. Working on a major program to upgrade the software used in your country's airspace system to make it far easier for the air traffic controllers to use and also to avoid incidents of their falling asleep at times when there is limited activity or having tremendous stress when there is a lot of activity, you are facing many challenges in your role as a program manager. You have seven projects on your program and expect to add others. One project is about to close. You need to make sure before it does close that—

    a. Deliverables are complete, and scope is compliant with the functional overview
    b. Deliverables have exceeded the original requirements, and there is universal agreement upon all stakeholders about the project's success
    c. The detailed administrative procedures for program closure have been followed, which are managed by your Program Management Office
    d. The program manager and team have been reassigned to other projects now that this project is complete

20. Program management is new to your company. You are managing the first program as you have taken program management training and have a track record of successfully managing complex and multiple projects. Your team is new to program management, and no one on the team has been exposed to it. Some team members have questioned the new approach, and others have asked why the organization has decided to manage projects as programs rather than as standalone projects. The project managers on your program are concerned they may lack visibility in this concept, limiting their opportunities for advancement and benefits. This shows that you must—

    a. Persuade them that program management is desirable and becoming a program manager then can be the next step in their career
    b. Set up a training session for your project managers and team members to explain the benefits of program management
    c. Establish an open-door policy and invite anyone who has concerns to meet individually with you or to call you without any fears that in doing so their performance may be criticized
    d. Establish a policy of "no surprises" and provide your team with the same status information that the executives receive

Answer Sheet

1.	a	b	c	d	11.	a	b	c	d
2.	a	b	c	d	12.	a	b	c	d
3.	a	b	c	d	13.	a	b	c	d
4.	a	b	c	d	14.	a	b	c	d
5.	a	b	c	d	15.	a	b	c	d
6.	a	b	c	d	16.	a	b	c	d
7.	a	b	c	d	17.	a	b	c	d
8.	a	b	c	d	18.	a	b	c	d
9.	a	b	c	d	19.	a	b	c	d
10.	a	b	c	d	20.	a	b	c	d

Answer Key

1. d. Ask a sponsor to make the business case to approve this new component

   Although programs have a wide scope that may require changes to meet the organization's benefits expectations, this request is for a new component to the program. Therefore, it requires a component initiation request with a business case to evaluate whether it should be included according to the approved selection criteria.

   PMI®, *The Standard for Program Management*, 2013, 87

2. a. Define and apply a mandatory common time-reporting process

   In executing a program, it is important for each team member to record his or her time in accordance with a well-defined, common standard. Cultural norms and country holiday schedules have little to do with the number of hours or days someone works on a program.

   PMI®. *Program Management Professional (PgMP)® Examination Content Outline*, 2011, 10

3. a. Program manager

   The program manager must set clear goals, assess readiness, plan for the change, monitor the change, and address those who are not fully embracing the change. Change management is a core knowledge and skill area for program managers.

   PMI®, *The Standard for Program Management*, 2013, 22, 147

4. d. Define the program data naming conventions

   To avoid confusion and the proliferation of numerous naming conventions across projects, the program should have a standard naming convention for all data, and the application of such conventions should be consistent across all projects. This will increase efficiency and productivity across the program team.

   PMI®. *Program Management Professional (PgMP)® Examination Content Outline*, 2011, 10

5. a. Use your program management office (PMO) for support with this software

   Programs tend to have a supporting infrastructure that includes specific processes and procedures as well as physical facilities. The infrastructure may include program-specific tools such as enterprise resource planning software.

   PMI®, *The Standard for Program Management*, 2013, 64–65

   PMI®. *Program Management Professional (PgMP)® Examination Content Outline*, 2011, 10

6. b. Align personnel aspirations to available roles

   Team members tend to be more motivated when they are working on projects or in roles in which they have strong interest. Therefore, a program manager should always consider someone's personal interest or desires when making assignments.

   PMI®. *Program Management Professional (PgMP)® Examination Content Outline*, 2011, 10

7. b. Finding the right fit between the role and the person

   Without the performance of people, the program cannot be completed. It is difficult to find the right fit between the role and the person as people will do their best work in the areas in which they excel. While values and abilities are unlikely to change quickly, additional skills can be acquired in a short time. The responsibilities of the role must complement how a person sees things and thinks.

   Herzog, Kim "Mobilizing the Organization: The Discipline of Execution", in Levin, Ginger. *Program Management A Life Cycle Approach*, 2012, Boca Raton, FL: CRC Press, 221

   PMI®. *Program Management Professional (PgMP)® Examination Content Outline*, 2011, 10

8. b. Manage and integrate the program components

   The purpose of Program Delivery Management is to manage and integrate the program components throughout benefits delivery. Therefore, components need to be initiated, change requests must be acted upon, and components will transition as appropriate.

   PMI®, *The Standard for Program Management*, 2013, 86–87

9. b. Preparing a human resource plan

   In Resource Prioritization, human resource planning is useful to identify, document, and assign program roles and responsibilities to individuals and groups. Resources should be allocated to meet key program needs.

   PMI®, *The Standard for Program Management*, 2013, 95

10. a. The ability to coordinate use of external resources

    Use of contractors is common on programs, and managing their inputs and contributions is fundamental to program success. To ensure external resources add value, it is necessary to coordinate effectively the input of different third parties in a seamless and integrated manner.

    Williams, David and Parr, Tim. 2006. *Enterprise Programme Management Delivering Value*. Hampshire, England: Palgrave MacMillan, 282–283

11. d. Ensure there are unambiguous contract management procedures

    Unambiguous contract management procedures are essential if the program team is to manage the overall program as an integrated program using common processes. Each contractor, for example, requires comparable acceptance criteria that fit in with the agreed-upon program processes. If an organization has standard supplier contracts in place, they may require substantial changes to be effective for the program. It is important not to contract too early and to make sure procedures are not ambiguous. Successful buyer-seller relationships depend on such factors as trust and good working relationships, both of which are best addressed at the program level.

    Williams and Parr, 2006, 194–195

12. a Interactions and realignment of this project must be managed

    In the Program Benefits Delivery Phase, the program manager is responsible to maintain alignment from components with the program to deliver the program's benefits. At the program level, interactions with components are essential to accomplish goals to position the program for success. The program manager must manage each component in a consistent and coordinated way and oversee the performance of the program's components.

    PMI®, *The Standard for Program Management*, 2013, 69–70

13. b. Issue requests for proposals (RFPs) or requests for quotations (RFQs)

    Qualified seller lists are used when RFPs, RFQs, or requests for information (RFIs) are issued. They can save time in the overall program procurement management process, because they list only known sellers who can provide needed products and services.

    PMI®, *The Standard for Program Management*, 2013, 91

14. b. Formalized procurement evaluation criteria

    Program managers have many tools and techniques available to conduct program procurements and must set standards for the program's components. Formalized proposal evaluation criteria are a best practice to follow.

    PMI®, *The Standard for Program Management*, 2013, 91

15. c. Promoting integrity in all interactions

As PMI® members according to the "Code of Ethics and Professional Conduct", honesty is a critical component as one must "understand the truth and act in a truthful manner both in our communications and in our conduct". By promoting integrity in all interactions, the emphasis is to behave honestly, provide facts, confront dishonesty, and challenge any system that encourages dishonesty or rewards. Ethical behavior must be practiced on programs.

PMI®, IPMI Code of Ethics and Professional Conduct. *Available from http://www.pmi.org/codeofethics/PDF*, 4

Levin, Ginger and Ward, J. LeRoy. 2011. *Program Complexity A Competency Model*. Boca Raton, FL: CRC Press, 77

16. c. A component initiation request is approved

Component planning is performed in the Program Benefit Delivery Phase. The component must properly support the program's outcomes before it is authorized. A new component initiation request must be submitted and approved.

PMI®, *The Standard for Program Management*, 2013, 60–61, 69

17. b. Setting up a master schedule that has some early milestones, which you know you can meet

It is easy for team members to lose motivation especially on large programs. One approach is to celebrate success among your team and maximize their contribution to achieving program goals. If the master schedule has early milestones set up that are ones that can be met, this then provides an opportunity to celebrate success and build a winning team.

PMI®. *Program Management Professional (PgMP)® Examination Content Outline*, 2011, 10

Levin and Ward, 2011, 67

18. d. Evaluate the program status while maintaining current program information

    Key Performance Indicators are a best practice in program management especially to show how the program remains in alignment with strategic goals and objectives, and the Balanced Scorecard is helpful in setting performance targets. The purpose is to be able in executing to evaluate the program's status in order to monitor and control the program while maintaining current program information.

    PMI®. *Program Management Professional (PgMP)® Examination Content Outline*, 2011, 10

19. a. Deliverables are complete, and scope is compliant with the functional overview

    Before the request to close a project is approved, the program manager must ensure the project's deliverables are complete. The scope should be compliant with the functional overview so requirements are met as well as the success criteria in the scope statement.

    PMI®. *Program Management Professional (PgMP)® Examination Content Outline*, 2011, 10

20. b. Set up a training session for your project managers and team members to explain the benefits of program management

    Program management is used because through it more benefits can be achieved than if the projects were managed in a standalone fashion. There is a far greater emphasis therefore on strategic alignment, benefits realization, stakeholder engagement, and governance than in project management. As a program manager, one must lead by training among other things in order to improve team engagement and achieve commitment to the program's goals.

    PMI®. *Program Management Professional (PgMP)® Examination Content Outline*, 2011, 10

Controlling the Program

Study Hints

The Controlling the Program questions on the PgMP® certification exam, which constitute 10 percent of the exam, or 17 questions, continue to focus on phase four of the program life cycle from the *Examination Content Outline* and more specifically on monitoring and controlling the program and its components. The expected benefits need to be in line with the original plan, the level of risk must remain acceptable, and accepted best practices must be followed.

The *Examination Content Outline* focuses on the need to analyze variances in costs, schedule, quality, and risks to identify corrective actions or opportunities to the program because of these variances. The Program Management Plan and other plans may need updating as a result of corrective actions that are implemented. It also emphasizes the need to manage issues on the program to identify and select a course of action consistent with the program's scope, constraints, and objectives to achieve the programs benefits. Impact assessments for various possible changes may need to be conducted and decisions made. Additionally, risks require monitoring, following the risk management plan.

In the *Standard for Program Management*—Third Edition (2013), monitoring and controlling is part of the Benefits Delivery Phase of this life cycle. Questions then cover program performance reporting, program financial monitoring and control, program performance monitoring and control, program procurement administration, program quality control, resource interdependency management, program risk monitoring and control, and program scope control.

You should expect to answer questions on earned value and should be familiar with the various earned value terms and formulas. You should also expect to answer some questions about program trends and the need to communicate these trends to the program's stakeholders. Stakeholders are emphasized in the Manage Program Stakeholder Expectations process, covered in the stakeholder domain in this book. Other work involves governance oversight and managing benefits, covered in the respective domains in this book.

Because monitoring and controlling involves preventive and corrective actions, some questions include scenarios in which the program manager and the core program team must decide on the best course of action. Because the program manager is responsible for managing program issues, the use of an issue register is required, and its contents may be reviewed by the Governance Board. Many of these processes will occur throughout the program's life cycle, from initiation to closure. Furthermore, it is essential to focus on monitoring and controlling the program's scope, schedule, and budget, and if contracts are to be awarded, to focus on administering program procurements.

Following is a list of the major topics covered in Controlling the Program. Use this list to focus your study efforts on the areas that are most likely to appear on the exam.

Major Topics

Program Benefits Delivery

- Program Performance Monitoring
  - Preparing contract and sponsor related data reports
  - Requesting customer feedback
  - Preparing periodic reports, presentations, and key performance indicators

- Program Financial Monitoring and Control
  - Monitoring program finances and coordinating expenditures within budget
  - Managing changes as they occur
  - Making payments to contractors
  - Closing component budgets
  - Updating the budget baseline
  - Approving change requests
  - Using earned value
  - Implementing corrective actions

- Program Performance Monitoring and Control
  - Collecting, measuring, and disseminating performance information
  - Assessing program trends
  - Providing information to determine the program's status, trends, and areas in need of realignment
  - Determining if requests for preventive or corrective action are needed
  - Preparing status reports
  - Preparing forecasts

- Program Procurement Administration
  - Ensuring the budget is being spent to deliver benefits
  - Using performance/earned value reports
  - Using progress reports from contractors with key performance indicators

- Program Quality Control
  - Monitoring deliverables to see if quality requirements are fulfilled
  - Implementing quality change requests
  - Using quality control checklists
  - Using quality test reports and measurement results

- Resource Interdependency Management
  - Controlling the schedule for scarce resources
  - Focusing on interdependent resources

- Program Risk Monitoring and Control
  - Identifying, analyzing, and planning for new risks
  - Tracking identified risks
  - Reanalyzing existing risks
  - Executing risk responses
  - Documenting lessons learned

- Program Schedule Control
  - Tracking and monitoring start and finish of milestones
  - Managing the master schedule planned timelines
  - Identifying slippages and opportunities
  - Reviewing the program master schedule
  - Updating the roadmap

- Program Scope Control
  - Determining scope changes with significant impact
  - Establishing a scope change control system
  - Determining when updates to the scope statement and PWBS are needed

Preventive and corrective actions
Proactive and reactive cost control
Managing and controlling changes

- Change requests
- Coordinating changes
- Change control board
- Change request log
- Impact analysis
- Approved change requests
- Variance analysis

Meetings and reviews

- Presentations
- Status review meetings
- Lessons learned reviews

Program management controls

- Standards
- Policies and procedures
- Program plans
- Performance reports
- Forecasts

- Program performance analysis
- Issue analysis
- Program metrics
- Impact assessments
- Time and cost reporting systems
- Inspections
- Reviews
- Oversight
- Audits
- Contracts
- Documentation
- Regulations

Earned value

- Schedule and cost variance
- Schedule performance index and cost performance index
- Estimate at completion
- Estimate to complete
- Budget at completion

Trend analysis
Variance analysis
Impact assessments
Issue register

Practice Questions

INSTRUCTIONS: Note the most suitable answer for each multiple-choice question in the appropriate space on the answer sheet.

1. As a program manager on the next generation nuclear submarine, you have six projects so far in your program, and this is only year one. You know additional projects and non-project work will be added as the program continues since it is scheduled to last for at least seven years. One of your responsibilities is to ensure that common activities among projects are coordinated to maximize the use of resources and achieve results that would not be possible if the projects were managed in a standalone fashion. This is done in—

   a. Program Performance Monitoring
   b. Benefit Management
   c. Resource Prioritization
   d. Resource Interdependency Management

2. You know from your work on programs, that change is inevitable on both on the overall program and its projects. As a program manager for this nuclear submarine program, you use a change management system as part of the program management information system (PMIS). You do this during part of your work in—

   a. Integrating overall change control
   b. Working to deliver incremental benefits
   c. Managing scope
   d. Monitoring and controlling program performance

3. Your program, which designs, develops, and manufactures a class of farm equipment that can be used above the Arctic Circle, has been requested to consolidate data and status for a key stakeholder. Part of your work involves maintaining a spare parts inventory and fulfilling spares requests for clients. In consolidating your report, you—

   a. Do not include the spares data because they are really not part of the defined program and do not fit the definition of a project
   b. Include the spares data, even though they are non-project work, because they are part of the program
   c. Include the spares data because you can reasonably define fulfilling a spares order as a project
   d. Ask the stakeholder who requested the report whether he or she wants to see the spares data

4. You have been asked to assume the management of a program to rebuild the water desalinization plant for Haddad, Saudi Arabia. Much of the equipment on the job is being leased. The program has been under way for more than five years. You decided to conduct an audit of the hundreds of lease agreements, and you found that you are making payments on leases for equipment that are not being used. Your next step is to—

   a. Set up a system to alert your team to this problem on future leased resources
   b. Use a resource register
   c. Recommend corrective actions
   d. Inform your Governance Board because it is focused on the program's financial status

5. Your program to produce the first polycarbonate city car is making progress. The client is concerned that the cost to manufacture the car will cause the car to be priced at a level that the average consumer cannot, or will not, pay. The client has asked you to see whether you can reduce the cost of manufacturing the vehicle yet still meet the specifications. Such customer feedback requests are helpful and are part of—

   a. Establishing a cost change management system
   b. Preparing program performance reports
   c. Determining when to take corrective actions
   d. Implementing a lean Six Sigma manufacturing processes

6. You have been asked to assume the management of a program to rebuild the water desalinization plant for Haddad, Saudi Arabia. You are using earned value on your program. The schedule performance index indicates that you will not meet your proposed schedule, and you are only about 20 percent complete to date. You need to—

   a. Issue a revised schedule to your program team
   b. Update the program master schedule
   c. Update your budget baseline
   d. Inform your Governance Board

7. As program manager for development of a next-generation catalytic converter, you have a core team of six people. So far, you are in the first year of your program, scheduled to last four years, and you have three projects as part of your program. The project manager of the first project to design the converter has raised an issue to you as he feels it has far reaching consequences. You decide to use an issue register. After each issue is identified, your core program team records it in this register. The next step is to—

   a. Subject the issue to analysis by a reviewing authority
   b. Appoint a member of the program team to resolve the issue
   c. Ask the person who raised the issue to propose a resolution
   d. Determine a course of action

8. Assume you are managing a program for the judicial branch of your government, and you are reporting to the Chief Information Officer of the Administrative System of the Courts. The program is the number one priority on the Court's list of ongoing programs and projects in the portfolio. The purpose of your program is to manage a legacy system conversion program, and thus far, your team has identified a number of risks to monitor, which means at the program level, you should—

   a. Determine if the program's assumptions are still valid
   b. Appoint a member of your core team to be responsible for risk management on the program
   c. Ensure the planned risk responses are executed in a timely way
   d. Monitor the effects of the risk responses as they are executed to ensure they were effective

9. It is important to address and control scope changes on programs to ensure successful program completion. These scope changes can originate from many sources including—

   a. Risks
   b. Architecture issues
   c. Missed milestones
   d. Resource reallocations

10. One of the issues on your program is difficult to resolve because it concerns serious personality conflicts. Although it was raised by Project Manager A, it affects Projects B and C. Each of the three project managers has a different solution, and there is a stalemate. Therefore, a key performance competency for a program manager in monitoring and controlling the program is to—

    a. Establish an issue analysis process
    b. Recognize some of these solutions could be program opportunities
    c. Provide issue oversight at the program level
    d. Ask an expert for assistance before taking corrective

11. You realized in your work on the next generation nuclear submarine that since it will last seven years, you will probably have scope changes. You want to prepare for them and be able to exploit them as much as possible. However, because most scope changes have associated costs, every proposed change requires analysis to determine whether it should be implemented. If change requests are accepted and approved, the next step is to—

    a. Communicate the decision to the stakeholders involved
    b. Update the program management plan
    c. Revise the work breakdown structure (WBS)
    d. Work with the component manager to implement the change

12. A scope change request is approved for your program. It is estimated to require an additional $1 million. Your program Governance Board recommended to the executive sponsor that this scope change be approved to maintain a competitive advantage. Which of the following should you first update?

    a. Program management plan
    b. Budget baseline
    c. Program work breakdown structure (PWBS)
    d. Scope management plan

13. You are the legacy system conversion program manager in your company. You have a request now to update the company's business development/sales tracking system, which was not in your business case. Your Governance Board recognizes the importance of including this project in your program and asks you to prepare a cost estimate for this new project. The board approves your estimate. You now should—

    a. Update the program budget baseline
    b. Revise the cost management plan
    c. Prepare a resource management plan
    d. Identify staffing needs

14. Because of their size, complexity, and duration, programs tend to be more important than projects in most organizations, and program managers tend to interact more with senior management, often through the Governance Board or steering committee that oversees the program. Throughout the program, it is especially important to monitor and control program changes. It is helpful to—

    a. Conduct impact assessments
    b. Authorize funding for each change
    c. Update the scope statement
    d. Influence factors that lead to change with effective program metrics

15. You are the program manager on a mergers and acquisition (M&A) team that is responsible for integrating your company with the one it has recently acquired. The company you acquired has a history of failure in such mergers; your company is now its fourth owner, and unfortunately, things are not going well. In a meeting with your executive sponsor after the last governance review meeting, he suggested that you set up—

    a. Key performance indicators
    b. A different governance structure
    c. Benchmarking studies
    d. A program audit

16. In a program performance meeting, you asked the project manager of Project A what the status was on her program. She responded by saying that the total project budget of $600,000 was evenly allocated over the project's six-month life. She has just completed the second month of the project and has finished 50 percent of the work. What earned value method information is available thus far?

    a. Earned value
    b. Planned value
    c. Actual costs
    d. Earned value and planned value

17. Every program is planned on the basis of a set of hypotheses, scenarios, or assumptions. As a newly appointed program manager, you ask one of your core program team members to explore cost and contingency reserves. This is important as part of the—

    a. Forecasts
    b. Risk monitoring function
    c. Program procurement administration
    d. Program financial monitoring and controls

18. You are a program manager on an international program that relies on contractors for approximately 75 percent of its work. Some of the contracts apply to a specific project, but five contracts span six of the projects. You have one basic ordering agreement, which enables you to obtain temporary resources as required for this complex program. In terms of Program Procurement Administration, you should review the—

    a. Program reports
    b. Procurement register
    c. Contract management plan
    d. Change requests

19. Your program is beginning to miss key milestones because of delays by your customer, with whom you have a contract. Your goal is to ensure that corrections are made as quickly as possible, so you decide to conduct a contract performance review earlier than planned. At the program level, it is your responsibility now to—

    a. Prepare a change request
    b. Document the causes for the delay and bring it to your attorney's attention
    c. Ensure the budget is being spent properly
    d. Document the delay and discuss it with the steering committee

20. You are preparing for a meeting of your program's Governance Board. On your program, you are using earned value for monitoring, control, and forecasting. The planned value is $30,587, and the earned value is $26,365. You are working on a customer-imposed schedule for the completion of the program. Looking at the schedule variance (SV), you conclude that—

    a. The SV is –$4,222, and the program is behind schedule
    b. The SV is 1.16, and it appears that the schedule will be met
    c. The program is behind schedule, and the tasks on the critical path are affected
    d. The budget at completion is $46,475, but the delays are insignificant

Answer Sheet

1.	a	b	c	d	11.	a	b	c	d
2.	a	b	c	d	12.	a	b	c	d
3.	a	b	c	d	13.	a	b	c	d
4.	a	b	c	d	14.	a	b	c	d
5.	a	b	c	d	15.	a	b	c	d
6.	a	b	c	d	16.	a	b	c	d
7.	a	b	c	d	17.	a	b	c	d
8.	a	b	c	d	18.	a	b	c	d
9.	a	b	c	d	19.	a	b	c	d
10.	a	b	c	d	20.	a	b	c	d

Answer Key

1. d. Resource Interdependency Management

   Resources must be shared across the program, and the program manager controls the schedule for these shared resources.

   PMI®, *The Standard for Program Management*, 2013, 95

2. c. Managing scope

   Scope control is necessary to ensure the program delivers its intended benefits. To administer and manage scope, a change management activity is necessary.

   PMI®, *The Standard for Program Management*, 2013, 106

3. b. Include the spares data, even though they are non-project work, because they are part of the program

   At the program level, in preparing performance reports, these reports summarize progress of components in the program. The summarization incudes both the projects and the non-project work.

   PMI®, *The Standard for Program Management*, 2013, 87

4. c. Recommend corrective actions

   To avoid penalties or ongoing lease payments, leased resources should be tracked to ensure that they are returned when the lease expires or when they are no longer needed. Based on the audit findings, it is now necessary to request changes or recommend corrective action requests. A program whose costs exceed budgets may no longer justify its business case. Even minor overruns must be justified.

   PMI®, *The Standard for Program Management*, 2013, 81–82

5. b. Preparing program performance reports

   Program Performance Reporting coordinates performance data to provide stakeholders with information on resource use to determine effectiveness in delivery of program benefits. Customer feedback requests are an output of this activity.

   PMI®, *The Standard for Program Management*, 2013, 77

6. d. Inform your Governance Board

   At this point, it is obvious the program will not meet its schedule. The first step is to inform your Governance Board and then make a decision as to the next steps and the corrective actions to be performed.

   PMI®, *The Standard for Program Management*, 2013, 81

7. d. Determine a course of action

   After an issue is identified, it should be recorded in the issue register. This is an example of a program-level issue, and the program manager now must select a course of action consistent with scope, constraints, and objectives to achieve planned benefits.

   PMI®, *Examination Content Outline,* 2011, 11

8. a. Determine if the program assumptions are still valid

   In program risk monitoring, often it is necessary to review the initial program assumptions and determine if they are still valid as assumptions are a key source of risks.

   PMI®, *The Standard for Program Management*, 2013, 100

9. b. Architecture issues

   Controlling scope is critical to program success. These scope changes may originate from stakeholders, program components, previously unidentified requirements, architecture issues, or external sources.

   PMI®, *The Standard for Program Management*, 2013, 105

10. a. Establish an issue analysis process

    A performance competency for program managers is to identify issues and risks continuously and take corrective actions as required. As part of this competency, an issue analysis process should be established to assess the impact and severity of issues, and an issue log should be maintained.

    PMI®, *Examination Content Outline,* 2011, 11

    Levin, Ginger and Ward, J. LeRoy. 2011. *Program Management Complexity A Competency Model.* Boca Raton, FL: CRC Press, 50

11. b. Update the program management plan

In Program Scope Control, a change management activity is a necessity. When change requests are accepted and approved, the program management plan and the program scope statement are updated.

PMI®, *The Standard for Program Management*, 2013, 106

12. b. Budget baseline

The program budget baseline is updated as an output of Program Financial Monitoring and Control. Monitoring finances and controlling expenditures are critical aspects of ensuring the program meets its funding goals. A change of this magnitude requires the need to update the budget baseline.

PMI®, *The Standard for Program Management*, 2013, 81

13. a. Update the program budget baseline

As an output of the Program Financial Monitoring and Control, updates to the program budget baseline are needed when there are significant cost impacts. These updates are communicated to program stakeholders as appropriate.

PMI®, *The Standard for Program Management*, 2013, 81

14. a. Conduct impact assessments

Impact assessments should be conducted for program changes in order to recommend decisions and obtain approval according to the program's governance model.

PMI®. *Program Management Professional (PgMP)® Examination Content Outline*, 2011, 11

15. a. Key performance indicators

In Program Performance Reporting, performance data on the program are consolidated and conveyed to stakeholders to provide information about the program's performance. As an output, key performance indicators should be established.

PMI®, *The Standard for Program Management*, 2013, 77

16. d. Earned value and planned value

For the earned value (EV) of the project, note that half the work has been completed, for an EV of $300,000. The planned value (PV) through month two is $200,000. Remember that the estimate was $600,000 spread evenly over six months (or $100,000/month).

PMI®, *The Standard for Program Management*, 2013, 77

Pritchard, Carl L., 2003. *The Project Management Drill Book: A Self-Study Guide*. Arlington, VA: ESI International, Chapter 1

17. b. Risk monitoring function

Risk monitoring includes evaluation of whether cost or schedule contingency reserves need to be modified in line with the risks of the program as program risk responses are continuously monitored for new and changing risks.

PMI®, *The Standard for Program Management*, 2013, 100

18. c. Contract management plan

The contract management plan is used to administer contracts for significant purchases and acquisitions. It covers contract administration activities throughout the life of the contract and is used effectively to manage a variety of suppliers. It is an output of Program Procurement so it should be followed in Program Procurement Administration.

PMI®, *The Standard for Program Management*, 2013, 91

19. c. Ensure the budget is being spent properly

As contracts are awarded during Program Procurement Administration, it is the program manager's responsibility to maintain visibility in the procurements to ensure the budget is spent properly to obtain program benefits.

PMI®, *The Standard for Program Management*, 2013, 91

20. a. The SV is –$4,222, and the program is behind schedule

Schedule variance (SV) is calculated by subtracting the planned value (PV) from the earned value (EV); that is, SV = EV – PV. At this point, the SV is –$4,222. The program is behind schedule; however, without additional information, the effect on the critical path is not known.

PMI®, *The Standard for Program Management*, 2013, 81

PMI®, *PMBOK® Guide*, 2013, 224

Closing the Program

Study Hints

The Closing the Program questions on the PgMP® certification exam, which constitute three percent of the exam, or five questions, emphasize the last phase in the program life cycle according to the *Examination Content Outline*, Program Closure. This phase formalizes the acceptance of products, services, or results that brings the program or one of its projects to completion. The program's work is complete, and benefits from the program are accruing and will continue to do so in the future.

In *The Standard for Program Management*—Third Edition (2013), closing is covered in the Program Closure phase of its life cycle with the purpose to execute a controlled closure of the program. This phase concentrates on program transition as well as program closeout and includes program financial closure, program transition and benefits sustainment, program closure, and program procurement closure.

This phase tracks to the benefits transition phase in the program benefits management life cycle. At this time, the benefits from the project and non-project activities are consolidated, and the ongoing responsibility to sustain the benefits is transferred in accordance with the program transition plan. Many associated ongoing activities are involved with ensuring and sustaining benefits, and these activities differ in each organization. Benefit related questions primarily are covered in the Benefits section of this book

You should recognize that administrative closure is ongoing and should not wait until the program is complete. Each project within the program is closed at different times, as are the associated contracts. If a project is terminated for any reason, it may be closed earlier than scheduled or anticipated. Lessons learned are collected throughout the program life cycle. Closure activities, therefore, occur throughout the program and not just at completion of the program.

Following is a list of the major topics covered in Closing the Program. Use this list to focus your study efforts on the areas most likely to appear on the exam.

Major Topics

Program Closure Phase

- Program Transition
  - Meeting the program's benefits
  - Completing transition work
  - Requiring a new program to oversee transition activities
- Program Closeout
  - Program financial closure
  - Sustainment budgets
  - Financial closing statements
  - Closed program budget
- Program Transition and Benefit Sustainment
  - Ensuring benefit sustainment
- Program Closure
  - Final reports
  - Knowledge transition
  - Resource disposition
  - Program closeout
- Program Procurement Closure
  - Closed contract reports
  - Lesson learned updates
  - Closed contracts
- Program Performance Analysis Report
- Stakeholder Support for Closure
- Execute Transition and Closeout of Program and Component Plans

Conduct a Post-Review Meeting
Report Lessons Learned and Best Practices
Intellectual Property Requirements
Communication of Program Results

Practice Questions

INSTRUCTIONS: Note the most suitable answer for each multiple-choice question in the appropriate space on the answer sheet.

1. You have been managing a major software program for six years under contract to a Fortune 500 company. You have been helping this company move to Cloud computing. Finally, you completed the last project in this program, and it is time to officially close the program. Although you have completed your program, your customer requires telephone and e-mail support in case an issue arises or a defect is detected. Such assurance is—

   a. An activity to be done as part of closing the program
   b. Outside the scope of the program
   c. An ongoing activity that is part of the program
   d. A standard best practice

2. You are managing a program for the first time in your telecom company. It is to convert all the existing phone lines in your city to ones that are underground to prevent outages during hurricanes and tornadoes, which are common to your region of the country. You realize that since you have seven projects in this program that various projects will close at different times during the life cycle of your program. These closing activities are—

   a. Limited to the project's life cycle
   b. Covered as you close the program
   c. Followed by a certificate of program completion
   d. Limited to closure of each project

3. As the closing manager for a program that has been under way for five years in your company, you must ensure that all deliverables were completed and that program objectives and measurable program success criteria were met. You meet with the former program manager, the Governance Board, key stakeholders, and members of the core program team. To further confirm that all the work has been completed, you review the—

   a. Program work breakdown structure (PWBS)
   b. Program charter
   c. Benefits register
   d. Program management plan

4. You are a program manager, and one of your component projects is complete. You work with the project manager to ensure that all closure activities are finished. The project manager has numerous tasks to complete; at the program level, you need to—

   a. Review relevant contract documentation
   b. Confirm that the project's benefits have been delivered
   c. Assess the project's budget
   d. Confirm that project closure has occurred

5. You are in the closing phase of managing a major program in your company. Your program included 11 separate contracts and was a significant endeavor for your organization. Your Governance Board has asked your PMO to conduct an individual review to make sure all procurement closure activities are complete. It should focus on—

   a. Those contracts that were terminated for convenience or default
   b. The procurement management plan
   c. The contract management plan for each of the 11 contracts
   d. The procurement process for outstanding issues

6. You have been managing a program to deliver a new tractor that will use 75 percent less fuel. The program is ready to close, and activities then to sustain the benefits will be transitioned to the product support group. During this transition, you need to make sure—

   a. The operations group has been involved in the program as a key stakeholder
   b. Estimates of the cost to sustain the benefits are finalized
   c. Stakeholders have signed off on product acceptance criteria
   d. Component transition requests have been submitted

7. You establish a program support function to provide ongoing product support for the heating, ventilating, and air-conditioning (HVAC) program for the new class of amphibious warfare vehicles. Prior to transitioning your program's work to this group, you need to ensure—

   a. Successful, on-time product delivery
   b. The Governance Board is consulted
   c. That attention is paid to benefits sustainment
   d. That all documented benefits are realized as planned

8. Finally, it is time to close your program. You need to now execute the transition plan to the operations group in your company. When you are executing your transition plan you focus on—

   a. Ensuring the program has satisfied all requirements
   b. Managing the redeployment of all project resources
   c. Conducting reviews of your suppliers
   d. Archiving lessons learned

9. You work with numerous contractors and suppliers on your program. Your company considers two of the contractors to be valued partners; however, three of the contractors have not worked on any previous programs or projects for your company. Furthermore, one supplier and two contractors have worked with competitors, and one contractor uses a competitor as a supplier. In closing your program, you need to ensure—

   a. Each contractor has signed a nondisclosure agreement
   b. A final performance review is held with each contractor
   c. A decision is made to determine whether any of the three new contractors should be added to the qualified supplier list
   d. All deliverables are completed satisfactorily

10. You are the Business Change Manager on a mobile workforce initiative to decrease the costs associated with office space. As a result of this initiative, 2,000 employees now work in their homes, thereby saving the company millions per year in lease fees. Now that the culture change has been complete, you are working to close this program. You realize program closure activities are distinct from those of other phases of program management because closure activities—

    a. Do not require involvement with sellers or suppliers
    b. Occur at the end of the program life cycle
    c. Are handled by someone who is appointed as the closing manager
    d. Occur throughout the program

11. Assume it is time to prepare your final report to close your new product development program. This means you need to describe in it—

    a. Actual work performed
    b. Contractors to be added to the qualified supplier list
    c. Program documentation archive plan
    d. Knowledge transition

12. Resource Disposition is an important aspect of program closure so the resources can be used elsewhere in the organization. Releasing resources is handled by—

    a. The program manager
    b. The program sponsor
    c. PMO Director
    d. Program governance

13. Lessons learned can be reported in various ways. For consistency and quality, each program should adopt a standard approach. In the closing phase of the program, the program manager should—

    a. Address the advantages and disadvantages of the methods used to gather and report on lessons learned
    b. Share lessons learned with team members
    c. Survey the customer and the team for overall program satisfaction
    d. Report these lessons learned to the chief knowledge officer

14. You have been appointed closing manager for a program that has been under way for eight years. You have met with the program manager to talk about lessons learned. You have also met with the core program team members and reviewed the lessons learned that were documented by each of the six projects in this program. Your next step is to—

    a. Select the key lessons learned and archive them
    b. Add any additional lessons learned to the program's final report
    c. Index each project's records
    d. Assign metadata tags to the records so they can be easily located using a content management system

15. As program manager, you follow a detailed closure process that was developed by the enterprise program management office (EPMO). You have customized this procedure somewhat to fit the unique requirements of your program. Project C is now in its closing phase. This means it is your responsibility to—

    a. Conduct a performance review with the project team members
    b. Reallocate resources to other program components
    c. Perform a final performance review
    d. Update personnel records

16. You are a program manager for an aerospace company that is developing the C888 aircraft. Each of the component projects is scheduled to end at a different time. Each time a project closes to initiate closeout activities, it is necessary to—

    a. Obtain stakeholder support
    b. Ensure all project procurements are closed
    c. Meet with your team to discuss lessons learned before team members are released
    d. Ensure operations management is ready to handle sustainment activities

17. You are managing the development of a series of heating, ventilation, and air-conditioning (HVAC) products. Each product is being managed as a separate project. Because the products will be completed at different times, you have a product support group. Your team has also established a configuration management system as a subsystem of the overall program management information system (PMIS). Changes have been requested to the product that was delivered in Project A. These changes affect the product from Project B, which is in production. You focus on—

    a. Responding to customer complaints regarding the product already delivered from Project A
    b. Ensuring that support is properly scheduled for Projects A and B
    c. Ensuring that a policy of zero defects is implemented as part of the quality assurance and control activities
    d. Conducting a thorough audit and extensive testing of future products before they are delivered

18. Each project in your program, Program B, is developing a specific product. Together your program will have eight separate products once it is complete. You establish a product support group to provide ongoing support for all the products in your program. A critical success factor is to ensure that—

    a. Staff members are physically collocated with the project team
    b. Support is available on a 24/7 basis
    c. Support is properly scheduled when changes are made
    d. Knowledge transfer activities are performed

19. You are the program manager responsible for product development for your company's Class C vehicles. You have six projects in this program. After five years, the program is finally in the closing stage. It is time to begin program financial closure when—

    a. Benefits are delivered
    b. A financial closing statement has been prepared
    c. All contractors have been paid
    d. Budget allocation reconciliation is complete

20. A critical part of program management is managing the intellectual property that is created. One of your senior engineers left the company three weeks before your program was complete. A key scientist departed a year early. For program success you need to ensure that—

    a. Lessons learned are readily accessible
    b. Program staff are not able to join competing firms at any time
    c. The organization conducts exit interviews with anyone who leaves the program
    d. Knowledge assets are transferred into the organization's knowledge repository

Answer Sheet

1.	a	b	c	d
2.	a	b	c	d
3.	a	b	c	d
4.	a	b	c	d
5.	a	b	c	d
6.	a	b	c	d
7.	a	b	c	d
8.	a	b	c	d
9.	a	b	c	d
10.	a	b	c	d

11.	a	b	c	d
12.	a	b	c	d
13.	a	b	c	d
14.	a	b	c	d
15.	a	b	c	d
16.	a	b	c	d
17.	a	b	c	d
18.	a	b	c	d
19.	a	b	c	d
20.	a	b	c	d

Answer Key

1. a. An activity to be done as part of closing the program

   The activities in the Program Closure lead to transition of artifacts, benefits monitoring, and ongoing operations to other groups. One key activity, which is generally defined by contract, is to provide customer support to an operational support function to ensure that guidance and maintenance are available in case any issues arise, or any defects are detected after release.

   PMI®, *The Standard for Program Management*, 2013, 70, 88

2. b. Covered as you close the program

   Component Transition and Closure occurs as each component closes. All of its areas are reviewed to ensure benefits are delivered and the transition to other projects and sustaining areas is complete. Final component status is reviewed with the program sponsor and the Governance Board before authorizing formal closure. Closure activity occurs throughout the program.

   PMI®, *The Standard for Program Management*, 2013, 70

3. b. Program charter

   The program ends if its charter is fulfilled or conditions arise that bring the program to an early close. The charter is reviewed before the program is closed.

   PMI®, *The Standard for Program Management*, 2013, 88

4. b. Confirm that the project's benefits have been delivered

   Program component closure focuses on closure issues at the program level. It involves ensuring that closure has taken place at the project level, but it is not a substitute for normal project closure activities. The program manager is responsible for executing the transition or closeout of all program and component project plans.

   PMI®. *Program Management Professional (PgMP)® Examination Content Outline*, 2011, 11

5. d. The procurement process for outstanding issues

   Key activities are performed in Program Procurement Closure. They include ensuring each contract has been formally closed, all deliverables have been completed satisfactorily, all payments have been made, and to see if there are any outstanding contractual issues.

   PMI®, *The Standard for Program Management*, 2013, 91

6. b. Estimates of the cost to sustain the benefits are finalized

   As part of Program Financial Closure, estimates may be required to determine costs of sustaining the benefits of the program. While many of these costs may be captured in the benefit delivery phase as components are delivered, there may be some residual activities required to oversee the ongoing benefits.

   PMI®, *The Standard for Program Management*, 2013, 82

7. b. The Governance Board is consulted

   Prior to program transition the program manager should meet with the Governance Board to determine if the program has met its desired benefits, the transition work has been performed successfully, and there is a sustaining activity to oversee the benefits from the charter.

   PMI®, *The Standard for Program Management*, 2013, 70

8. d. Archiving lessons learned

   The program transition plan is executed, and the program and project plans are closed. During this process, administrative and PMIS program closure activities are performed, program documents are archived, lessons learned are documented, and the ongoing activities are transferred for sustainability.

   PMI®. *Program Management Professional (PgMP)® Examination Content Outline*, 2011, 11

9. d. All deliverables are completed satisfactorily

   In Program Procurement Closure, each contract must be formally closed after confirming all deliverables have been satisfactorily completed, all payments have been made, and there are no outstanding issues.

   PMI®, *The Standard for Program Management*, 2013, 90

10. a. Occur throughout the program

Program closure activities do not occur only at the end of a program; rather, they occur throughout the program, each time a project is completed. All components must be completed, and all contracts must be closed before the program closes.

PMI®, *The Standard for Program Management*, 2013, 89

11. c. Program documentation archive plan

The program's final report contains information to be applied to future programs and projects and information senior management requires for corporate governance. Among other things, it should include a program documentation archive plan.

PMI®, *The Standard for Program Management*, 2013, 88

12. d. Program governance

Efficient and appropriate release of resources is essential. At the program level, program governance handles resource releases as part of a number of activities leading to program closure approval.

PMI®, *The Standard for Program Management*, 2013, 70, 88–89

13. b. Share lessons learned with team members

Lessons learned are a key part of Knowledge Transition in program closure. As part of this activity, the program manager assesses overall performance and shares lessons learned with team members.

PMI®, *The Standard for Program Management*, 2013, 88

14. b. Add any additional lessons learned to the program's final report

Upon program completion, a meeting should be held with the team to discuss lessons learned. If there are any others than the ones the program manager identified, they should be added to the program's final report.

PMI®, *The Standard for Program Management*, 2013, 88

15. b. Reallocate resources to other program components

At the program level, resources that become available from one project may be reallocated to other components that are active in the program or to another program in the organization.

PMI®, *The Standard for Program Management*, 2013, 89

16. a. Obtain stakeholder support

    Before beginning to close the program or any components in it, stakeholder support to initiate the closing activities is required to ensure the stakeholders are satisfied that the program has successfully delivered its benefits.

    PMI®. *Program Management Professional (PgMP)® Examination Content Outline*, 2011, 11

17. b. Ensuring that support is properly scheduled for Projects A and B

    After a product is deployed, any support must be scheduled to avoid interruption to the customers' use of the item to the greatest extent practicable. Benefit sustainment may be handled through operations, maintenance, new projects, or other efforts.

    PMI®, *The Standard for Program Management*, 2013, 88

18. d. Knowledge transfer activities are performed

    As benefits are transitioned to other organizations for sustainment, it is necessary to include knowledge transfer activities to support ongoing benefit sustainment. This is handled by providing the new supporting organization with documentation, training, or materials,

    PMI®, *The Standard for Program Management*, 2013, 88

19. a. Benefits are delivered

    Program financial closure begins when sustainment budgets are developed, benefits are delivered, and sustainment has started.

    PMI®, *The Standard for Program Management*, 2013, 82

20. a. Lessons learned are readily accessible

    Lessons learned should be identified and documented throughout the program management processes. As people leave and when the program closes, lessons learned should be regularly accessible to existing and future programs to avoid any pitfalls and for continuous learning.

    PMI®, *The Standard for Program Management*, 2013, 88

Benefits Management

Study Hints

Benefits management is the third domain in program management according to the *Examination Content Outline.* These questions constitute 11%, or 19 questions, on the PgMP® exam. Since programs are established in order to obtain greater benefits than if the projects and other work that comprise them were managed in a standalone fashion, it is essential to focus on benefits management from the time the program was set forward in its business case, as a candidate to be in the organization's portfolio, until the program is officially closed, and the realized benefits then are transferred to others.

This area, therefore, focuses on the importance of the benefits realization plan and the criteria that are used to determine whether the benefits in the plan actually are met. This plan requires detailed and ongoing communications with stakeholders, especially if there are changes to the plan during the life of the program. Any changes, especially when benefits are realized as described in the plan or if they need to be modified, must be communicated to stakeholders, especially to the Governance Board and to the sponsor.

Additionally, a benefits transition plan and a benefits sustainment plan are needed. This means that once the program ends, its benefits then are transitioned to customers, end users, or to a product or an operations support group. These stakeholders require involvement in the program and a detailed understanding of the benefits of the program so they are able to sustain them once a project in the program is complete as well as the entire program.

Metrics then must be monitored to make sure the benefits are realized as stated in the plan and are communicated to stakeholders often in terms of a benefits realization report. Some benefits will be tangible and easily quantifiable, while others will be intangible and difficult to quantify but may be of equal or greater importance depending on the specific program. These benefits also must be continually reviewed to make sure the program remains in alignment with the organization's overall strategic objectives.

As risks (both threats and opportunities) and issues arise, or as new projects are added, and others are completed, the benefits realization plan requires review and update to see if changes are required.

Benefits management, therefore, is ongoing throughout the life of the program, and its life cycle also requires review. The benefits domain in *The Standard for Program Management—Third Edition* (2013) discusses these items in greater detail and is titled Program Benefits Management. It describes the program life cycle and the relationship to a benefits management life cycle and shows the relationship in Figure 4-1. It also describes the importance of maintaining a benefits register during the program and its suggested contents. Figure 4-2 explains cost and benefit profiles across the generic program life cycle. The relationship between benefits management and the roadmap is explained along with program benefits and governance. Study this section of the Standard thoroughly.

Major Topics

The Importance of Benefits Management to Program Management

- Major activities
- Types of benefits
- Defining and delivering benefits

Program Life Cycle and Benefits Management

- Benefits Identification
  - Identify and qualify business benefits
  - Activities in benefits identification
  - The business case and benefits identification
  - Benefit register
  - Purpose
  - Contents
- Benefits Analysis and Planning
  - Purpose
  - Major activities
  - Quantifying incremental delivery of benefits
  - Cost and benefit profiles across the life cycle
  - Benefits and program governance
  - Benefits realization plan
  - Purpose
  - Contents
  - Measurement criteria
  - Communications to stakeholders
  - Benefits and the program roadmap
  - Updating the benefits register
- Benefits Delivery
  - Purpose
  - Major activities
  - Reports and metrics
  - Methods to monitor the metrics
  - Benefits and program components
  - Benefit realization criteria
  - Achieving strategic objectives
  - Analyzing and updating the benefits realization plan
  - Benefits and governance
  - Strategic alignment
  - Value delivery

- Benefits Transition
  - Purpose
  - Major activities
  - Benefits transition planning
  - Receivers of program benefits
- Benefits Sustainment
  - Purpose
  - Major activities
  - Process
  - Metrics
  - Tools
  - Planning ongoing sustainment
  - Business case
  - Analyzing and updating the sustainment plan

Practice Questions

1. Assume you are leading a consortium of four other firms. This is the second time your consortium has worked for this specific client, and it seems that the interpersonal relationships between the people on your team and the client's team are positive, and there is trust between the two groups. You hope for future business with this consortium and this client once your program is complete. Your success is measured primarily according to—
   a. Payback period
   b. Sustainment of benefits
   c. Products delivered according to specification
   d. Products delivered on time and without the need for additional funding

2. As you lead this consortium, XYZ, in its program work for company DEF, you have a large team and a large number of stakeholders. Since the consortium is of interest to the senior executives of all four firms, you and your core team seem to be in constant meetings and briefings with the executives and submitting reports to them, not to mention the meetings and briefings with the points of contact in company DEF. The person who is ultimately responsible for delivering the program benefits is—
   a. The program director
   b. Your Chief Executive Officer, since your firm leads the consortium
   c. The consortium program manager
   d. The program sponsor

3. Working on the next generation of computing since Cloud computing, as the program manager for the G6 program, you believe you have a major innovative, new development product. You are developing this new product for a client, firm MNO, and now you are at a point in your program where one of the projects in this G6 program is complete. You are delivering it to the MNO client representative, who wants to measure now how this benefit has helped MNO. Measuring benefits should focus on—
   a. The degree to which the benefit has been adopted and used by its intended recipients
   b. The level of customer satisfaction achieved, as measured by specific surveys
   c. The ability of benefits to translate into value
   d. The morale of the individual employees who are responsible for executing the new process or operation

4. In your work on the G6 program, which was set up with eight separate projects, since each project in it has inter-relationships with other projects especially in terms of the benefits to be delivered, you decided one best practice to follow was to track the benefits described in your benefit realization plan in a benefit register and make this register visible not only to your entire team but also to your client, firm MNO. In terms of the program benefit management life cycle, this register ends when—
   a. Benefits are delivered incrementally
   b. Benefits are transferred to product support
   c. Benefits planning is completed
   d. The program is terminated

5. Assume you prepared a benefits register for use on your program. You decide to review it with your key stakeholders to—
   a. Obtain buy in to begin developing the benefits realization plan
   b. Determine if benefit achievement is occurring within key parameters
   c. Define and approve key performance indicators
   d. Determine how best to transition benefits to operations

6. Working on your personal helicopter program for company BCD, one of your first tasks as the program manager was to build on the benefits identified and recorded in the benefit register and prepare a benefits realization plan. Now, you are measuring how each benefit is realized, which means you are working in—
   a. Benefits management
   b. Executing
   c. Monitoring and controlling
   d. Benefits delivery

7. Finally, your program, G6, which has taken the concept of Cloud computing to the next level, and your eight separate projects as well as some ongoing work, is complete. As program G6 is closed, now benefit management is focusing on a number of key initiatives, including—
   a. Reporting planned versus actual benefits at the current point in time
   b. Ensuring that the benefits delivered are in line with the original business case
   c. Ensuring stakeholder agreement on the factors contributing to the benefits
   d. Verifying the program has met or exceeded benefit realization criteria

8. Your Governance Board decided to conduct a benefits review on your internal program. During such a review, it is important to analyze—

   a. Reasons for any deviation in the proposed benefits and the ones that were realized
   b. How new benefits affect the flow of operations
   c. The effectiveness of the transition plan
   d. Usefulness of the benefit reports to stakeholders

9. You are the Business Change Manager on a mobile workforce initiative to decrease the costs associated with office space. As a result of this initiative, 2,000 employees now work in their homes, thereby saving the company millions per year in lease fees. Assume you are working to transition the benefits of your program. A key activity is to—

   a. Dispose resources
   b. Plan for behavioral changes necessary for the at home employees
   c. Monitor performance to evaluate productivity improvements
   d. Monitor the need for logistical support for the at home employees

10. You have been appointed program manager for Program XYZ. You have assembled your team and have begun work on your benefits realization plan. The person who wrote the plan delivered it to you. After you read it, you told the team member that the plan was missing a key component. It did not describe—

    a. How the potential impact of any planned program change affects the benefits outcome
    b. A method to identify interdependencies of benefits within program components
    c. A way to link the outputs to the planned program outcomes
    d. An assessment of the value and organizational impact of the program

11. Assume you are the program manager for the next generation of parachutes for your Department of the Army. Each of the new parachutes must have a reliability rating of 99.99%, and certain types of parachutes will be deployed in certain conditions given climate and terrain. In total, your program has five projects; all work is to be done in three years. As you regularly report on the status of the benefits of this program, you must measure the benefits that have accrued to date and communicate the information to your program sponsor and the program Governance Board. The metrics and procedures you are using for this reporting are stated in—
    a. Program charter
    b. Benefits realization plan
    c. Program management plan
    d. Key performance indicators

12. Assume your government is in serious financial difficulty and may even default on some government issued funds. However, you are managing a program to cut the spending of the National Park Service in your Department of Interior by 50%. You and your team have seven projects in your program. Finally, you have completed this program and have made the spending cuts, which were approved by the Secretary of the Interior. Now that the program is closed, benefits sustainment focuses on a number of key initiatives including—
    a. Facilitating the ongoing realization of benefits
    b. Ensuring that the benefits delivered are in line with the business case
    c. Reviewing the operational and program process documentation for needed updates
    d. Ensuring the capabilities provided continue

13. Working in your processed cheese company, project management has been successfully introduced over the past seven years. A member of your PMO recently attained her PgMP®. She has recommended that a new initiative to modernize the process cheese factory be managed as a program because it is so complex and will have a number of projects associated with it that have interdependencies. She needs to—
    a. Follow a repeatable process
    b. Identify and qualify benefits
    c. Quantify benefits in the business case
    d. Focuses first on benefits realization

14. Because a program is responsible for delivering benefits to the organization, the program manager, members of the program team, project managers and team members, and other program stakeholders all have key roles and responsibilities in benefits management. These roles are set forth in the—

    a. Benefits register
    b. Benefits realization plan
    c. Benefits management plan
    d. Responsibility assignment matrix

15. As the manager of a new program to develop the next-generation heating, ventilation, and air-conditioning (HVAC) system, you have three projects in your program, and it is only the first year. You expect the program to last at least three years, and you are hopeful you will have a PMO for support. You also are sure more projects will be added as the program ensues. Therefore, you establish a process to monitor your program benefits. Following the standard benefits management life cycle, you develop this process during the—

    a. Benefits identification
    b. Benefits analysis and planning
    c. Benefits realization
    d. Benefits delivery

16. As you move to establish program management in your processed cheese company, you are facing a lot of questions especially from project managers and the other members of the PMO since this is a culture change from the organization. A first step is to—

    a. Define program critical success factors
    b. Meet with key stakeholders
    c. Establish processes for benefits realization
    d. Set up individual project deliverables to ensure that they align with organizational objectives

17. Assume you have just completed a program to design and develop a new Park for your City of 10,000 people. The purpose was to provide benefits to the residents of all ages. You are working to transition the benefits from your program to your City. It Is important to recognize as you do so that these activities are—

    a. One part of program transition
    b. Updated in the program roadmap
    c. Ones that ensure benefit sustainment
    d. Monitored to ensure the benefits provided are those expected

18. You are the program manager for a six-year program that is in its second year. You are in the early phases and are working to identify your benefits. A best practice is to prepare a benefits register using the—

    a. Identified and qualified benefits
    b. Business case
    c. Program's key performance indicators
    d. Target dates in the roadmap for benefit achievement

19. Your company is a leader in the pharmaceutical industry. It has received approval from the Food and Drug Administration (FDA) for a new drug that will cure all glaucoma conditions. Although the demand for this product is high, the company has many other drugs to manufacture. You are managing a program to upgrade the manufacturing process. Because you recognize the potential benefits associated with this new product, as the program manager, you should regularly monitor the—

    a. Organizational environment
    b. Benefits realization plan
    c. Benefits register
    d. Extent to which each benefit is achieved prior to program closure

20. You have worked hard on your four year program. As it is about to close you want to execute your sustainment plan. It is prepared—

    a. During the performance of the program
    b. As a subsidiary plan to the program management plan
    c. As part of the benefit realization plan
    d. As an activity in benefit transition

Answer Sheet

1.	a	b	c	d	11.	a	b	c	d
2.	a	b	c	d	12.	a	b	c	d
3.	a	b	c	d	13.	a	b	c	d
4.	a	b	c	d	14.	a	b	c	d
5.	a	b	c	d	15.	a	b	c	d
6.	a	b	c	d	16.	a	b	c	d
7.	a	b	c	d	17.	a	b	c	d
8.	a	b	c	d	18.	a	b	c	d
9.	a	b	c	d	19.	a	b	c	d
10.	a	b	c	d	20.	a	b	c	d

Answer Key

1. b. Sustainment of benefits

   While all are good measures of success, programs are established in order to obtain greater benefits than if the projects that comprise them were managed in a standalone fashion. The benefits are stated in the benefits realization plan, and success is measured in terms of the continued realization of benefits once the program is complete.

   PMI®. *Program Management Professional* (PgMP)® *Examination Content Outline*, April 2011, 13

   PMI®, *The Standard for Program Management*, 2013, 34

2. d. The program sponsor

   The program sponsor is the group or person who champions the program initiative and is responsible for providing resources and for the ultimate delivery of program benefits.

   PMI®, *The Standard for Program Management*, 2013, 62

3. c. The ability of benefits to translate into value

   Value delivery is essential in benefits delivery. Value delivery focuses on ensuring the program delivers the benefits, and they translate into value. There may be only a small window of opportunity to accomplish the realization of a planned benefit, and the program manager, Governance Board members, and other stakeholders need to ensure if this window of opportunity can be met successfully.

   PMI®, *The Standard for Program Management*, 2013, 41

4. d. The program is terminated

   A program may be terminated without transition to operations especially if the charter has been fulfilled, and operations is not a consideration in realizing benefits, or if the program is no longer of value to the organization. Each component and the program as a whole must still be viable.

   PMI®, *The Standard for Program Management*, 2013, 40, 42

5. c. Define and approve key performance indicators

   The benefits register is updated during benefits analysis and planning. It is reviewed with appropriate stakeholders to define and approve key performance indicators and other measures to monitor program performance.

   PMI®, *The Standard for Program Management*, 2013, 39

6. d. Benefits delivery

   In Benefits Delivery, the emphasis is to ensure the program delivers the expected benefits as stated in the benefits realization plan. It also involves preparing a defined set of reports or metrics and providing them to stakeholders to monitor the program and its actions to ensure successful benefits delivery.

   PMI®, *The Standard for Program Management*, 2013, 39–40

7. d. Verifying the program has met or exceeded benefit realization criteria

   During Benefits Transition, the benefits are transitioned to operational areas and can be sustained once they are transferred. A key activity is to verify that the integration, transition, and closure of the program has met or exceeded the benefit realization criteria established to achieve the program's strategic objectives.

   PMI®, *The Standard for Program Management*, 2013, 41

8. b. How new benefits affect the flow of operations

   For an internal program, the benefits realization process measures how new benefits affect the flow of operations in the organization. The emphasis is to review how the change is introduced and how negative impacts and the potential disruptiveness of introducing the change may be minimized.

   PMI®, *The Standard for Program Management*, 2013, 41

9. a. Dispose resources

   A key activity of the Benefits Transition is to dispose all related resources since the program is closed and integrated into other elements.

   PMI®, *The Standard for Program Management*, 2013, 42

10. c. A way to link the outputs to the planned program outcomes

    There are a number of key components in the benefits realization plan, which is prepared in Benefit Realization Plan. One is the need to link the component project outputs to the planned program outcomes as part of achieving the program's planned benefits.

    PMI®, *The Standard for Program Management*, 2013, 38–39

11. b. Benefits realization plan

    The benefits realization plan is drafted early and maintained throughout all phases of the program. Among other things, this plan defines the metrics including key performance indicators and the process to use to measure benefits.

    PMI®, *The Standard for Program Management*, 2013, 39

12. d. Ensuring the capabilities provided continue

    A number of activities are performed during Benefit Sustainment. One is to implement the required changes to ensure the capabilities provided by the program continue as it is closed and as its resources are returned to the organization.

    PMI®, *The Standard for Program Management*, 2013, 43

13. b. Identify and qualify benefits

    The purpose of Benefit Identification is to analyze available information about organizational and business benefits, internal and external influences, and program drivers. This is done in order to identify and qualify the benefits the program stakeholders expect to realize from the program.

    PMI®, *The Standard for Program Management*, 2013, 35

14. b. Benefits realization plan

    A key component of the benefits realization plan is a description of roles and responsibilities for benefits management.

    PMI®, *The Standard for Program Management*, 2013, 39

15. d. Benefits delivery

    A process for benefits monitoring is established in benefits delivery. This includes monitoring components, maintaining the benefits register, and reporting benefits.

    PMI®, *The Standard for Program Management*, 2013, 35

16. a. Define program critical success factors

    In Benefit Identification, the program manager uses the program mandate and the business step. A key, and usually the first, activity is to define the program's objectives and its critical success factors.

    PMI®, *The Standard for Program Management*, 2013, 35–36

17. a. One part of program transition

    Benefits transition planning is extremely important, however, they are only one part of the complete transition process.

    PMI®, *The Standard for Program Management*, 2013, 41

18. b. Business case

    The benefits register is developed based on the business case, strategic plan, and other relevant program objectives.

    PMI®, *The Standard for Program Management*, 2013, 36

19. a. Organizational environment

    A major activity in Benefits Delivery is to monitor the organizational environment, considering both internal and external factors. This is done to ensure the program remains aligned with the organization's strategic objectives.

    PMI®, *The Standard for Program Management*, 2013, 39

20. a. During the performance of the program

    Ongoing sustainment of the program cannot wait until the program closes. Sustainment of program benefits is planned by the program manager and component managers during the performance of the program.

    PMI®, *The Standard for Program Management*, 2013, 43

Stakeholder Management

Study Hints

The Stakeholder Management questions on the PgMP® certification exam, which constitute 16% of the exam, or 27 questions, focus on the importance of stakeholder identification, management, and engagement throughout the program's life cycle and even when the program is first being proposed. They also emphasize the link between stakeholders and effective communications, since communications is the key competency for program managers, and so much of the program manager's time is spent in communications given the large and diverse numbers of stakeholders on programs. Therefore, other questions focus on communications planning and distributing information to stakeholders in the format needed, at the desired frequency, and with the desired level of detail.

Throughout the program, stakeholders will have different levels of influence and interest in the program at different phases of the life cycle. A stakeholder analysis, therefore, is essential and is ongoing. The program manager and his or her core them must work diligently with some stakeholders, who may not be program supporters, to gain their confidence and turn them into advocates for the program. A stakeholder matrix is a useful tool to prepare and maintain.

Stakeholder engagement is essential for program success and is a way to generate and maintain program visibility. As a result, defining communications needs for different types of stakeholders and providing it as required also promotes their support for the program.

While the *Examination Content Outline* titles this domain as Stakeholder Management, *The Standard for Program Management*—Third Edition (2013) calls the domain Stakeholder Engagement recognizing that stakeholders cannot be managed but instead only stakeholder expectations can be managed. This domain in the Standard has three key activities: Program Stakeholder Identification, Stakeholder Engagement Planning, and Stakeholder Engagement. From the Standard, in the Supporting Processes, Program Communication

Management is another area of focus in terms of Communications Planning and Information Distribution.

Following is a list of the major topics covered in Stakeholder Management. Use this list to focus your study efforts on the areas that are the most likely to appear on the exam.

Major Topics

Importance of Stakeholder Management

- Definition of a stakeholder
- Types of stakeholders—internal and external
- Customer engagement management
- Bridging the gap between the "as is" to the "to be" state
- Necessity in terms of organizational change

Program Stakeholder Identification

- Identifying stakeholders
- Types of stakeholders
- Stakeholder register
- Stakeholder matrix
- Stakeholder analysis
- Prioritized list of stakeholders

Stakeholder Engagement Planning

- Collecting information about stakeholders
- Stakeholder engagement plan
- Negotiating stakeholder support
- Metrics to measure performance of stakeholder engagement activities
- Guidelines for components

Stakeholder Engagement

- Ensuring stakeholders are adequately and appropriately engaged
- Generating and maintaining visibility of the program
- Confirming stakeholder support
- Evaluating risks identified by stakeholders
- Developing and fostering stakeholder relationships
- Capturing issues and information
- Using communication, negotiating, and conflict resolution skills
- Using an issue log
- Prioritization mechanisms
- Addressing issues and concerns
- Stakeholder metrics

Program Communications Management

- Differences from project communications management
- Communications skills
- Influencing skills

Communications Planning

- Determine stakeholder information and communication needs
- Define communications requirements
- Cultural and language differences
- Working with virtual teams
- Communication methods
- Program communications plan

Information Distribution

- Providing stakeholders with timely and accurate information
- Information channels
- Status information
- Notification of change requests
- Budget information—internal and external
- Government and regulatory filings
- Public announcements and press releases
- Media information and benefit updates
- Types of communications methods

Communication Considerations

- Communication and presentation skills
- Defined and documented strategy for communications requirements

Information Gathering and Retrieval Systems

- Different media
- Using data bases
- Storage and retrieval systems

Information Distribution Methods

- Communicating required information to stakeholders in a timely way
- Face-to-face meetings
- Electronic communications and conferencing tools
- Electronic program management tools

- Social media
- Informal communications
- Keeping information in the program's control

Lessons Learned Data Base

- Acquiring lessons learned
- Using lessons learned to develop the communications management plan
- Updating lessons learned
- PMIS
- Data archiving and retrieval instructions

Program Performance Reporting

- Providing information on resource use to deliver benefits
- Communication as a two-way flow
- Using information distribution

Practice Questions

1. As the program manager to develop a new source of energy that can be used in the northern and southern hemispheres when solar power is not readily available, you have a large number of stakeholders, both internal and external. You also are working with a virtual team, and many team members represent different cultures. You recognize since you are the program manager the importance of keeping all of your stakeholders informed in a timely manner by distributing various types of information. One piece of information that stakeholders need but that is often overlooked by program managers is a—

   a. Receipt of proposals
   b. Notification of responses to change requests
   c. List of preventive actions
   d. Record of training

2. You are working on a complex five-year program that has a minimum of four projects under way at any given time. A major scope change to Project L has resulted in a need to rebaseline its schedule. Consequently, because of dependencies with Project L, Project D also had to revise its schedule. You have informed your Governance Board and key stakeholders about the revisions. Some stakeholders have asked questions regarding the rebaselining. Your next step is to—

   a. Capture and publish questions and answers
   b. Ask the project managers to meet with their key stakeholders
   c. Hold meetings with key stakeholder groups to listen to their concerns an answer questions
   d. Follow your defined communications strategy

3. The president of your company has selected you to be the head of all eLearning and has asked that you launch a program to develop new media for delivering your company's content. The program has a number of stakeholders, some of whom are supportive and some of whom are skeptical, and you anticipate many debates concerning the program's objectives. As the program manager, you recognize that you need to rely on—

   a. Leadership skills
   b. Conflict resolution skills
   c. Environmental awareness skills
   d. Diplomatic skills

4. As program manager for all eLearning in your company, BBB, you are launching your program to develop new media for delivering your company's course content. You have a diverse group of stakeholders, and your program has active involvement by BBB's Chief Executive Officer. As the program manager, you must ensure the performance data on your eLearning program are consolidated and routed to the intended recipients to provide a clear picture of overall program performance and especially to show how resources, which already are constrained in BBB, are being used effectively. This is done through—
   a. Targeted communications messaging
   b. Information distribution
   c. Program performance and status reports prepared in reporting program performance
   d. Stakeholder engagement as identified in the stakeholder management strategy

5. As the program manager to develop a new source of energy that can be used in the northern and southern hemispheres when solar power is not readily available, you have a large number of stakeholders, both internal and external. You also are working with a virtual team, and many team members represent different cultures. You have eight projects so far in your program and are in the planning phase. This means in regard to project and program communications with your stakeholders you should be—
   a. Determining who needs to be receiving the communications and when
   b. Distributing communications messages to stakeholders
   c. Implementing the feedback loops developed earlier in the program
   d. Building your communications infrastructure

6. On your program, you have identified over 50 internal and external stakeholders, and have three projects in your program. You are providing regular updates on the status and specific requirements of your program to these stakeholders. A key focus in performance reporting is information on—
   a. Cost and schedule status
   b. Use of resources to deliver program benefits
   c. Issues to be discussed at program Governance Board meetings for decisions to move to the next phase
   d. Activities to determine whether specific work results have been completed

7. Meeting stakeholder expectations is vital to program success; therefore, participation of stakeholders must be monitored to ensure that their expectations are met. You are managing a large program with diverse stakeholder groups. On this program, you have found that you often need to—

   a. Meet one-on-one with each of the 200 stakeholders on the program
   b. Facilitate negotiation sessions between stakeholders
   c. Have your enterprise program management office (EPMO) take over responsibility for stakeholder expectations management
   d. Use your stakeholder analysis chart as a key tool and technique to assist in managing expectations

8. You have been managing a complex and major program in your company, BBB. Your program has 11 separate contracts and also two projects using in-house resources. Your team is a virtual, and because of budget constraints, you could not have a face-to-face meeting. Because of the large number of stakeholders to best address the urgency of their issues, you decide to—

   a. Hold a focus group
   b. Set up a prioritization mechanism
   c. Conduct an impact analysis
   d. Determine the frequency and rate of communications on the program

9. You are now conducting a phase-gate review with your Governance Board to determine if you can close the program. You and two of the Board members, who are not in the CEO's inner circle, are having a disagreement as to whether the phase has been completed successfully, and your program can now advance to the closing process. One way this can be determined is to—

   a. Take a vote of the members of the program board
   b. Compare performance to date against the exit criteria for the phase
   c. Try to reach consensus among all stakeholders
   d. Use fact-based decision making

10. In the most recent program performance meeting as part of the program closeout phase, you reported that the earned value data were favorable, that all performance metrics were in line with stated criteria, and that stakeholder requirements were met. Yet several stakeholders reported that the program fell somewhat short of their expectations. You assert that the program is successful because it has met all objective criteria. Your assessment is—

   a. Incorrect. Expectations are as important as requirements.
   b. Incorrect. Although expectations should be considered, they are not as important as requirements.
   c. Correct. There is no difference between expectations and requirements.
   d. Correct. The stakeholders should have expressed their expectations as requirements during the requirements-gathering phase.

11. Recently, your City has been experiencing numerous power outages because of excessive heavy rainfall and numerous hurricanes. Many residents have purchased gas generators, but they tend to not last long enough so people are also purchasing generators that use propane. Your propane company has decided that it should set up a program that would be put in place to use natural gas instead. You are the manager for this program. You also have a large number of interested stakeholders, and they are monitoring your progress to see if this new natural gas approach will be ready before the next hurricane season. Your goal is to—

   a. Assess the degree to which the program satisfies needs and benefits
   b. Set clear stakeholder engagement goals
   c. Work to turn stakeholders who are negative about the program to be positive or at least neutral to it
   d. Communicate actively to your stakeholders as to your progress and your program's benefits

12. You are the program manager on a highly controversial e-mail retention program for your company, AEI. More than 75 percent of the people in AEI are opposed to the program because they realize all of their e-mail messages will be archived. AEI management has informed everyone someone will review each e-mail to make sure it pertains to company business and is not a personal one. All e-mails are to be written in a professional way and must be ethical. You now have many conflicts as you and your team execute the five projects in your program. This program represents a major culture change for AEI as in the past it was common to discuss anything with anyone. Generally accepted methods of organizational change management are required for this program, and the person in charge of this change is—

    a. The program director
    b. The program sponsor
    c. The program Governance Board
    d. You, the program manager

13. As a program manager, you recognize the importance of stakeholder engagement. To support your efforts, especially with key stakeholders whose displeasure might hinder the program's success, you prepare a stakeholder engagement plan You know that stakeholders must see the benefits of the program. Therefore, you need to have strong skills in—

    a. Strategic planning
    b. Leadership
    c. Enterprise resource management
    d. Customer relationship management

14. Each program has stakeholders. At the time you were appointed as program manager, you and your core team immediately identified 50 key stakeholders. Now the number of stakeholders has increased according to your stakeholder analysis to 88. You seem to feel as if all you do all day is communicate with stakeholders and have meetings with groups of them. As part of stakeholder engagement planning, you need to identify how the program will affect stakeholders in areas such as—

    a. The organization's culture
    b. Management of operations
    c. Corporate governance
    d. Legal policies, standards, and regulations

15. When you worked as a project manager, you learned that most project managers spend about 90 percent of their time in communications. Now as a program manager you know you are spending almost 100% of your time in communications. It seems to never end. You have set presentations now for different groups of stakeholders but then you must continually update them to show progress, and new stakeholders seem to become interested in your progress as the program ensues. Communication planning in program management therefore focuses on—
    a. Reacting to stakeholder concerns
    b. Taking corrective actions in response to program issues
    c. Determining the information and communications needs of each stakeholder
    d. Identifying suitable technologies for distributing program information

16. You are the program manager responsible for implementing salesmagic.com, a highly complex but powerful tool for customer relationship management. You and your team have spent three days identifying the metrics against which you will measure stakeholder engagement activities. Your next step is to—
    a. Meet with key stakeholders to gain agreement
    b. Include the metrics in the stakeholder register
    c. Test the effectiveness of the metrics through a focus group
    d. Include the metrics in the stakeholder engagement plan

17. You are a program manager for a city transit authority. Your program has a number of projects under way to upgrade the infrastructure to current technologies and to implement a process improvement program. The transit authority's chief financial officer (CFO) has left to assume a position in a different city, and a new person has been appointed CFO. You should—
    a. Update your stakeholder inventory
    b. Appoint one of your core team members to interact with the new CFO
    c. Meet with the new CFO to explain the importance of the program
    d. Update the stakeholder register

18. You are a program manager for a new line of children's toys called The Destroyer. Your stakeholders—especially the members of your program Governance Board—have requested an analysis of any opportunities that can be leveraged as you collect and analyze performance on your program. Also, you want to identify any adverse impacts that must be corrected. After you prepare this information and consolidate it, you—

    a. Meet with your key stakeholders to inform them of your program's progress according to their specific areas of interest
    b. Make the information available through the information distribution activity
    c. Follow the process outlined in your communications management plan
    d. Contact your Governance Board about any adverse trends that require immediate action to meet the required delivery date

19. Stakeholders play a critical role in the success of a program or project. As program manager for development of a next-generation motorcycle to be available in 2020, you know it is a best practice to determine a strategy to engage stakeholders. This should be done—

    a. During overall program planning
    b. While the business case for the program is made
    c. As the program is being initiated
    d. After the projects and other ongoing components of the program are determined

20. You are managing a program under contract with a major motion picture studio. The Statement of Work noted that you needed to interface with ten different groups of people within the studio. After your company, KSI, won this contract, you and your team recognized the importance of performing a detailed stakeholder analysis based on the Statement of Work. To conduct such an analysis, you plan to hold interviews, use focus groups, and perhaps conduct a survey. This approach enables you to—

    a. Develop a stakeholder communications strategy
    b. Prioritize stakeholders in terms of their ability to influence the program
    c. Develop a stakeholder register
    d. Identify stakeholders' attitudes toward the program

Answer Sheet

1.	a	b	c	d	11.	a	b	c	d
2.	a	b	c	d	12.	a	b	c	d
3.	a	b	c	d	13.	a	b	c	d
4.	a	b	c	d	14.	a	b	c	d
5.	a	b	c	d	15.	a	b	c	d
6.	a	b	c	d	16.	a	b	c	d
7.	a	b	c	d	17.	a	b	c	d
8.	a	b	c	d	18.	a	b	c	d
9.	a	b	c	d	19.	a	b	c	d
10.	a	b	c	d	20.	a	b	c	d

Answer Key

1. c. Notification of responses to change requests

   Distributed Information includes notifications of change requests to the program and project teams of the corresponding responses to those requests.

   PMI®, *The Standard for Program Management*, 2013, 75

2. a. Capture and publish questions and answers

   It is important to engage and interact with stakeholders. As some stakeholders are curious about the program and ask questions, a best practice to follow is to capture the questions and answers to them and publish them in a way that will allow multiple stakeholders to benefit from the exchange.

   PMI®, *The Standard for Program Management*, 2013, 49

3. b. Conflict resolution skills

   In Stakeholder Engagement, the program manager requires skills in conflict resolution as different stakeholder groups will have different interests and influence about the program. The program manager must define how conflicts will be managed among stakeholders and should include an escalation path to ensure that stalemates do not occur.

   PMI®, *The Standard for Program Management*, 2013, 50

4. b. Information distribution

   The purpose of information distribution is to convey information to program stakeholders to provide them with needed status and deliverable information. It provides timely and accurate information to stakeholders in useful formats.

   PMI®, *The Standard for Program Management*, 2013, 74–75

5. a. Determining who needs to be receiving the communications and when

   As part of communications planning, determining the information and communications needs of stakeholders is based on who need what information, when it is needed, how they will receive it, and who will provide the information to the stakeholders.

   PMI®, *The Standard for Program Management*, 2013, 74

6. b. Use of resources to deliver program benefits

   In Program Performance Reporting the purpose is to consolidating performance data to provide information to program stakeholders about the use of resources to deliver program benefits. It provides information on overall program performance.

   PMI®, *The Standard for Program Management*, 2013, 77

7. b. Facilitate negotiation sessions between stakeholders

   Negotiation skills are necessary in Stakeholder Engagement. These skills can help diffuse any stakeholder opposition to the program and its stated benefits. On large programs, the program manager may need to facilitate negotiation sessions among stakeholder groups when expectations conflict.

   PMI®, *The Standard for Program Management*, 2013, 50

8. c. Conduct an impact analysis

   Stakeholder issues and concerns will address different aspects of the program. Impact analysis techniques are useful to understand the urgency and probability of stakeholder issues and to determine whether they will be risks to the program.

   PMI®, *The Standard for Program Management*, 2013, 50

9. d. Use fact-based decision making

   It is always preferable to have an objective measure of success as opposed to relying on peoples' opinions if at all possible. Fact-based decision making is required to ensure that all program work is complete and that the intended benefits are being realized in order to make decisions on programs when stakeholders have conflicting opinions.

   Levin, Ginger and Ward, J. LeRoy. 2011. *Program Complexity A Competency Model* Boca Raton, FL: CRC Press, 85

10. a. Incorrect. Expectations are as important as requirements.

    Successful program managers are as concerned with meeting stakeholders' expectations as they are with meeting their requirements.

    PMI®, *PgMP® Examination Content Outline*, 2011, 14

11. b. Set clear stakeholder engagement goals

    Successful program managers recognize the importance of stakeholder engagement. They use strong leadership skills to set clear stakeholder engagement goals for the program to address the changes that will occur on the program.

    PMI®, *The Standard for Program Management*, 2013, 46

12. d. You, the program manager

    Program managers are the champion for change in the organization. Each program represents some type of change, and the program manager must work with those stakeholders to overcome their resistance to change proactively. The program manager must expect change and be prepared to manage it.

    PMI®, The Standard for Program Management, 2013, 8, 46

13. b. Leadership

    Stakeholders play a critical role in determining program success. Because they can help or hinder a program, the program manager needs to have strong leadership skills to work with them.

    PMI®, *The Standard for Program Management*, 2013, 46

14. a. The organization's culture

    In stakeholder analysis and engagement planning, the organizational culture and acceptance of change are two key areas to address in the stakeholder engagement plan.

    PMI®, *The Standard for Program Management*, 2013, 49

15. c. Determining the information and communications needs of each stakeholder

    The emphasis of communications planning is to clearly define communications requirements to facilitate the transfer of information to each stakeholder. It is necessary to determine the stakeholder's information and communications needs.

    PMI®, *The Standard for Program Management*, 2013, 74

16. d. Include the metrics in the stakeholder engagement plan

    The stakeholder engagement plan defines the metrics to measure the performance of stakeholder engagement activities. It includes measures of participation in meetings and other types of communications and the effectiveness of stakeholder engagement in meeting its goals.

    PMI®, *The Standard for Program Management*, 2013, 49

17. c. Meet with the new CFO to explain the importance of the program

    The CFO is a significant stakeholder on programs since funds are typically limited. As a new person in this role, he or she may be unaware of this program. The program manager must then spend time and energy with this new CEO to address any concerns, especially if they relate to program benefits, objectives, or outcomes.

    PMI®, *The Standard for Program Management*, 2013, 45

18. b. Make the information available through the information distribution activity

    During Program Performance Reporting, performance information is collected, measured, and consolidated, and measurements and trends are assessed to generate improvements. Information about how resources are being used to deliver program benefits is consolidated, and the consolidated information is then made available to program stakeholders through the information distribution activity.

    PMI®, *The Standard for Program Management*, 2013, 77

19. c. As the program is being initiated

    Stakeholders are persons who have an interest in or influence over the program. They may be internal or external to the organization, and their expectations must be managed from the beginning to the end of the program. Stakeholder considerations are stated in the program charter, which is developed during Program Initiation and should include an initial strategy to manage them.

    PMI®, *The Standard for Program Management*, 2013, 84

20. c. Develop a stakeholder register

    The stakeholder register is prepared during Program Stakeholder Identification. Stakeholder analysis is used to create the register to list stakeholders, their relationship to the program, their ability to influence its outcome, their degree of support, and other characteristics and attitudes that may affect the outcome.

    PMI®, *The Standard for Program Management*, 2013, 46

Governance

Study Hints

Governance is the fifth domain in program management. It represents 14% of the 170 questions, or 24 questions, on the PgMP® exam. Governance transcends program management from the beginning of the program when it is first approved to be part of the portfolio to the closure of the program.

In program management, there can be several types of governance structures—one used for program approval, one used to oversee the program at the stage gates and for periodic reviews of program progress, and one used by the program manager to oversee the projects in the program. These Governance Boards, often called Steering Committ4es, Oversight Groups, or Boards of Directors, each require a defined structure to promote efficiency and consistency among programs and their respective projects. In smaller organizations, a senior executive often performs these functions. A program governance plan is a best practice to describe policies, procedures, and standards that the Governance Board will follow and how the stage-gate reviews will be conducted, including the requirements for each one.

An issue escalation process also is a best practice as the program manager may wish to escalate risks and issues to the Governance Board for resolution, and project managers may wish to do the same to the program manager.

Key performance indicators (KPIs) are useful to measure program success and to help monitor benefits throughout the life cycle. They may include items such as risks, financials, compliance, quality, safety, and stakeholder satisfaction. The program management information system is used to help facilitate tracking these KPIs. A best practice to follow is to regularly evaluate new and existing risks that impact strategic objectives and update the risk management plan as required, presenting it to the Governance Board for approval. Also, the business environment should be monitored in order to ensure the program remains in alignment with the organization's strategic objectives.

Further, emphasis is placed on contributing to an information or knowledge repository with program-related lessons learned, processes, and documentation to support organizational best practices. These lessons learned then are identified and applied to support and influence the existing program and future programs or improvements in the organization.

Note that in the *Examination Content Outline,* this domain is referred to as Governance, while in the *Standard for Program Management*—Third Edition (2013), it is titled Program Governance.

Following is a list of major topics covered In this domain. Use this list to focus your study efforts on the areas that may appear on the exam.

Major Topics

Governance Importance

- Governance and the program life cycle
- Practices and procedures
- Support to program success
- Governance at different levels
- Phase-gate reviews and the life cycle
- Aligning program goals with the strategic goals and objectives of the organization
- Ensuring value promised by the program is realized, and benefits are delivered
- Ensuring effective stakeholder communication
- Setting up measures to ensure compliance with policies
- Ensuring appropriate tools and processes are used in the program

Program Governance Boards

- Staffing
- Governance model
- Positioning the Board to address issues and questions
- Usefulness of a single Governance Board for the program
- Need for multiple Governance Boards

Program Governance Board Responsibilities

- Program governance and the organization's vision and goals
- Program approval, endorsement, and initiating
- Program funding

Establishing a program governance plan

- Summary of the program's goals
- Structure of the Board
- Definition of roles and responsibilities
- Planned meetings
- Phase-gate reviews
- Initiation and closure or transition criteria
- Periodic health checks
- Issue and risk escalation processes
- Success criteria, communications, and endorsement
- Key performance indicators
- Approving plans and the program's approach
- Program performance support

- Reporting and control processes
- Quality standards and planning
- Monitoring progress and determining changes
- Other decision reviews
- Approving component initiation and transition
- Program closure

Program Governance and Program Management

- Collaborative relationship
- Shared responsibilities
- Program and project management standards

Individual Governance Roles

- Program sponsor
- Governance Board members
- Program manager
- Project managers
- Program team members

Governance of Components

- Component governance
- Program manager responsibilities

Other Governance activities

- PMO
- PMIS
- Program management knowledge management
- Identifying and applying lessons learned
- Audit support
- Evaluating new and existing risks
- Education and training
- Monitoring the business environment
- Developing and supporting the integration plan

Practice Questions

1. Within the Acme Bearing Company, management uses the terms project management and program management interchangeably, and there is no consistency across programs. Furthermore, there is no executive support to facilitate issue resolution, no direction or leadership provided to program teams, and little control over work initiatives. As an external consultant, you have been asked to provide recommendations for improvement. You prepare a report with a prioritized list of actions for Acme management. Number one on your list is to establish—

    a. A portfolio management information system
    b. Enterprise project management across all divisions
    c. A program governance model
    d. A program delivery model with supporting competencies

2. As the program manager for a new curricula of training products, you will need to work with numerous divisions within your company, many of which are located in other countries. Additionally, other projects and programs in the organization are linked to your program at various levels. Because you realize the importance of gate reviews and health checks, you need to develop a(n)—

    a. Interface management plan
    b. Integration plan
    c. Governance plan
    d. Program roadmap

3. As your organization's troubled program recovery specialist, you have been called in to take over a program that has had difficulties from the start. An initial assessment revealed that the project-level requirements had not been completed nor had those at the program level. Of course, they need to be finalized before work can be done. You also found that even though your program management methodology requires a Governance Board for a program of this magnitude that it had been set up. You realize this is a necessity, and stage-gate reviews must be conducted. The governance processes, procedures, and templates for programs are defined and managed by the—

    a. PMO
    b. Program office
    c. Program manager
    d. Program Governance Board

4. Assume you now have a Governance Board set up for this troubled program that has had difficulties from the start. You worked with your core team and developed program-level requirements. When you inherited the program, you learned it already had three projects, so you have had your project managers define the project-level requirements succinctly. You have been working with the project managers now on overall program planning and also on planning for their projects. You are scheduled now to meet with your Governance Board in two weeks to see if you can pass Gate Review 3 and officially begin the executing process. You realize these gate reviews are a necessity to—
   a. Obtaining customer support for your work to date
   b. Ensuring the customer acceptance criteria for the end products of the program will be met as planned.
   c. Delivering benefits according to the benefits realization plan
   d. Assuring the ability to sustain program benefits in the long term

5. The program Governance Board on your program is considered to be the best in the organization because of its approach to monitoring performance. Not only do its members monitor progress reports on a routine basis, but they also specifically employ the best practice of—
   a. Meeting with you quarterly to discuss status
   b. Conducting client satisfaction surveys to determine whether quality is being achieved
   c. Hiring an outside consultant to monitor progress reports to get an objective view
   d. Providing support when changes are needed in the program's approach

6. You have been managing a program to run the clinical trials for a new class of drugs that will forever eliminate prickly heat in the subtropics. Partway through the trials, you discovered that a competitor had already achieved regulatory approval to begin manufacturing and selling an identical class of drugs that will be sold at half the cost of the drug that you are developing. You met with your Governance Board to discuss the situation. The next step is to—
   a. Prepare a program closure recommendation
   b. Conduct an audit
   c. Prepare a performance report
   d. Terminate the program

7. You are working on a complex five-year program that has a minimum of four projects under way at any given time. A major scope change to Project L has resulted in a need to rebaseline its schedule. Consequently because of dependencies with Project L, Project D also had to revise its schedule. These two revisions required that your overall program schedule be revised as well. The program schedule change has been approved, and the program and its components' schedules have been updated. As a result of these schedule changes, your original estimate is now totally out of date. Your program Governance Board now asks you to prepare revised—

   a. Forecasts
   b. Estimate at completion
   c. Approach to pursue goals
   d. Earned value scorecard

8. Finally, your program to rebuild the water desalinization plant for Haddad, Saudi Arabia is complete. You asked your Governance Board to approve a recommendation to close this program. To do so, the Board confirms that conditions warranting closure are satisfied as possibly defined in the—

   a. Business case
   b. Benefit realization plan
   c. Program charter
   d. Closure procedures

9. You are preparing for a meeting of your Governance Board. This meeting is a decision point review based on the need to—

   a. Approve initiation of a component
   b. Confirm stakeholder satisfaction with current performance
   c. Confirm that a component has satisfied its business case
   d. Determine if benefits are being realized as stated in the benefit realization plan

10. You are the program manager for your city's initiative to put all electrical, cable, and telephone lines underground to prevent outages during tornados and hurricanes. You have a number of subcontractors working for you, and you also have a small core team of five people. So far, you have four projects in your program, but given its complexity, you expect to have more as the program ensues. You are getting ready for a review by your Governance Board for your program. One purpose of this review is to—

    a. Request approval to initiate another project into the program
    b. Manage the program resources
    c. Identify needed training for your program team members
    d. Prepare for an external audit by the City's Finance Director

11. You are the program manager on a highly controversial e-mail retention program. More than 75 percent of the organization is opposed to the program because it means that all their e-mail messages will be archived and reviewed for inappropriate, unethical, or illegal statements. You know that there will be many conflicts as you and your team execute the component projects. You inform your team that, in the case of any conflict, the first point of escalation is—
    a. The program director
    b. The program sponsor
    c. The program Governance Board
    d. You, the program manager

12. Although your company has been active in project management for many years, it is relatively new to program management. One of the executives knew about the usefulness of governance and stage-gate reviews from his previous work in new product development, and he recommended all programs have a Governance Board. Since the company is following the Project Management Institute's guidelines, this Governance Board approves each program's approach. To do so it—
    a. Approves the business case
    b. Ensures the PMO sets up consistent process that each program follows
    c. Approves the roadmap
    d. Follows the governance plan

13. Although your company has been active in project management for many years, it is relatively new to program management. You became certified as a PgMP® and suggested to your supervisor that two of your current projects would be better managed as a program. Your supervisor in turn met with some members of the executive team, and collectively, they realized a number of the existing projects in the company would be better handled through a program structure. One of the executives recommended all programs have a Governance Board. The recommended governance structure is stated in the—
    a. Program charter
    b. Program management plan
    c. Benefits realization plan
    d. Business case

14. Your program to develop the next-generation helium automobile has been completed. Your Governance Board suggested that audits be held throughout the program, and while you realized the audits were time consuming for you and your team, you found they were—

    a. A best practice
    b. An indicator of benefits realized
    c. A measure of program quality
    d. A way to take proactive actions

15. Your program is part of a company portfolio that includes two other programs as well as three projects that are not part of any specific program. The portfolio also includes additional ongoing work. You will have a number of phase-gate reviews of your program's initiatives. These reviews will be—

    a. Carried out within the context of the corresponding portfolio
    b. Held at the key go/no-go decision points of your program
    c. Used to assess periodic project performance
    d. Held when you request them in your role as program manager

16. You are the program manager for a new version of a MP3 player. The players are manufactured by third-party companies operating plants in five countries. You have a project manager on site in each of these five countries and a total of seven projects in your program to date. Your company is working diligently to be the first to market with these new players as they are using the latest technology, and it differs significantly from that of the competition. You have a Governance Board for your program and it supports program success by—

    a. Ensuring goals are aligned with the strategic vision
    b. Setting key performance criteria for the program and project managers
    c. Setting up a PMO for direct program support
    d. Establishing the benefits the program is to deliver

17. You are the program manager for the development of a new slot machine for the Sand Dunes casino in Macau. Your company is using program management more frequently as it realizes the benefits associated with it but operates with a balanced matrix structure. You meet regularly with members of your Governance Board for periodic health checks, which provide the Board an opportunity to—

    a. Formally review program performance
    b. Assess progress toward benefit realization and sustainment
    c. Focus on the phase that was just completed to determine whether the next phase should begin
    d. Review and approve required program changes

18. You are a program manager under contract to a government agency that is responsible for issuing visas and passports. You have been working on this program for eight years and are responsible for all the information and telecommunications functions for the agency. Your company realizes this program is essential to its success, and this is the first time it has worked for this agency. Therefore, it established a Governance Board to oversee the process. You helped prepare a governance plan and a key part of it is—

    a. A summary of the program's goals
    b. An overview of the business case
    c. Schedules for audits
    d. A description of the knowledge management system

19. You are preparing for a major review by your program's Governance Board. They are especially interested in progress on Project A, because it sets the stage for two other projects. Your program control officer informs you and the Board that Project A has a pessimistic estimate of being completed within 136 days, a most likely estimate of 121 days, and an optimistic estimate of 116 days. They are concerned that the pessimistic estimate will occur and are therefore considering—

    a. Recommending that this component be terminated since it cannot meet its schedule
    b. Adding resources to Project A
    c. Working collaboratively with the program manager to provide support for needed changes
    d. Requesting a program audit

20. You are the program manager for a manufacturing program. This program has been under way for three years. You are using a virtual team to manage the program, and you are unable to have face-to-face meetings of your team because of the financial situation. You have five projects in your program thus far. You just learned you needed to take immediate action in response to a quality metric. This metric indicated that the manufacturing process, Project A, exceeded parameters and therefore would affect Projects B, C, and D and the entire program. You decided you needed to meet with your program's Governance Board because of the severity of this issue. Your next step should be to—

    a. Issue a change request
    b. Use the governance decision register
    c. Update the quality management plan
    d. Allocate to the program a resource who is a certified Six Sigma Black Belt

Answer Sheet

1.	a	b	c	d
2.	a	b	c	d
3.	a	b	c	d
4.	a	b	c	d
5.	a	b	c	d
6.	a	b	c	d
7.	a	b	c	d
8.	a	b	c	d
9.	a	b	c	d
10.	a	b	c	d

11.	a	b	c	d
12.	a	b	c	d
13.	a	b	c	d
14.	a	b	c	d
15.	a	b	c	d
16.	a	b	c	d
17.	a	b	c	d
18.	a	b	c	d
19.	a	b	c	d
20.	a	b	c	d

Answer Key

1. c. A program governance model

   In the context of a program or a portfolio, there are five main functions of governance: facilitate decision making, provide program teams with leadership and direction, exercise program/project control, ensure consistency, and provide support for issue resolution. It is used to promote efficiency and consistency on programs.

   PMI®. *Program Management Professional (PgMP)® Examination Content Outline*, 2011, 15

   Williams, David and Parr, Tim. 2006. *Enterprise Program Management Delivering Value*. Hampshire, England: Palgrave MacMillan, 61

2. c. Governance plan

   The governance plan describes the goals, structure, roles and responsibilities, and logistics for the governance process.

   PMI®, *The Standard for Program Management*, 2013, 55

3. a. PMO

   As part of its oversight, the PMO provides support for the organization's programs, including its governance function. It often is tasked with providing centralized and consistent program management expertise.

   PMI®, *The Standard for Program Management*, 2013, 64

4. c. Delivering benefits according to the benefit realization plan

   A phase-gate review is an objective assessment against the exit criteria of each phase to determine whether the program should proceed to the next phase. These reviews also assess the program in terms of achieving goals at the time of the review and to ensure benefits are being delivered as stated in the benefit realization plan.

   PMI®, *The Standard for Program Management*, 2013, 56

5. d. Providing support when changes are needed in the program's approach

   One responsibility of the program Governance Board is to monitor program progress and the need for change. The Governance Board establishes thresholds for changes the program manager can make on his or her own and working with the program manager provides support when changes need to be made in the program's planned approach or activities.

   PMI®, *The Standard for Program Management*, 2013, 58

6. d. Terminate the program

   This situation is an example in which the Governance Board would terminate the program because of changes in the environment eliminated the need for the program to continue.

   PMI®, *The Standard for Program Management*, 2013, 62

7. c. Approach to pursue goals

   The Governance Board approves the overall approach by which individual programs pursue their goals. In this situation, these changes mean the approved approach needs revision and approval by the Governance Board.

   PMI®, *The Standard for Program Management*, 2013, 57

8. c. Program charter

   The last phase in the program life cycle is Program Closure. To determine whether to recommend closure, the Governance Board may confirm that it is warranted based possibly on review of the program charter.

   PMI®, *The Standard for Program Management*, 2013, 61

9. b. Confirm stakeholder satisfaction with current performance

   The Governance Board can review programs at various decision points and can be held to request updates of program progress. These reviews are held for various reasons and to discuss a variety of items including stakeholder satisfaction with current program performance.

   PMI®, *The Standard for Program Management*, 2013, 59–60

10. a. Request approval to initiate another project into the program

    Reviews by the program's Governance Board are an opportunity for senior management to assess program performance before the program moves to the next phase or before another project is initiated in the program. The criteria for approval are defined in the governance plan.

    PMI®, *The Standard for Program Management*, 2013, 60–61

11. d. You, the program manager

    Program managers are the first escalation point for issues, changes, risks, interfaces, and dependencies from component managers and teams.

    PMI®, *The Standard for Program Management*, 2013, 56

12. a. Approves the business case

    By approving the business case, the Governance Board confirms the projection of the value the program is to deliver and justifies the resources required to do so.

    PMI®, *The Standard for Program Management*, 2013, 54

13. a. Program charter

    The primary output of Program Initiation is the program charter. Among other things, it includes the recommended governance structure to manage, control, and support the program as well as the governance structure for the program's components.

    PMI®, *The Standard for Program Management*, 2013, 85

14. c. A measure of program quality

    While audits can be time consuming, they often are valuable measures of program quality and assist the program manager and team to avoid the need for later corrective actions.

    PMI®, *The Standard for Program Management*, 2013, 65

15. b. Held at the key go/no-go decision points of your program

    Planned phase-gate reviews are described in the program governance plan. They enable the Governance Board to approve the program to pass from one significant phase to the next phase.

    PMI®, *The Standard for Program Management*, 2013, 56

16. a. Ensuring goals are aligned with the strategic vision

    Program governance supports program success in numerous ways, one of which is to ensure the program's goals remain aligned with the strategic vision, operational capabilities, and resource commitments of the sponsoring organization.

    PMI®, *The Standard for Program Management*, 2013, 51

17. b. Assess progress toward benefit realization and sustainment

    Periodic health checks are held between phase gate reviews and enable the Governance Board to assess ongoing performance and progress toward benefit realization and sustainment.

    PMI®, *The Standard for Program Management*, 2013, 56

18. a. A summary of the program's goals

    This section of the governance plan lists the program's goals and those of each of its components and the planned delivery of benefits. The section then describes how the goals will be monitored and measured by the Governance Board.

    PMI®, *The Standard for Program Management*, 2013, 55

19. c. Working collaboratively with the program manager to provide support for needed changes

    The Governance Boars is uniquely positioned to monitor the progress of the program and the need for change. By working collaboratively with the program manager, the Governance Board can provide support when changes are needed in the programs' planned approach.

    PMI®, *The Standard for Program Management*, 2013, 58

20. b. Use the governance decision register

    Decisions of the Governance Board should be formally documented because these decisions are critical feedback used to improve the results of the components and the program.

    PMI®, *The Standard for Program Management*, 2013, 59

Practice Test 1

This practice test is designed to simulate PMI®'s 170-question PgMP® certification exam. You have four hours to answer all questions.

INSTRUCTIONS: Note the most suitable answer for each multiple-choice question in the appropriate space on the answer sheet.

1. Assume you are working to change the culture of your organization to one that views its programs and projects as strategic assets and critical to overall success. You have been working on a team to define the long-term objectives of the organization and to set forth vision and mission statements for employees that are meaningful and informative. In your efforts you recognize and your team has agreed that one of the indicators of the organization's risk tolerance is found in its—
   a. Program management office (PMO)
   b. Portfolio
   c. Strategic plan
   d. Program charter

2. Your team is located on three continents. Many team members are struggling to use the new project and portfolio management (PPM) system, and training is required. You have a PPM expert on your staff, and the PPM vendor also offers training courses. Team members work six days a week. In this circumstance, the most appropriate training approach is to—
   a. Dispatch your PPM expert to each site for individualized training
   b. Conduct synchronous webinar training so that everyone receives information at the same time
   c. Have your vendor prepare eLearning modules that team members can access at their convenience
   d. Provide audio recordings of training sessions that team members can download to their MP3 players

3. You are managing a program to develop a new source of energy in the extreme northern latitudes when solar power is not available. You have a core team and a Program Management Office to support you and the nine projects that are under way. However, your power company, DCE, is resource constrained. You are finding it difficult to obtain the key subject matter experts you need for this important program. You have been working diligently with your stakeholders to gain their support as you know stakeholder engagement is critical to program management. Your approach is to have effective and ongoing communications with your stakeholders. You have prepared a communications management plan for your program, and it has been approved by your sponsor and Governance Board. To complement this plan, you should prepare a(n)—

   a. Stakeholder register
   b. Information distribution plan
   c. Communications log
   d. Knowledge management plan

4. Assume your organization submitted its proposal to government agency ABS. One requirement was that the program manager be certified as a PgMP®. You were listed in the proposal as the program manager and plan to take the exam in three weeks; there is plenty of time as it is June 1, and the contract is not to be awarded until July 1. Your company is convinced it will win this opportunity, and you are working on the charter. You passed the exam, and the company won the contract. But, you just learned you did not pass the MRA. You should—

   a. Complete the charter so the program can commence
   b. Hold a kick-off meeting with your team
   c. Inform your sponsor about the MRA issue
   d. Inform the ABS point of contact about the MRA issue

5. You are preparing for a meeting of the Governance Board for your program. Board Member A told you in a pre-meeting that she believes some recent issues were not in line with your benefits realization plan. She also says that the level of risk in your program is unacceptable. She plans to request a change during the Board meeting. Your best course of action is to—

   a. Review your benefits register and resolve any issues
   b. Update your benefits realization plan and present the revised version at the Governance Board meeting
   c. Proceed as planned with your meeting, as other Board members have not expressed any concerns
   d. Consider her proposed change may be an opportunity to respond adaptively

6. Assume you are on a selection committee to determine which programs and projects your organization should undertake in the next year. Resources in terms of both people and funding are major constraints. One program is for an organizational change program in which for one project in this program, its output is a new personnel information system, with an outcome a new resource management and compensation policy, which is documented in the—
   a. Benefits realization plan
   b. Business case
   c. Program goals and objectives
   d. Program management plan

7. You are excited because upon achieving your PgMP®, you have been assigned to manage a program in your motorcycle company, BCD, to design the 2025 program of vehicles to be produced. Each motorcycle is to be able to be used without helmets. Also, the motorcycles must have other safety features to make sure even in heavy traffic or inclement weather that the rider is protected, and the motorcycle must be able to travel for at least 500 miles without the need to refuel. You just prepared your benefits realization plan for this program. It will be helpful because—
   a. Your performance plan is tied to the benefits realization plan through the balanced scorecard approach
   b. The benefits realization plan will involve all the key stakeholders in the program to get their buy in to each specific project
   c. You and your team can monitor the agreed-upon benefits until the program is completed
   d. It will define how and when benefits will be delivered

8. On your motorcycle program, you and your team are actively tracking the benefits identified in your plan. Your Governance Board asked you to revise your plan after they saw that there were so many intangible benefits and asked you to also include more tangible ones that were easier to track and then report to your stakeholders. You made a strong case for retaining your intangible benefits as you also felt the plan was useful as it—
   a. Served as a baseline for the program with the existing metrics in it
   b. Was prepared through a brainstorming session with some of the key stakeholders who then would question why some of the intangible benefits were omitted
   c. Helped to better define the specific project deliverables
   d. Was set up in a fashion that all the benefits would be realized at the end of the program

9. You are the program manager for your city's initiative to put all electrical, cable, and telephone lines underground to prevent outages during tornadoes and hurricanes. As program manager, you will select subcontractors to support your program. You prepare criteria for the make-or-buy decisions, as well as the criteria to select the subcontractors to—
   a. See how much cheaper it is to buy rather than to make
   b. See how much cheaper it is to make rather than to buy
   c. Outsource as much as possible in accordance with company policy
   d. Determine the optimal supply chain strategy based on a wide variety of factors

10. Because your program has the highest priority in the organization's portfolio, your Governance Board meets each month, and each member receives a weekly status report. The executive sponsor requests these reports to enable him to stay current on program activities and assist you with any issues that need resolution. Your customer also requests monthly meetings and a weekly teleconference. To ensure that your list of these meetings and communications is up-to-date, you should develop a(n)—
   a. Communications log
   b. Information distribution plan
   c. Communications capability matrix
   d. Communications strategy

11. Assume your executive management team has requested that a standard process be put in place for a business case for new programs and projects to pursue in the organization. You are the leader of a cross-functional team that is designing this process. Your executives have stressed they wish to analyze each proposal from multiple business perspectives and want a balanced view of the business opportunity to be realized as well as the business risk to do so. The first step in this generic process should be to—
   a. Determine the key milestones in the program
   b. Define the high-level requirements
   c. Establish authority, intent, and philosophy
   d. Analyze program complexity and strategic alignment

12. You are managing a program with a long duration for the water management district in your county. At this time, it is scheduled to last nine years, but you believe the timeline could even be longer. You have seven projects in your program at this time, and you are only in year two. You and your program management team need to analyze any environmental or legislative changes during execution that may affect your program. This is a key activity to perform during the—

    a. Benefits Identification phase
    b. Program Financial Monitoring and Control
    c. Program Setup phase
    d. Program Risk Monitoring and Control

13. You are a program manager for a software services company. This new software will bring your company into Cloud computing. It also will replace your company's legacy finance and accounting systems. You are to complete your program in two years. Your sponsor has asked you to develop metrics for program success. This is done as part of the development of the—

    a. Program charter
    b. Program roadmap
    c. Program plan
    d. Program management plan

14. You are a program manager for a software services company. This new software will bring your company into Cloud computing. It also will replace your company's legacy finance and accounting systems. To formalize scope, you should use the—

    a. PWBS
    b. Program charter
    c. Business case
    d. Financial framework

15. As executive sponsor of a major program to restore coral reefs off the coast of the Maldives, you have observed conflict between the program manager and her project managers, stakeholders, and peers. Although the conflict is manageable, you are concerned about her long-term future with the organization. She is a very bright and talented individual, and you want to keep her in the organization. Therefore, you—

    a. Tell her to take a well-deserved vacation to reduce her stress level
    b. Send her to a training class on conflict management
    c. Have her go through a 360-degree feedback analysis
    d. Assign her a personal coach to uncover the causes of conflict

16. On your motorcycle program, you and your team are actively tracking the benefits identified in your benefit realization plan. You found, though, that employee satisfaction, which was in the first plan, was not really useful so you decided to delete this benefit and not track it. Now, you have a new plan in place. Your next step is to—

    a. Begin a process to revise your benefit report and benefit register
    b. Update the roadmap
    c. Discuss the new plan at your upcoming, regularly planned program status meeting with your Governance Board in two weeks
    d. Distribute your plan to your key stakeholders

17. Assume your company has fully embraced program management. It has recognized its value and has changed its Project Management Office into an Enterprise Program Management Office. You are the Director of this Enterprise Program Management Office and report directly to the CEO. You have a program life cycle, which is followed, and you and your team developed a standard but scalable program management methodology. You also have set up a process where each program has a Governance Board with stage-gate reviews. Such an approach—

    a. Is focused on control
    b. Ensues the program sponsor makes all final decisions
    c. Enables a focus on changing strategies
    d. It requires monthly meetings for increased effectiveness

18. Assume you are the sponsor for a program for helping your government become a member of the Asian Union, which will be set up like the European Union. You know this will take some time to achieve so you have—

    a. Prepared a funding framework
    b. Prepared a roadmap
    c. Assessed costs and benefits
    d. Focused on business value

19. Working as the program manager for the Asia Union program has proved to be a challenging assignment to say the least. Not only do you have a number of stakeholders located in many different countries, you now have seven projects in your program and fortunately a PMO for support. You find it is necessary to—

    a. Differentiate between the resources assigned to the program and those at the project level
    b. Implement a team-based reward and recognition system
    c. Prepare a team charter and present it to the team
    d. Establish one person to be the sole contact with each of the different stakeholders

20. On your program, you are continually spending the majority of your time communicating with stakeholders at all levels and in varying locations and coordinating activities. You also are preparing a number of status reports for different stakeholder groups and also for your Governance Board with its numerous program reviews and more rigorous stage gate reviews. Working as a program manager, you recognize the key distinctions between a project life cycle and a program life cycle. One of these distinctions is—

    a. Some projects may need to be integrated with others to provide program benefits
    b. The life cycle assists in the control and management of the project deliverables
    c. Programs have a distinct life cycle that is not extended
    d. The way the life cycle is set up means that project benefits cannot be realized immediately

21. As one of the industry's leading program management consultants, you have been asked by the Global Financial Corporation to help establish a program governance structure and then to put in place a management-by-program culture in the organization. You now are establishing your core team and your first step it to—

    a. Negotiate with functional managers for key resources
    b. Identify competency requirements for each role and responsibility
    c. Establish a training program for core team members to address skill gaps
    d. Conduct a 360-degree assessment on each team member to better understand his or her strengths and weaknesses

22. Assume as you continue with this program to put in place a management-by-program culture into the Global Financial Corporation, you realize there are not that many in this worldwide corporation that possess actual experience in program management. But, your first program will be in the area of portable financial transactions by any type of device—a phone, PDA, tablet, eReader, or computer. You recognize that with this program an expert in your corporation will be needed by two of the projects in the program at approximately the same time. Both project managers have included this person in their project management plans, resource assignment matrices, and project schedules. This is an example of—

    a. An assumption
    b. A constraint
    c. Critical chain analysis
    d. An issue to be resolved by the Governance Board

23. One of the projects in your program has reported actuals to date of $1 million against a planned value of $500,000. You suspect that the project will run out of money soon. If it runs out of money, it will place financial constraints on your other projects and also on the entire program. Therefore, as the program manager for this program, you should—

    a. Prepare a program operational cost estimate
    b. Issue a request to terminate this project
    c. Hold a status review
    d. Calculate the schedule performance index (SPI) to see how far behind schedule you are

24. You work as a program manager for a medical device company. Extensive clinical trials are typically managed as individual projects during and after product development. This is done to assess any flaws in the products before they are submitted for regulatory approval. As a program manager, you recognize that—

    a. You must define the life-cycle phases for each of these projects
    b. The major project life-cycle phases and the activities in them will remain similar
    c. The purpose of your program life cycle is to produce deliverables
    d. Each project should have a different life cycle to ensure that there are no problems with the devices that are being manufactured

25. You are managing a business process management program for a large insurance company. After six months of effort, you have noticed that the key stakeholders seem to be losing interest in the effort and that friction has surfaced between your key staff members and key client contacts. You look into the root causes to uncover the reasons for these apparent issues. You advise your deputy program manager to have lunch with her client counterpart at least once a week; likewise, you will start taking the client's vice president out to dinner every month. This activity can be viewed as—

    a. Positive, because you will be building stronger relationships with your client
    b. Positive, but bordering on being unethical
    c. Negative, because it is a calculated attempt to gain information that could be obtained through more direct means
    d. Ineffective, because clients can see through such actions

26. You are the executive sponsor for a proposed program to be presented in two weeks for approval from your Portfolio Review Board in your automotive company, ABC. Your program is to develop a next generation vehicle that will not require gasoline, ethanol or electricity. In your presentation in your business case, you want to differentiate this product. To do so, you should first—

    a. Demonstrate an understanding of the needs of the customer
    b Define the program success criteria
    c. Describe the business opportunity
    d. Analyze program risk

27. Assume you are managing a program for the National Oceanic and Atmospheric Agency (NOAA) in your country. Scientists in NOAA have been doing extensive research on global warming and have noted that the current warming of the world's oceans can cause serious diseases in the next three years. You and your team prepared a benefit realization plan. This plan is one of the key documents that now are being used by your Governance Board members in NOAA to—

    a. Determine specific projects to pursue in the program
    b. Present the business case for the program to the Agency Administrator
    c. Determine whether changes are required to components
    d. Determine the Governance Board's roles and responsibilities

28. Assume a new program to increase the use of social media in your engineering company was approved by the Portfolio Review Board. A number of people have expressed interest in managing this program. The program manager should be—
    a. The person with the knowledge, skills, and competencies best suited for the position
    b. An individual who has attained the PgMP® and has excellent interpersonal skills in engaging stakeholders
    c. Appointed by the Portfolio Review Board members
    d. Assigned by the program sponsor

29. In your program to manufacture a new series of hybrid vehicles for the 2016 year, you initially thought you would have seven projects. As you worked to develop your program charter, however, you now know you will need instead 15 component projects. You have prepared a business case for each of these projects. However, you have not been successful in recruiting the specific team members you want for your program. People have been assigned to your team by other managers who contend that these people have the necessary skills for the job. Your first step is to—
    a. Complete a skill set inventory
    b. Conduct a kickoff meeting
    c. Have an informal meeting to get to know the team members
    d. Align personnel aspirations to available roles

30. So far, you have three projects identified in your program to manufacture the new series of hybrid vehicles. However, you are only in year one of this program. You recognize that at the program level, your role involves exploiting and embracing change. Also, at the program level, analysis of change requests involves identifying, documenting, and estimating the work that the change would entail. In addition, as program manager, you must—
    a. Document the rationale for the decision
    b. Meet with the program Governance Board for approval, rejection, or deferral of the request
    c. Convene a meeting of the project's configuration control board
    d. Prepare a status report

31. Finally the hybrid vehicle program is almost complete. As an experienced program manager, you know it is a best practice in program management is to identify and document lessons learned throughout the program as it moves through the various phases of its life cycle. The next step in this process is to—

    a. Formally document these lessons learned in the knowledge management system
    b. Have experts examine each one to determine whether it should be included in the organization's process asset library
    c. Make them readily accessible for continuous learning
    d. Appoint one of the core program team members as a knowledge broker to pass on these lessons learned

32. You are responsible for developing a new line of printers using advanced laser jets for the consumer market. The customers for your products are large retail outlets and certain online outlets. As program manager, it is critical that you have a good understanding of the needs of the end user. Therefore, you—

    a. Meet with customers to obtain a profile of the buying habits of their shoppers
    b. Meet with customers to understand the wants and needs of their clients with respect to printer capability
    c. Conduct market research to see what your competitors are offering
    d. Meet with as many end users as is feasible to understand what features they would like in a printer

33. Assume you are working as a program manager under contract to the company developing the advanced laser jet printers for the consumer market. Even though you believe you have a good working relationship with the program manager at the printer company, your client has not paid its last invoice of £500,000, and it is now more than 90 days overdue. Your company's accounting policy states that any invoice that is more than 90 days late becomes bad debt. You now need to—

    a. Rebaseline your budget
    b. Update your cost management plan
    c. Take corrective action
    d. Issue a change request

34. Risk management is continual in program management. It is important in the early stages, even when approval to authorize a program has not yet been obtained. Assume you are the sponsor of a possible new program in which all asphalt on your nation's highway system would be totally replaced with a new product that would never require any maintenance. However, obviously there are going to be risks with such a new product to be developed, and you need to identify some of them to obtain approval to proceed. Therefore, a key question to be able to answer when you request approval to proceed is—

    a. What are the assumptions that are part of your analysis?
    b. How much do we need to set aside for contingency in our budget should the risks occur?
    c. How will these risks affect the ultimate sustainability of the product?
    d. What is the probability of success for this program?

35. Working to prepare the business case for your proposed program to develop a new product to replace asphalt on your nation's highways so maintenance will not be required, you realize the members of the Portfolio Review Board will be interested in a cost/benefit analysis, which means, you should—

    a. Identify tangible benefits as they can be easily quantified
    b. Identify direct benefits to your nation that will result from this program
    c. Identify tangible and intangible benefits, expressing the intangible benefits in quantifiable terms
    d. Identifying the tangible and intangible benefits showing the intangible benefits through market analysis techniques

36. As manager of a program for the Federal Trade Commission that involves changes to existing regulations throughout the agency concerning mergers and acquisitions, you have a number of key stakeholders—both internal and external—because these regulations have not been reviewed for more than 20 years. The Commission has established a Governance Board, and you meet with this Board monthly to review progress. Because the Commission practices government in the "sunshine," each meeting is open to the public to attend. This means that—

    a. Public announcements concerning the program do not need to be prepared
    b. Board meeting minutes can substitute for any notifications to the public concerning the program
    c. Public announcements should be prepared
    d. A member of the core team should interface regularly with every public interest group

37. You are pleased to be appointed as the Program Manager for the development of a new ballpoint pen program. This pen will never need replacement and is to be physically appealing and available in a variety of colors. It also is to be fun to use but practical for those in a business setting. Therefore, you are developing a series of these pens and so far the program is considered to be on track. Your only key issue is that each of the stakeholders on this next-generation ballpoint pen program has different communications needs. To ensure each stakeholder receives the appropriate information he or she need in a useful format and in a timely manner, you ask a core team member to prepare a(n)—

    a. Lessons-learned process
    b. Stakeholder register
    c. Information-retrieval system
    d. Information-gathering system

38. As the program manager for a new line of children's toys, called The Destroyer, because your requirements tend to be constantly changing and because some key subject matter experts have been reassigned, you realize that you already are in a position in which a portion of your budget may be depleted, and you are not yet to the halfway point of your program. Some of the toys do not pass inspection. You are becoming concerned. You need to therefore consider—

    a. Submitting component transition requests to your Governance Board
    b. Requesting a quality assurance audit
    c. Formalizing a quality policy
    d. Reviewing and updating the financial management plan

39. One of your project managers (Project Manager A) has identified an issue that has implications for three projects (A, B, and C). You met with this project manager and concurred with her estimate of the importance of the issue. You then convened a meeting of your Governance Board to determine the best way to resolve it. The Governance Board decided that proposed Project B is not required and that existing Project C should be terminated. It decided to add Project D. Your next step should be—

    a. Revisit and update your program documentation as required
    b. Inform the client of this issue and its impact
    c. Meet with all the project managers and the core program team to discuss next steps
    d. Officially recognize and reward Project Manager A for bringing this issue to your attention

40. Assume you have a Governance Board overseeing your program in your government agency. It is comprised of the top executives and political appointees as the program is ranked in the top five in the portfolio. You have had to reduce some of the features originally planned for your program deliverables because of funding cuts. The Governance Board must determine—

    a. How corrective actions were applied
    b. Whether the window of opportunity was compromised
    c. Actual resource use versus that projected
    d. The number of issues escalated to you, as the program manager, and their effect on other aspects of the program or other programs in the agency

41. You are the program manager for a sixth-generation cell phone product. A number of component projects are associated with this program. You were on the core program team for the fifth-generation phone, so you can apply the lessons learned from that program. The schedule is the dominant constraint, and there is a chance that you will miss the user-acceptance test milestone even though it is six months away. Your next step is to—

    a. Implement your plan
    b. Inform the executive team that you will miss this critical milestone unless preventive action is taken
    c. Revisit the program master schedule
    d. Ask your program steering committee for additional resources to ensure that you can meet the milestone

42. In your role as program manager for your country's food safety department to ensure the safety of imported food in your country, you are facing a number of challenges. It seems as if more imported food is arriving rather than producing the food domestically. You lack the needed number of inspectors who have expertise in some of the exotic food that now is being imported, and you are implementing a Hazard Analysis Critical Control Program approach as part of this important program. You are working hard to keep your stakeholders, internal and external, informed of your progress and upcoming milestones in a timely manner, and you distribute a variety of different reports based on the category of stakeholders and their information requirements. However, one type that often is overlooked is—

    a. Needed corrective actions
    b. Notification of change requests
    c. List of preventive actions
    d. Resource prioritization decisions

43. Your company has been the leader in Segway® production since they were first made available to consumers. However, their popularity has increased tremendously since the product was first made offered, and they are less expensive to manufacture. Therefore, sales have increased dramatically. However, recently your company has been getting a large volume of customer complaints as the battery life is only 20 miles. You have been appointed as the program manager to develop a new line of Segway® products in which the battery life will be 100 miles, yet the production process still will be one that focuses on lean manufacturing so the products can be offered to customers at a reasonable price. To document the relationship between the program activities and expected benefits, you have prepared a—

    a. Roadmap
    b. Charter
    c. Benefits realization plan
    d. Statement of the program's goals and objectives

44. Assume your company has fully embraced program management. It has recognized and has set up a process where each program has a Governance Board with phase-gate reviews. Working with program managers, members of the Governance Board can monitor progress to maximize program success. Obviously changes will occur. The most significant requests involve—

    a. Program issues
    b. Resource use
    c. Quality
    d. Program benefits

45. As the program manager for the development of the next-generation catalytic converter, you have several major challenges. First, it is the first program in your company, second, it is highly complex, and third resources are limited. To handle these challenges you plan to—

    a. Assign program roles and responsibilities
    b. Establish an easy to use and comprehensive program management information system
    c. Set up a program control framework
    d. Use enterprise resource planning tools

46. You have had several issues on your next-generation catalytic converter program. But, finally it is in the closing stage. You want to make sure there is operational sustainability from your program that is ongoing. To do so effectively, you should—
   a. Update the program document repository
   b. Document lessons learned
   c. See if residual activities are required
   d. Hold a final meeting with key program stakeholders

47. You manage a program to develop a new e-commerce program for automotive parts distributors. Your organization has established this program to keep up with competitors and to increase market share, but it has recently acquired a competitor that already has a highly regarded e-commerce program in place. Your next step is to—
   a. Convene a meeting of your Governance Board to terminate your program
   b. Meet with each of your project managers to discuss an orderly transition to redeploy resources
   c. Revisit and update your program plans
   d. See if you can learn from the competitor

48. Your professional association in business development is increasing in terms of its membership. You have a core team of people to help you in your program to certify its members, but other team members are volunteers. Recently the Executive Director authorized you to hire some consultants to help on a full-time basis. The stakeholders, who are volunteers and members of the association, knowledge and expertise are vital to the outcome of this program. However, especially since so many volunteers are involved, you have had to reach negotiated compromises with some of these stakeholders to respond to their concerns. They are part of—
   a. The stakeholder engagement strategy
   b. Stakeholder analysis and planning
   c. The communications log
   d. Stakeholder engagement

49. You are sponsoring a program to digitize all of the records in your nation's archives. Some of these records are extremely important but are difficult to digitize, because they are ones when your country was established, approximately 500 years ago. However, it is essential that they be preserved, and the effort of your undertaking is far larger than originally anticipated. But, now your government is in financial difficulty, and you wonder if your program will be able to be funded. You must—

    a. Prepare an impact analysis to show the results if the program does not receive needed funding.
    b. Conduct a benchmarking study to see how other countries have handled this type of project
    c. Estimate the high-level financial and non-financial benefits
    d. Perform a SWOT analysis

50. You have been managing a program to restructure your department within your government agency. The head of the agency informed your sponsor that she wants to change the scope of the program so that you will be working to restructure the entire agency instead. This means you—

    a. Are working on a strategic program
    b. Must resubmit a new business case and receive approval from the Portfolio Review Board
    c. Should terminate work to date following the standard closure process
    d. Submit a formal change request as your next step

51. Assume you are in charge of reorganizing your government agency because its funding has been cut by 50% based on the shortfall of the overall available funds in your government. To cut the funds, a number of projects and programs were terminated, and in doing so, many staff members lost their jobs. In making the decisions as to which programs to terminate, one of the considerations was—

    a. The number of staff members involved
    b. The overall schedule status
    c. The funds already allocated
    d. The benefits report

52. Your company established a Governance Board, and it meets at least monthly to review progress to date on your program, not just at stage-gate reviews. You and your team worked to identify stakeholders who may have an interest in or an influence over your program and to analyze them to see if they are positive or negative. Your next step is to—

    a. Develop a stakeholder engagement strategy
    b. Prepare an interest/power stakeholder map
    c. Prepare a stakeholder register
    d. Develop a project stakeholder engagement plan

53. You are the program manager for the development of a new slot machine for the Sand Dunes casino in Macau. Your organization operates with a balanced matrix organizational structure, and you have resources supporting your program from a variety of functional departments. Some of these people report to you as well as to their respective departmental managers. You should—

    a. Work with the functional managers so you can provide input into the performance of these individuals
    b. Set up a team-based reward and recognition system
    c. Ask the team to develop a team charter to serve as their commitment to the program
    d. Release resources when they are no longer needed

54. Assume you have been appointed as a program manager for an internal restructuring of your government agency. It has not been reorganized for 10 years, and many new programs and projects are under way. Also, some of the existing Divisions do not seem to relate to the new five year strategic plan the agency issued six months ago, and on the surface, without detailed analysis, it is questionable that they remain necessary. As you initiate the program, you want to reveal and explain any gaps; therefore, it is important to—

    a. Prepare a benefits analysis plan
    b. Perform an initial identification of program risks
    c. Develop a financial framework
    d. Develop a program roadmap

55. Assume your organization has approved an internal improvement program and has identified key stakeholders. It is now deciding whether or not it should focus on the Software Engineering Institute's Capability Maturity Model for Integration (CMMI) to obtain Level 3 and have the opportunity to bid on more U.S. Federal Government projects. The other option is to establish a program to pursue best practices in portfolio, program, and project management using the Project Management Institute's *Organizational Project Management Maturity Model (OPM3)®*. Since the area to be addressed is understood, the next step is to—

    a. Qualify the business benefits
    b. Conduct a feasibility study
    c. Use the voice of the customer (VOC) approach for a market analysis
    d. Prepare a high-level approach

56. Assume your organization selected *OPM3®*, and you hired an external consultant to perform the assessment. The consultant prepared an assessment report and an improvement report. As there are 488 Best Practices in *OPM3®*, your company is so new to program management and portfolio management, it only achieved 75 of these Best Practices. You are now leading an internal program to address the consultant's prioritized improvement program. You have seven projects now in your program. As each project manager begins to identify the work to be done on their projects, you want to make sure the program's scope encompasses all benefits to be delivered so you should—

    a. Follow the PMO's project management standard
    b. Make sure the context and framework are documented is a scope statement
    c. Use a program work breakdown structure
    d. Prepare a benefits realization plan

57. As the contract program manager to integrate the back office components of your customer's system into a single system that contains data on accounting, finance, sales, business development, personnel, and portfolio, program, and project management, you have a core team of six people and six project managers. You are working to obtain information from stakeholders to better understand the organizational culture and decide to—

    a. Use questionnaires and surveys
    b. Hold a focus group
    c. Conduct interviews
    d. Use open-ended questions

58. You and your core team have identified within the organization 17 key stakeholders, and there are approximately 33 that have a peripheral interest in your program. You know you will have other stakeholders to add to this list as program progresses. The person, or group, who is responsible for providing project resources on this program is—
    a. Program director
    b. Program manager
    c. Program sponsor
    d. Governance Board

59. Because of extreme droughts in Ferguson, Jordan, water restrictions have been imposed. Your company is awarded a contract to eliminate the need for these restrictions. The program includes a project to formulate and implement policies and procedures that ensure continuity of operations and performance of associated equipment. Another project will oversee improvements and modifications to existing treatment methods and facilities. A third project will design modifications to increase productivity and effectiveness. You expect other projects to be added later. Your company has a Governance Board in place for your program, which conducts phase-gate and other periodic reviews. You meet regularly with this board, and these meetings are necessary because they—
    a. Are program performance reviews
    b. Assess performance against the need to realize and sustain program benefits for the long term
    c. Approve required changes to the program
    d. Assess performance of the program against expected outcomes

60. Finally, after three years of planning, your detailed design for the next-generation missile system of your country is complete. You were appointed the program manager for this program, and you now have also prepared your program management plan and schedule, as well as your subsidiary plans. Last week, your program's Governance Board approved your program management plan. The next step is to—
    a. Assign project managers and appoint your core team
    b. Prepare charters for component projects
    c. Set up your PMO
    d. Authorize components

61. Assume you are managing a high visibility program that is global with stakeholders located on four continents. You have performed a thorough identification of your program's benefits with your team and have set up a benefits register. In order to develop appropriate performance measures for these benefits, you should—

    a. Review the business case
    b. Meet with stakeholders
    c. Take the qualified benefits and turn them into ones that can be measured quantitatively
    d. Assign each benefit to an owner and empower the owner to set up metrics and discuss them at the scheduled core team meeting

62. You are pleased to be the first program manager in your company to manage a virtual team. While the company has managed programs for several years, in the past, it tended to hire subject matter experts or ask people from its offices in four other continents to meet in one place in order to work as a collocated team. It also relied extensively on contactor support. Finally, your executives have recognized that it will be cost beneficial to use a virtual team for your new program to develop a new product that combines the capabilities of a smart phone, an eBook reader, and a tablet in a single device that is less expensive with a higher quality of resolution than possible with the existing products on the marketplace. Such an approach is one in which you should consider—

    a. Using focus groups to obtain a picture of the various attitudes of your stakeholders
    b. The cultural backgrounds of the team members
    c. Changing culture
    d. Using market analysis

63. Your company has a career path in program management and has established standard competencies for the various positions. You were a project manager on the company's virtual team in which your program developed a new product combining the capabilities of the smart phone, eBook reader, and a tablet in a single device. You managed the integration project in your program, and you were commended by the executive team and the program manager for outstanding work. Now, you are transitioning into your first program management position. The guiding rule in your new job is to—

   a. Provide as much support as needed to project managers in their daily activities
   b. Training, coaching, mentoring, and recognizing your team
   c. Actively manage each project until you have confidence in the project manager's ability to do so without your continual involvement
   d. Mentor project managers in their roles by working with them throughout their projects

64. As the program manager for the new landfill program for your county, you are facing a number of challenges. You have identified a large number of stakeholders, mostly in the county and the residents who have this "not in my backyard" syndrome about the landfill program, along with environmental activists. However, you recognize you need to engage each stakeholder group, even if they are negative, to ensure overall success. Recently, at some key meetings, you and your team realized some of the active stakeholders were missing. You realized some also missed the previous meeting. To identify and assess causes of nonparticipation, as a program manager, one tool to use is—

   a. Root cause analysis
   b. Cause-and-effect diagrams
   c. Variance analysis
   d. Conflict resolution strategies

65. Assume you have decided to sponsor a new program to develop a new way to determine whether or not an organization should bid on any opportunity, and the steps it should follow to predict whether the submitted proposal will be selected. This will be a quantitative model that basically can transform the way business development is handled. It will show areas of strength, areas in need of improvement, and an approach to improve an organization's chances of winning the opportunity. As the sponsor, you received approval to move to the initiating phase from your Portfolio Review Board. It now is appropriate to—

    a. Define the program's scope and benefit strategy
    b. Identify the program's benefits
    c. Quantify business benefits
    d. Prepare a program governance plan

66. Your company has established a program to manage the development of new pet food products, and you have been appointed manager of this program. It is the first program of its kind in your company; its structure was set up because numerous projects in the planning stage have dependencies and require some of the same resources. You realize that there are some commonalities among the benefits in the projects. Your program will be the first in your company to have a Governance Board throughout its life cycle. It has led to the company establishing program governance as a standard process, and it then addresses—

    a. Endorsing or approving recommendations for programs
    b. Aggregate performance of components of the program
    c. Value indicators for program components
    d. Models to ensure that the portfolio makes the best use of resources

67. You are the program manager for the International Air Traffic Association (IATA). The executives, representing all the airlines in the world, want to set up a global program for loyalty to airlines rather than the myriad of separate reward programs that now exist. They have built a business case for this program that shows in doing so benefits will accrue as there will be fewer disruptions to passengers and to the airlines if a flight is canceled, and the passenger could have taken a non-stop flight from his or her home airport rather than needing to travel to another airport just for the loyalty program. You have been asked to document thresholds for evaluating achievement of key performance indicators. This should be in—

    a. The business case
    b. The benefit register
    c. The benefit realization plan
    d. The benefit report

68. Your organization has a defined process that it follows to determine which programs and projects should be in the portfolio, and this process is followed before leadership approval is received officially to authorize a program or project. In the past 10 years, your company, XYZ, has focused on projects. It has set up a project management methodology, which project managers are to follow, and it also has a Project Management Office. However, you recently attended a conference, and you realize since you are a member of the XYZ's Portfolio Review Board that many of the projects you are considering at your next meeting might be better managed if they were a program. After this conference, you met with other members of the Portfolio Review Board and explained how many of the existing projects in XYZ might be better organized as a program so they could then obtain more benefits than if the projects were managed in a standalone fashion. Now, with the upcoming Portfolio Review Board meeting, of the following possible key initiatives, which one would benefit by being managed as a program?

    a. Expanding a ski area
    b. Setting up a career path for people in the project management profession
    c. Upgrading the nation's airspace system
    d. Introducing a new project planning tool in a large organization

69. You are managing a program under contract with a major motion picture studio. Your contract is for three years with annual renewal possible if the program is completed on schedule. Payment terms in your contract are 60 days. You need to hire several subcontractors to assist with the program. To protect your financial position and cash flow on the program, you should set the payment terms for your subcontractors at—

    a. 30 days
    b. 45 days
    c. 60 days
    d. 90 days

70. On your program, two key members of your Governance Board are not attending any meetings. The three other members are pleased with your progress, but you are concerned because these Board members are not participating, sending substitutes, or communicating with you when you send status updates. To avoid incorrect assumptions about their lack of participation, you should—

    a. Request a face-to-face meeting
    b. Ask a core team member to meet with some of their staff members
    c. Talk with the other Board members about their lack of participation
    d. Conduct a thorough analysis of the situation

71. Although each program has its own Governance Board, there are times when issues arise that a program manager may need to interface with executive management and external stakeholders. If this needs to be done—
    a. Escalate the issue first to the Governance Board before going elsewhere
    b. Obtain needed information to inform the Governance Board
    c. Follow the issue escalation process explicitly
    d. Ensure the issue is one that has major implications outside of the program

72. As your government agency moves toward performance-based management, the senior executives issue a five-year plan with a number of initiatives. Each program and project will have key performance indicators (KPIs). Programs and projects will not be pursued without a detailed business case that is approved by a Governance Board composed of senior managers from each of the functional units. You are appointed as program manager to develop processes for these initiatives and are working on your charter. But, the agency now has undergone a 50% reduction in its budget, and no changes are expected in the near future. As the program manager, you should—
    a. Seek guidance from your sponsor
    b. Complete the charter
    c. Update the business case
    d. Expand your roadmap so initial milestones will not be met for at least two years

73. Your program to develop a 7G phone is being terminated early because your competition already has a 7G phone model on the market. This early closing has resulted because of—
    a. Poor performance
    b. Inability to deliver benefits
    c. A technology change
    d. Realignment of strategic goals

74. Your company is a worldwide leader in Six Sigma and the ISO 9001. Because of the importance of quality management, you appoint a member of your core program team to be responsible for quality planning on your program. At Governance Board meetings, he will often describe whether quality standards for the program are being met. The Governance Board is interested because—
    a. It approved the quality plan
    b. Quality issues are covered in reporting and control processes
    c. It ensures consistency in program management
    d. These standards must be met before approving component transition

75. You are the program manager for an updated enterprise resource planning system that also will include business development and knowledge management modules. Time to market is critical, and as the program manager you know other competitors' products tend to take an extremely long time to implement so with your new products you also are emphasizing ease of implementation and training end users. You will be using external contractors for part of the work. As you administer procurements, your company's program management methodology requires you to follow which of the following—
    a. Contract management plan
    b. Contract administration plan
    c. Procurement management plan
    d. Contract procurement plan

76. You are Company A's program manager for the development of an online banking system for your community bank, for which your company will realize $20 million in US dollars. To track the various stakeholders, you and your team set up a stakeholder register and prepared a stakeholder engagement plan. The individual or organization responsible to ensure program goals are achieved is—
    a. Executive sponsor
    b. Governance Board
    c. Program sponsor
    d. Program manager

77. You are the program manager for a water-alleviation program in Ward, Florida, that requires extensive equipment. Some of this equipment represents new technology. As the program manager, you are preparing regular program performance reports, and each one discusses this equipment. In these reports, they should include—
    a. Risk analysis
    b. Resource use
    c. Approved change requests
    d. Audit recommendations

78. Your water alleviation program in Ward, Florida, is progressing. You have a core team of six people, and you have seven project managers. You were fortunate this year in that while Ward got a lot of heavy rain during the rainy season, it did not get any hurricanes. However, the Lake levels are still low, and residents cannot water more than two hours once a week until your program is complete. The City also is limited to watering only once a week as well but for four hours. You have a number of key stakeholders in the City government as well as the residents plus your own company. Therefore, you realize the importance of influencing throughout the program but especially as you work to—

    a. Manage program resources
    b. Negotiate with stakeholders
    c. Lead with stakeholders
    d. Maintain program strategic alignment

79. As a program manager for the 888 series of aircraft being produced by your company, you are preparing for an important meeting of your Governance Board to assess progress in coordinating deliverables. Because of an acquisition by your company, the Board includes two new executives. This will be their first Board meeting. The other organization did not follow governance processes. To explain the governance approach, you need to—

    a. Aggregate performance information about your program for these new members
    b. Personally provide a copy of the governance plan to these new members
    c. Ask your sponsor to meet with these new members to discuss their roles and responsibilities
    d. Meet with these two new Board members to discuss your program prior to the Board meeting

80. You are a member of your company's Program Selection Committee, which is trying to decide which one of four programs to launch. Your company prides itself on superior quality in the automobile parts field. Each program has prepared its business case. Proposed Program A will overlap and combine its phases, milestones, and activities. Proposed Program B will delay its schedule if necessary in a trade-off situation to ensure that quality is achieved. Proposed Program C will have a flexible structure to ensure innovative features at a minimal cost. Proposed Program D will focus on the technical features, cost, and schedule in its metrics. You select—

    a. Program A
    b. Program B
    c. Program C
    d. Program D

81. When your program is complete, it will generate more than 80 percent of the revenue earned by the company. Thus, it will have a major impact on the balance sheet. To assist you in your work, you prepared a program financial plan and established a budget baseline. Now you are tracking, monitoring, and controlling funds and expenses. Not to be overlooked in this process is—
    a. The profit the company earns
    b. The balance between profit and loss
    c. The operational costs
    d. A summary of the revenue, direct cost, indirect cost, operating profit, and net profit of a company at a given point in time

82. You are the program manager for the International Air Traffic Association (IATA). You also are about to complete a project to determine how many points will be transferred from people in existing programs to the new loyalty program. You have just prepared a request to close this project to present to your Governance Board. The Governance Board members and your sponsor have indicted before approving the transition, they want to review—
    a. Sign offs on completed deliverables
    b. Business case
    c. Delivery and transition of benefits
    d. Project management plan

83. Your company is noted for its maturity and excellence in program management. It has received awards for its successes in program and project delivery. Last year, it received the Project Management Office of the Year Award, even though it really calls its PMO a Program Management Office, which it established about 12 years ago. One reason your company is a leader in the field is the PMO provides support in—
    a. Recognizing the use of environmental enterprise factors
    b. Defining quality standards
    c. Ensuring alignment to organizational strategy
    d. Adhering to standards of professional conduct and responsibility

84. You meet with your Governance Board on the 888 aircraft series program. Your program is on schedule, but the Board wants to accelerate production to beat a competitor's 480 aircraft to market. The Board provides you with an additional 100 aerospace engineers to perform concurrent engineering in the design phase. This shows the importance of the Governance Board in—

    a. Conducting periodic health checks
    b. Setting program success criteria
    c. Program funding
    d. Program performance support

85. You have been a program manager for three years. You realize that a common understanding of program scope among the stakeholders leads to greater program success. Throughout the past three years, you have communicated extensively with your stakeholders and believe you are meeting most of their expectations, but some still have some doubts as to overall success. Therefore, in your last program review with your Governance Board, you noted this concern and now want to document a common understanding of the overall scope and have the key stakeholders sign off on it. This understanding is best documented as part of the—

    a. Stakeholder management plan
    b. Program scope statement
    c. Program scope management plan
    d. Program charter

86. For your program, you prepared a detailed stakeholder analysis. Stakeholder A thought that the program objectives were to deliver a detailed plan for your city's growth and development over the next 10 years; Stakeholder B thought that the purpose was to design a water-retention process to ensure that each citizen would have adequate water in the future; Stakeholder C thought that the program was to provide services to the city for its overall management by outsourcing its information technology (IT) services, personnel, and procurement functions; and Stakeholder D thought that the program was to provide a detailed workflow for all the city's functions. In the face of this lack of common understanding of the requirements, you need to prepare a—

    a. Feasibility study
    b. Stakeholder management plan
    c. Benefits realization plan
    d. Program scope statement

87. In a meeting with your program's Governance Board, you discussed ongoing and completed risk responses. You have been working to minimize risks, and a member of your core program team is responsible for overall risk management as her primary activity. You recently held a risk review meeting for your program, and many risks have occurred that were not identified and analyzed. This was followed by a meeting with your Governance Board, which directed you to prepare a comprehensive update on all risks. This decision by the Governance Board in its role in—

    a. Establishing an issue escalation process
    b. Program reporting and control
    c. Program performance support
    d. Monitoring progress and determining if changes are needed

88. You are a member of your insurance company's Program Selection Committee, which is considering a number of potential programs. Program A is estimated to cost $100,000 to implement and will have annual net cash inflows (ANCI) of $25,000. Program B is estimated to cost $250,000 to implement and have ANCI of $75,000. Program C is estimated to cost $600,000 to implement and have ANCI of $125,000. Program D is estimated to cost $125,000 to implement and have ANCI of $50,000. Your selection criteria are based on the shortest payback period. You recommend that your company select—

    a. Program A
    b. Program B
    c. Program C
    d. Program D

89. As an energy company "upstream" program manager, you use your program work breakdown structure (PWBS) to build your schedule. You have seven projects in your program, and it is to be completed in three years. The best approach is to—

    a. Hold an off-site meeting in which project managers and your core program team work together to complete the schedule
    b. Have the project managers build the detail for their projects and then roll it up into the control points and PWBS program packages
    c. Work with your core program team to develop the program schedule and then ask the project managers to use this schedule as they prepare more detailed project schedules
    d. Have the first draft of the program schedule identify the start and end dates of the components

90. Your molecular biology program is scheduled to last three years. Project A has been under way since the program began and is scheduled to be complete at the end of year 2. Project B is scheduled to begin in year 2. Project C has just begun and requires some domain-specific resources in molecular biology from both Projects A and B. Project Manager A is concerned that Project Managers B and C will require some of her key scientists; if these resources are reassigned, then the end date for Project A will slip. She has been practicing a philosophy of "no secrets" with the client and has informed Project Managers B and C that she is not willing to let any of her molecular biologists leave Project A until it is officially closed. You receive a call from the client requesting a meeting to discuss resource issues and the status of Project A. At this point, you—

    a. Meet with Project Manager A and tell her to first talk with you before she informs the client of any concerns in the future
    b. Tell Project Managers B and C that you support Project Manager A's decision not to release any of her key scientists
    c. Meet with all three project managers and inform them that you will manage any resource redeployment issues
    d. Meet with all three project managers and empower them to reach consensus on how the resources should be redeployed before you meet with the client

91. You are managing Program BBB for your manufacturing firm. You have one subprogram and seven projects thus far, and the program is just beginning. You need to set up a governance structure for these components. You have your PgMP® and have managed successfully two other programs for your firm. The best approach to follow is—

    a. Use the same governance structure as that for your program
    b. Ask your PMO to provide the governance function
    c. Manage a component Governance Board
    d. Have your sponsor provide oversight and determine when the program Governance Board should be consulted

92. You are managing a program whose budget at completion (BAC) is €420,000. The program is 10 percent complete and has an earned value of €42,000. The actual costs (AC) are €50,000. This means that—

    a. Although the program is over budget, the overrun is insignificant at this time
    b. The program is over budget by –€8,000, which is a major problem
    c. You need to calculate a new estimate to complete (ETC)
    d. The CV is €378,000, and immediate action is necessary

93. You are managing Program BBB for your manufacturing firm. Program EEE is experiencing severe resource shortfalls. The executive sponsor is the same for both programs. Your Governance Board holds an emergency meeting to decide what you can do to assist Program EEE. The Board asks you to transfer seven of your manufacturing engineers to Program EEE and gives you the authority to contract with an outside firm for the engineering support that you need. With the change in your program BBB to use contractors for much of the manufacturing engineering work, you should—
    a. Notify your stakeholders
    b. Update your roles and responsibilities matrix
    c. Prepare a contracts administration plan
    d. Approve a change to the outsourcing company's contract

94. Your company is new to program management, but it has practiced a management-by-projects culture for many years. Many people now have their PMPs® as well as advanced degrees in project management. Recently, you took a seminar at a PMI® conference on program management and suggested to your manager that the company should consider adopting program management because of its benefits to the organization. Before proceeding to take this idea to the Executive Committee, he asked you to perform an initial assessment as to why a focus on program management would add benefits. You need to therefore—
    a. Define the vision statement
    b. Show the link to organizational program management
    c. Identify integration opportunities
    d. Define the objectives

95. You manage a program in the Ministry of Education. Your seven-year program is designed to ensure mandatory testing requirements for high school students throughout the country. Your program receives funding soon after the start of each fiscal year. Funds that are not spent during a fiscal year cannot be allocated to other programs or agency activities; rather, they revert to the general fund. As a program manager, you ensure that—
    a. Your program focuses on reserve analysis
    b. You spend all the money allocated in each fiscal year
    c. All available financial information and all income and payment schedules are listed in detail as the budget is prepared
    d. You add at least a 10 percent margin to the budget in anticipation of the reductions by the Ministry's budget office

96. Assume you are a member of a program team that is working to provide a better way to notify citizens in your City about the possibility of tornadoes. Now, the warning allows them only minutes to seek safety, and everyone believes a system such as that available for hurricanes and cyclones is necessary. As a resident of this city, you are pleased to be on the core team. Your program manager has asked you to be responsible for ensuring the program's stakeholders, of which there are many, receive information in a timely manner. Among other things, you must—

    a. Show "what's in it for me"
    b. Collect stakeholder feedback on information timeliness
    c. Be proactive in terms of both preventive and corrective actions
    d. Prepare a stakeholder engagement plan

97. Your organization is embarking on a program to establish a culture of knowledge management. You established a lessons-learned register on your last project. The enterprise program management office (EPMO) was impressed and suggested to the CEO that a program focusing on knowledge management is needed. The CEO concurred, and you were appointed program manager. Two people from the EPMO have been assigned to the core program team. This is important because—

    a. The organization lacks available resources
    b. The two members from the EPMO have expertise in this field
    c. The EPMO Director is the program sponsor
    d. The EPMO provides knowledge management support

98. Assume you are managing a program in your country which now allows people to buy in each state a pass to enable them to avoid the need to stop at toll booths on highways and bridges. However, each state in your country has a different type of pass so if you are in a different state, you cannot use it. As the program manager, your program's goal is to have an identical pass that every state can use on its highways and bridges. Additionally, your program will enable the pass to be used as well in airports at parking lots and garages. As you work on your program, you find there are a number of issues involved as states are reluctant to change to a new system, and various stakeholders have different concerns and issues. You are working to identify, track, and close each issue as it arises. It is important to select a course of action consistent with—

    a. Resource control
    b. Program scope
    c. Risk management
    d. Organizational strategic goals

99. You are an executive with a major recording studio. Four new groups have auditioned for a record contract, but you can select only one. The program to launch any group consists of Web site development, music videos, a nationwide tour, T-shirts, and a fan club. Your head of Marketing has done a net present value (NPV) for each group. Which do you choose?

Group A NPV at	*Group B NPV at*	*Group C NPV at*	*Group D NPV at*
5% = 5,243	5% = 2,320	5% = 6,400	5% = 3,000
10% = 2,841	10% = 1,254	10% = 3,275	10% = 2,755
15% = 1,563	15% = 688	15% = 1,679	15% = 700

You recommend that your company select—

a. Group A
b. Group B
c. Group C
d. Group D

100. You are the program manager for development of a next-generation personal digital assistant (PDA) that can be used on computers, airplanes, trains, and phones. You are in the early stages of your program, but it is ranked number 5 on your company's portfolio list. You have been asked to determine the organization's overall financial environment for the program and are doing so as part of—

a. Developing your charter
b. Establishing the program's financial framework
c. Developing the program's financial plan
d. Developing the infrastructure for the program

101. You now have five projects in your next-generation PDA program. So far, you are pleased with your core team and its progress, and you have a Governance Board in place to oversee your progress. They also are responsible for gate reviews. You have just completed the PWBS for this program. Your next step is to—

a. Generate the program schedule
b. Develop the issue resolution process for Governance Board Involvement
c. Negotiate for project team members
d. Identify key milestones

102. You are the program manager for the International Air Traffic Association (IATA). The executives, representing all the airlines in the world, want to set up a global program for loyalty to airlines rather than the myriad of separate reward programs that now exist. A number of benefits were identified in the business case and then in the benefits realization plan, which was approved by the Governance Board. You have a core team member who is maintaining a benefits register to track the status of each benefit, and you have assigned a person on your team to be the owner of each benefit. In a way, you have set this register up so it resembles the risk register you are using on your program. You found this has been a useful approach because—

    a. You need to regularly review your transition plan
    b. Some corrective actions may be required as a result of risk mitigation activities
    c. The same person who owns the benefit tends to also be a risk owner to minimize the responsibilities of your team members
    d. It is then easier to communicate benefit status to your Governance Board

103. Assume your county government decided to move into program management as it found that a number of projects under way had interrelationships and interdependencies in terms of the benefits they were to deliver to the citizens in the county. While the county has a project management methodology, it did not have one for program management so it decided to build on the best practices in the Project Management Institute's *Standard for Program Management.* As you reviewed the guidelines in *The Standard for Program Management,* you noted some activities are performed throughout the course of the program; an example is—

    a. Program Schedule Control
    b. Benefits Realization
    c. Program Performance Monitoring and Control
    d. Manage Program Issues

104. As the program manager, you have prepared your stakeholder register. However, you want to have a deeper understanding of the impacts of your program concerning your stakeholders' attitudes about it so you decide to use—

    a. Interviews
    b. Focus groups
    c. Questionnaires and surveys
    d. Brainstorming

105. You are managing a program that comprises new systems applications development and maintenance activities. These applications are critical to your company, as they involve access to proprietary data. The systems must be available to your clients on a 24/7/365 basis. Much of the work is to be outsourced. From a strategic perspective, your primary concern regarding this program is that—

a. The contractor has systems capable of accommodating the applications and that all hardware and software has been updated
b. Your legal team has reviewed all the contract's terms and conditions to ensure that your company is protected in case of default
c. Your organization has the necessary levels of skill and expertise to manage and administer a contract of this magnitude
d. The contractor has the appropriate tools and techniques to safeguard your intellectual property

106. Working as the program manager for a standard toll pass system, since there are about 30 such systems in existence now in your country to avoid the need for toll booths if people elect to buy these passes, you realized you needed to take the best practices of the various pass systems already in existence and incorporate them into your program. You found that one State, Virginia, had a quality plan for its pass program, while most of the other states instead were only focusing on inspection as a quality tool and technique. Your emphasis is to perform quality activities throughout the program. As you focus on quality control, you should ensure—

a. Checklists are completed
b. Quality audit recommendations are implemented
c. Perform health checks are performed
d. Service level agreements are established

107. The program sponsor for a new customer-focused program in your organization submitted a business case to the Portfolio Review Board, which was approved. Then, your company merged with Company ABC, and it already has a comparable product in its pipeline. No one has done an inventory of Company ABC's programs and projects to see if there are any overlaps with ones in your company, but you worked for ABC part-time last year before joining Company MNO. You should—

a. Inform the sponsor in MNO
b. Work with the sponsor in MNO to revise and resubmit the business case
c. Introduce the program manager in ABC to the MNO sponsor
d. Inform the Portfolio Manager in MNO

108. Members of your program Governance Board are complaining about performance information from your program. They claim that your reports are too detailed, are too many in number, and are produced on a shifting schedule. You met with each person on the Board early in the program and thought you were meeting their information requirements. You then asked your organization's Enterprise PMO for assistance. The Enterprise PMO Director recommends the development and use of—

    a. A program dashboard
    b. Standard metrics used in your industry
    c. A more comprehensive software tool
    d. The organization's standard financial reports

109. For seven years, you have managed a program that involved breakthrough scientific research. You are now in the closing stage. You have already met with each scientist involved in the program at the time his or her work was finished. You have also met with a member of your enterprise program management office (EPMO) who specializes in knowledge management to ensure that the intellectual property developed in the program is captured and documented for future reuse. You are—

    a. Ensuring legal protection of this valuable asset
    b. Promoting collaboration in the scientific community
    c. Recognizing individual efforts as well as the efforts of the entire project team
    d. Officially releasing each scientist to his or her functional organization

110. Recognizing the importance of benefits realization and management, as a program manager, it has been noted that a best practice to follow is to be able to quantify as many benefits in your benefits realization plan as possible and also to be able to communicate their status as required quickly to stakeholders. You and your core team decided that a best practice to follow in your program to develop a new drug to cure bone cancer with limited if any side effects and to beat your competitors to market even with all the federal regulations was to—

    a. Use tangible benefits in your benefit realization plan
    b. Have each stakeholder sign off on your benefits realization plan indicating his or her concurrence with it
    c. Invite each stakeholder to regularly scheduled benefit reviews, which are included in your program's roadmap
    d. Maintain a benefits register

111. As the program manager working on the development of an advanced polymer chemical for raincoats, you are in the process of initiating your program. You were selected as the program manager because in past program work, you excelled in some key performance competencies in initiation, one of which is—

   a. Identifying high-level risks
   b. Ensuring alignment of program objectives with organizational strategic goals
   c. Preparing a plan to initiate the program
   d. Engaging stakeholders in ensuring strategic benefits are understood

112. Finally, your program to develop the advanced polymer chemical for raincoats is near to completion. You have had seven projects in your program, and the last one should finish in two months. You have been involving the people in your operations support group to be part of your program team meetings now for the last year and earlier included them on the distribution list for your status reports so they felt they were part of the team for success as you recognize transition planning is the key to benefits sustainment in program management. As a program manager, you also recognize the importance of ensuring that component transition requests are prepared. It is especially important during—

   a. Transition Planning
   b. Direct and Manage Program Execution
   c. Develop Program Management Plan
   d. Program Benefit Delivery

113. As you work on your program to design, develop, and manufacture a class of farm equipment that can be used above the Arctic Circle, you are also maintaining a spare parts inventory and are fulfilling spares requests for clients in addition to the new work in this program. You met today with the spare parts project manager, and he had a change to his project that affected his scope dramatically. When you reviewed this change with him, you realized it also would affect the scope of the manufacturing project manager's project in your program. As a result of your work in Program Scope Control, this means you should—

   a. Authorize funding for these changes
   b. Issue an approved change request
   c. Convene your CCB
   d. Update the PWBS

114. On your program to design, develop, and manufacture a class of farm equipment for use above the Arctic Circle, you want to make sure that the benefits from the program will be sustainable ones. Your sponsor is interested in having regular status reports about the progress of your program especially since she is located below the Arctic Circle and rarely makes on site visits given the weather conditions to assess progress herself. To provide a clear picture of your program's performance as a while, you must—

    a. Forecast information on the significant project components
    b. Aggregate information across projects and non-project activity
    c. Provide detailed reports on component projects at regular intervals
    d. Monitor the status of the key deliverables

115. You are sponsoring a new program in your company. You have identified the benefits and objectives and submitted the documentation to the Portfolio Review Board two weeks before its next meeting. You are competing with two other possible programs, so you decide to contact the Board members to see if they have any questions about your program. Board Member A is very supportive; Board Member B has concerns about the competitive attributes of your program versus those of other programs in the pipeline; Board Member C is supportive but not enthusiastic; Board Member D is not available to talk to you; and Board Member E is skeptical about the overall program strategy. To try to increase the support of Board Members B and E, you—

    a. Align the elements of your program more closely with the company's strategy
    b. Refine your net present value (NPV) and internal rate of return (IRR) analysis
    c. Meet with the Enterprise Project Management Office director to obtain support
    d. Enlist greater support from the executive sponsor who personally knows the Board members

116. You manage the development of an off-shore liquefied natural gas facility. Several contractors will be used in the component projects, and you are creating specific procurement strategies. After you determine which program work breakdown structure (PWBS) elements can be handled internally and which can be contracted, your next step is to—

    a. Follow the program scope statement
    b. Determine the program requirements
    c. Prepare a procurement management plan
    d. Make sure contractors have comparable acceptance criteria

117. Assume you are leading a program in your gas company to promote more use of natural gas by customers. You have identified a number of benefits to the use of natural gas, and one of them is environmental since it is much cleaner. It also is more cost effective. However, everyone resists change, and people are having trouble understanding the benefits of this program and how to best present these benefits to consumers, especially when the natural gas production facilities in your company are fully operational. This means that as the program manager you need to convince stakeholders that the risks associated with natural gas are low. As you do so, it is important therefore to concentrate on—

   a. Solely financial benefits
   b. Both direct and tangible benefits
   c. Intangible benefits and tangible benefits
   d. Measurable benefits

118. You have set up measurement criteria for each of the benefits you identified in your benefit realization plan. You now want to establish a baseline for the benefits in the plan. As you establish your baseline, you have collected some key organizational, financial, and operational metrics against which you can measure improvements. A key task to consider as you establish the baseline is to—

   a. Devise a strategy to collect baseline data such as using questionnaires and interviews
   b. Review your cost estimates
   c. Assess process interdependencies
   d. Determine the appropriate infrastructure needs

119. Finally after four years of planning, your program management plan to convert customer relationship management software, supplier management software, human resource software, and telecom systems from legacy systems to an integrated platform was approved. At last, you are working to execute your plan, and you have four projects in your program thus far. Approved change requests are being implemented—

   a. Under the supervision of the individual project managers
   b. By the program manager, based on his or her scope of authority
   c. After approval by the program's Governance Board
   d. As directed by the program management methodology

120. Finally after four years of planning, your program management plan to convert customer relationship management software, supplier management software, human resource software, and telecom systems from legacy systems to an integrated platform was approved. At last, you are working to execute your plan, and you have four projects in your program thus far. As you build individual and group competencies to enhance the performance of your program, you should also—

   a. Conduct performance assessments and place reports in the Human Resources files
   b. Communicate personnel performance to each team member's line manager
   c. Communicate personnel performance to the Vice President for Human Resources
   d. Rely on the Chief Learning Officer to conduct competency assessments

121. You are preparing for a meeting of your program's Governance Board. Your program coordinator is using earned value (EV) to track and monitor performance and to forecast future performance. On your program, the planned value (PV) is $30,587, and the EV is $26,365. At this point, your program is 70 percent complete, so you can tell your Governance Board that your schedule performance index (SPI) is 0.86. The Governance Board therefore recognizes—

   a. You are not experiencing any schedule problems
   b. You will have problems meeting your scheduled end date but are able to allocate additional resources
   c. There are problems, but it is easy to recover from this performance
   d. It will be difficult to recover from this performance, and a decision now is needed to terminate the program

122. You are assuming a position in a company that has not had much experience with program management. You will be leading the program team and performing a business function for your program. The business case has already been made, and the program is scheduled to move into the Program Initiation phase. As the program manager, one competency that is embedded in your job is—

   a. Communication
   b. Political skills
   c. Strategic visioning
   d. Leadership

123. Assume you are managing a program at your University to establish a Master of Science degree in Program Management. Already, the University's Master of Science degree in project management is well recognized, and it has been accredited by leading organizations. Your business case for this program was approved by the University's trustees, and they asked for a benefits realization plan, which you prepared, and they signed off on and approved. However, they felt for reporting purposes to a Governance Board that it would be helpful to prioritize the benefits you have identified and will report on during meetings of the Governance Board. One approach to consider is to ensure—

    a. The identified benefits support best practices
    b. The benefits are aligned with the University's strategic objectives
    c. A benefit owner is assigned
    d. Realistic measures of these benefits can be prepared

124. Working on this program to establish a Master of Science degree in Program Management, assume you have a meeting coming up with your Governance Board in two weeks. You need to demonstrate at this stage gate review how you will report and track the benefits from your program. However, in your work in planning, you have identified a number of key factors external to your program that affect the proposed benefits, one of which is that your leading competitor in this field and located in your state also is looking into such a program and plans to offer it in an on-line fashion; your University only operates in a face-to-face mode. You know how important it is to track benefits and learning about this other University's plans to offer the degree on line is a key benefit that you had not planned for but now feel it is essential. The new benefit actually represents a—

    a. New project
    b. Risk opportunity
    c. Major issue
    d. New program

125. As a program manager, you recognize the importance of effective risk management. You want to maximize any risks that may be opportunities that can benefit your program and the organization. As you prepare your program risk management plan, you define risk profiles, which—

    a. Are collected through surveys
    b. You brainstorm with your team and other stakeholders
    c. Are expressed in policy statements
    d. You determine through interviews

126. As program manager for the development of a new drug, you are pleased that it has finally received regulatory approval, and you can move on to the manufacturing and distribution phase. You have been managing this program now for eight years, and you had six projects in it. As this program has been under way for eight years, it is a best practice to—

   a. Organize program knowledge as a reference
   b. Obtain a license for exclusive distribution
   c. Work to ensure a positive reception for the product from end users and the medical field using skills in customer relationship management
   d. Sign a nondisclosure agreement with the government

127. As the program manager for a new pipeline system that has as its goal no potential incidents of any type, you have a major challenge as your company in the past has had a poor safety record. This program is complex, and this goal will be difficult to achieve. However, after working to plan the program for three years, your Steering Committee met and approved your program management plan. As you move to approve components to be part of your program, you need to review the—

   a. Component charter
   b. Change requests
   c. Business case
   d. Component initiation requests

128. Your program management plan has been approved. So far, three projects have been chartered and authorized to be part of your program, and others may be added later. You have staffed your program team with a variety of in-house staff members, selected consultants, and several new full-time employees. It is now time to—

   a. Prepare your team development plan
   b. Update your program resource plan
   c. Prepare your resource management plan
   d. Update your staffing management plan

129. Assume you are working for a leading training company. Your leading competitor has just announced that it will launch in one month a new training approach using videos. Your CEO realizes such an approach will be highly beneficial and is superior to the on-line training your company offers, which is only asynchronous with people looking at slides, as the instructor discusses each slide. In fact, the CEO has had complaints about the boring nature of your firm's on line training. You have been selected as the program manager for this new video approach, and you need to have it available for all of your courses by the end of the year so you are not lagging that much behind the competition. You are working on your communication plan. You have found which of the following to be especially useful to you in this regard—

    a. Communications strategy
    b. Communications requirements analysis
    c. Lessons learned database
    d. Program charter

130. Finally, you Governance Board approved your communications plan for this program, and you now are addressing the best way to handle performance reporting and how to communicate this information to provide stakeholders with needed information. As you work in this area, you should consult the—

    a. Program management plan
    b. Program work breakdown structure (PWBS)
    c. Governance plan
    d. Organizational communications strategy

131. You are a member of your organization's Program Selection Committee, which is conducting an off-site meeting to review the company's five major strategic goals, all of which are weighted equally. Goal 1 is to produce the highest possible quality products; goal 2 is to provide outstanding customer relationship management; goal 3 is to reduce reliance on external supply sources and maximize internal resources; goal 4 is to reduce manufacturing costs; and goal 5 is to maximize productivity. You are considering four programs and will recommend one to the CEO. Program A partially supports goal 1, fully supports goals 2, 3, and 4, and does not support goal 5. Program B fully supports goals 1, 3, 4, and 5, but does not support goal 2. Program C fully supports goals 1 and 2, partially supports goals 3 and 4, but does not support goal 5. Program D partially supports goals 1, 2, and 5, and fully supports goals 3 and 4. Considering this information, your recommendation should be to select—

    a. Program A
    b. Program B
    c. Program C
    d. Program D

132. You are preparing for a major Governance Board review of your program. The program sponsor is especially interested in progress on Project A, as it provides the foundation for two other projects, and at the last meeting it was behind schedule. You want to ask the Board to approve the initiation of a new project. However, it is the Board's responsibility to—

    a. Request an audit of Project A
    b. Focus on overall performance at this meeting and convene another meeting to determine if the new project should be initiated
    c. Ask for data on Project A's performance to date and especially its use of resources
    d. Determine minimal acceptance criteria

133. As a program manager, you consider the interests and concerns of all your stakeholders for program success. You manage communications to ensure that your stakeholders are informed about what is happening on your program and so that you can resolve any issues of importance to them. This is done as part of your responsibilities in—

    a. Communications Control
    b. Information Distribution
    c. Stakeholder Engagement
    d. Communications Planning

134. Assume you are managing a program so your organization, a Fortune 50 company, has a standard program management system (PMIS) that all programs in all of its 90 business units will use. Such a common PMIS is a major internal program, and as a result, you have a limited budget to work with to make sure it is a success and is adopted by the heads of the business units and its program managers. You are following guidelines in the Project Management Institute's *Standard for Program Management* as you prepare this PMIS. You find as you monitor and control the program's finances you need to be both proactive and reactive. An example of being proactive is—
    a. Identifying impacts to the components from overruns or under-runs
    b. Responding to necessary but unplanned activities that negatively affect the budget
    c. Responding to necessary but unplanned activities that positively affect the budget
    d. Using cost forecasting techniques on a regular basis

135. You are Company A's program manager for the development of an online banking system for your community bank, for which your company will receive $20 million.. Your management at the highest level is totally committed to this program, and it is the number one program in Company A's portfolio. Your Governance Board is dedicated to its success. As a result, the chairperson of the Board is—
    a. The program sponsor
    b. The CEO
    c. The Portfolio Manager
    d. The Director of the Enterprise PMO

136. As a program manager in your country's food safety department, you are managing a program to ensure the safety of imported food in your country. This program resulted from many people becoming sick because of imported shrimp, poultry, and beef. This program is using public money and will last for several years; therefore, as the program manager, you need to—
    a. Have a thorough understanding of the financial environment
    b. Develop a plan for each of the components in your program
    c. Have your project managers use earned value management to track all expenses
    d. Set up a project management information system to track resource plans and use

137. Each of the projects in your program prepares a project risk management plan to describe how risk management is structured. Each project manager also prepares risk response plans for each of the key identified risks. As program manager, you review the risk response plans to—

   a. Establish triggers for the project risks
   b. Determine actions that could affect other components
   c. Identify intra-project risks
   d. Establish a contingency reserve

138. Your organization is ISO 9001 certified. As program manager, you have arranged for a member of your company's Quality Assurance Program (a Black Belt in Six Sigma) to support your program. This team member reports directly to you and by dotted line to the manager of the Quality Assurance Department. In his first audit, he finds that one of the projects includes several key service management activities that have not met quality requirements. Your next step is to—

   a. Facilitate an off-site meeting of your core program team to determine how best to handle this deficiency
   b. Convene a meeting of your program Governance Board to request that an additional resource be added to serve as a project manager for these activities
   c. Prepare a quality assurance change request
   d. Revisit the program's quality management plan and update it

139. You are Company A's program manager for the development of an online banking system for your community bank, for which your company will receive $20 million. One of your first tasks was to work with your sponsor and specify the purpose of the phase-gate reviews and when they will be held on this program. One goal of these reviews is to—

   a. Monitor the business environment for changes
   b. Assess strategic alignment of the program
   c. Ensure the program charter remains viable
   d. Identify the key decision makers and stakeholders associated with this program

140. You manage a program for the Occupational Safety and Health Administration (OSHA) to make all the agency's regulations performance based and applicable to any industry group. You identify 50 external stakeholders who are active participants in this process, and 30 who are interested but not active, along with 75 interested internal stakeholders. Initially, when you and our team identified these stakeholders, you used—

    a. Brainstorming
    b. Documentation reviews
    c. Questionnaires
    d. Interviews

141. As manager of a program for the Federal Trade Commission that involves changes to existing regulations throughout the Commission, you have a major challenge as the majority of the regulations have not been reviewed for more than 20 years. Others of course have been added. Your role is to make sure in your program that all of the regulations are current and also are easily accessible by all stakeholders. You have a total of seven projects in your program, and since your program is a government mandated one, you have a Governance Board for your program that meets at least monthly and at key stage gate reviews. The person who is responsible for ensuring program success is the—

    a. Program director
    b. Commission Chairman
    c. Program sponsor
    d. Director of the Enterprise Program Management Office

142. Assume you are working in a company, CDE, which specializes in new product development. The CDE executives are concerned because its last two products in the on-line music industry were late to market, and by the time they were on the market, competitors had products out with more attractive features to customers. As a result, CDE is in jeopardy of losing its market share in on-line music for mobile phones and tablets and also in games for these phones and tablets. You are now in process of working with your R&D team to determine a new product to propose to CDE's executives. Given the last two experiences, you believe you should include all of the following items in your business case but you especially need to focus on a—

    a. Existing work under way
    b. High-level net present value analysis
    c. High-level roadmap
    d. Competitive analysis

143. You are managing a program to develop a new source of energy in the extreme northern latitudes when solar power is not available. Working with your core program team and your Governance Board, you have identified a number of component projects. Your company has several key projects under way, and resources will be difficult to acquire for this new program. A key consideration is—

   a. The availability of key staff members
   b. Your ability to negotiate with functional managers for the needed staff
   c. Previous work by the staff as a successful team
   d. The availability of off-shore employees to drive down costs

144. In your role of program manager for this Masters of Science degree in Program Management, your benefit realization plan includes both tangible and intangible benefits. You recognize the demand for the degree, and it in turn will lead to new income to the University. It also will enhance customer satisfaction with the University and will demonstrate to the overall project management community that it is following the trends in the profession. You expect a large number of people to enroll in the program based on the interest now in obtaining the PgMP® credential. You have seven projects in your program and are fortunate to have a PMO, and it is determining an easy but meaningful way to report on the realization of benefits from your program and then to provide this information to your stakeholders—both internal and external. By tracking the benefits during the program rather than after the degree is in place and students have enrolled offers a number of benefits in itself, one of which is—

   a. Provides an opportunity to publicize the program
   b. Encourages ownership of the solution
   c. Ensures funding limits are not exceeded
   d. Ensures the available information is of the highest quality

145. As you work on your program to improve the economic growth of your country, you are following a program management methodology that your agency's Center of Excellence in Program Management prepared. Your organization therefore in defining all program management activity as well as that for every deliverable and service realizes the importance of—

   a. Program infrastructure development
   b. Benefit sustainment
   c. Stakeholder engagement
   d. Quality management

146. As the program manager for a multinational program headquartered in Sweden, you have adopted English as the common language for use on the program. However, most of your team members are located in Asia, and many of them do not speak English as their primary language. You have decided, therefore, to adopt the common English vocabulary of 4,000 words to facilitate the communication process. This decision should be stated in the—

   a. Communications requirements
   b. Program management plan
   c. Communications plan
   d. Program scope statement

147. Working on your program to improve the economic growth of your country, you know from the business case there are many risks and issues. However, the business case only presented a high-level view of them. You then held a risk planning meeting with your stakeholders to help prepare a risk management plan, and you have set up a process to track issues. Now, you and your core program team are working to identify risks that could affect your program building on those in the business case. You and your team are clarifying the definition of each risk and grouping them by cause. This means you are using which of the following techniques?

   a. Flowcharts
   b. Influence diagrams
   c. Root cause identification
   d. SWOT analysis

148. However, as you work on this program to improve the economic growth of your country, now you have another problem. A key member of your program staff has been complaining lately of the company's vacation policies. He would like to take more time off but has not yet accrued enough time to do so. You are concerned that he is going to leave the company, so you monitor his e-mail, in accordance with company policy, to see whether he is sending his resume to other companies. The act of sending out his resume would be called a—

   a. Risk trigger
   b. Risk event
   c. Misuse of the company's e-mail policy
   d. Violation of the company's code of ethics

149. You have a total of seven projects in your program, and since your program is a government mandated one, you have a Governance Board for your program that meets at least monthly and at key stage gate reviews. You and your core team have prepared a governance plan that you will present at the Board's next meeting in two weeks. As you prepared this plan, it was beneficial to review the—

    a. Governance structure and composition
    b. Gate review requirements
    c. Commission's quality standards
    d. Program charter

150. As part of your stakeholder engagement activities, your core program team meets with each of the stakeholders you have identified as critical to program success. During these meetings, the team members assigned to work with specific stakeholders try to gauge their attitudes toward risk, identify their perceptions, and better understand how they might respond. This approach is especially useful to you as you—

    a. Analyze risks
    b. Prepare the program's risk management plan
    c. Determine stakeholder issues that may lead to risks
    d. Prepare the stakeholder engagement plan

151. You are sponsoring a new program that will focus on a new product in which educators can immediately determine whether or not a student is plagiarizing, whether the student has cited the reference correctly, or whether it is an entirely new idea. The program will have a number of components, and the planned components have interdependencies between them. In this program you want to evaluate its program objectives, and you realize you need to address a number of concerns to satisfy all the involved and committed stakeholders. One of these considerations in this situation is—

    a. Cultural considerations
    b. Ethical concerns
    c. Sustainability issues
    d. Technological changes

152. Your government program to review and update existing regulations is to be completed in a year and a half, and you are now at the half-way point. You have three projects in your program plus a Governance Board for oversight. As you have been managing this program, it has been extremely helpful to you to—

    a. Have a program management information system
    b. Use your benefit delivery plan
    c. Have a change management specialist as a member of your core team
    d. Use benchmarking with other government agencies who have already conducted similar programs to update regulations

153. You have completed five of the seven projects in your program so far to establish a Master's Degree in Program Management. In the last meeting with the Governance Board, when it was time to transition one of the projects, this meant it was then time to hire the program director and a couple of people for supporting roles. This project had outlined all the support tasks that needed to be done and included items such as the job descriptions for the program director and his or her staff members, the criteria to use to select the program director and staff, and methods to evaluate their performance. Now the director has been hired. You therefore should as a best practice—

    a. Involve the new director in all meetings with all stakeholders
    b. Ensure the new director understands the benefits of this program and how they will be sustained
    c. Ask the director to serve as the project manager for the two remaining projects on the program
    d. Ask the Governance Board to add the new director to be a member to oversee the remaining projects on the program

154. Finally, your program to rebuild the water desalinization plant for Ferguson, Saudi Arabia is complete. This program has been under way for more than five years. You had a number of leasing agreements on the program, and you are confident all of them have been closed successfully. You also had several subcontractors, and you have had reviews with each of them. You are meeting with your Governance Board, to obtain approval for the final phase of the program. You have made a recommendation to the Board to close the program. The person who will make the official decision is—

    a. Executive director
    b. Program sponsor
    c. Governance Board
    d. Head of the PMO

155. Your organization has just announced that funds will be cut by 10 percent. Even though you are still in the planning phase of your program life cycle, and your program is considered a high priority in your company's portfolio, unfortunately, your program is not exempt from these budget cuts. But, you do have an advantage because your executive team is interested in your program because it is required for your company's continued viability in its product line of sport utility vehicles. Your executive team has mandated certain delivery dates, which you felt were feasible until these budget cuts were announced. Still, you must meet them so you have prepared a new program roadmap and a new master schedule. You now must communicate these changes to your stakeholders. As the program manager, you—

    a. Are the champion for change
    b. Should meet individually with your key stakeholders
    c. Must provide consistent messages to all stakeholders
    d. Empower the person listed in the stakeholder register to contact his or her stakeholders

156. You have been working on a new product development program for your company, which specializes in farm equipment. Your product is to combine an easy-to-use tractor with a more complex crawler so the customer does not have to purchase two separate items and can use the combination product to meet a number of unique needs. You just found out from your portfolio manager that the company plans to acquire a competitor that specializes in riding lawn mowers. You have now suggested to your Governance Board that you add a project to your program to also combine a mower into the new product of your program. You believe such an improvement will—

    a. Increase the benefits to be realized by the product
    b. Result in a longer timeline but will be one that customers should find of use
    c. Can position your company well in the marketplace
    d. Will lead to improved customer relationship management

157. You are ready to close a contract for a program-level contract that was set up to cover the requirements for any procurements by the components in you program. Before closing this contract, you should—

    a. Meet with each component manager
    b. Hold a meeting with this contractor for a performance review
    c. Document results according to the program plan
    d. Prepare a contract closeout report

158. Your program communications management plan shows the various items to be distributed to your stakeholders; their purpose, frequency, and format; and the person responsible for each. As you work on your program, you follow this plan for formal communication of program information. You now have your process in place to distribute information to your stakeholders at the time and frequency they require. It is important not to overlook the need to—

a. Update the communications requirements analysis
b. Update the lessons learned data base
c. Prepare standard information requests
d. Update the communications log

159. You are a program manager under contract to a government agency that is responsible for issuing visas and passports. You have been working on this program for eight years and are responsible for all the information and telecommunications functions for the agency. Your company realizes this program is essential to its success, and this is the first time it has worked for this agency. Therefore, it established a governance structure to oversee the process. A best practice to follow as approvals for program changes are made is to—

a. Update the governance plan based on decisions made
b. Record the outcome in the knowledge management repository
c. Meet with your core team and project managers and inform them of the results of the Governance Board meeting
d. Meet with your program sponsor to discuss your next steps

160. Assume you have been maintaining a benefit register once your program's benefit realization plan was prepared. Because of the importance of benefits management on programs, you are fortunate that a member of your core team has expertise in this area and have appointed her to serve as the business benefits manager of your program, working closely with the PMO in your company. She will work closely with you and the other core team members as she will be maintaining the register, preparing the benefit reports, and also conducting benefit reviews. One of the key purposes of the benefit reviews is to—

a. Create benefit ownership
b. Address the risk of operational areas that fail to commit to the benefits
c. Establish an approach to prioritize benefits that are in the realization plan
d. Review the benefits realization plan and implement improvements based on lessons learned to date

161. Your company, a member of the Fortune 500, is well known around the world as it is the leading producer of the top selling cereal. The cereal is nutritious, is one that both adults and children both enjoy, and has been on the market for over 40 years. Your company, though, is interested now in moving into the ice cream market. This will be a major change, and you have been asked to be the program manager for a new line of 12 different ice cream types. The development of this product is in your company's strategic plan, but it is so radically different from the cereal products for which you company is well known. Before going further and finalizing your charter, you feel it is important to talk with organizational leaders to address the program's—

    a. Attractiveness
    b. Readiness
    c. Vision
    d. Funding methods

162. Assume that your ice cream product line has been officially approved, and you are the program manager for this new program in your company. Because it is considered to be such a breakthrough program, it is ranked number three in your company. It has the support and visibility of the executive team. You are now helping to guide the initiating activities and are working on the financial framework. You have determined there will be a larger negative cash flow in the beginning than originally anticipated. This financial framework is useful for a number of reasons including—

    a. Preparing program funding schedules
    b. Serving as a cost baseline
    c. Determining constraints
    d. Describing management of risk reserves

163. You are working to plan your ice cream program for your Fortune 500 company, which is so well known around the world for its cereal products. Because it is venturing into ice cream, all resources are being provided internally, and everyone on the team is signing a confidentiality agreement so competitors are not aware of this new program. However, already resources are scarce although when you prepared your schedule you assumed the needed resources would be available. Now you realize you will need to do a lot of negotiating for resources. You decided since this program is ranked number three on the priority list that you should use—

    a. Market analysis
    b. Critical chain
    c. Resource leveling
    d. Resource optimization

164. You are enjoying your work as the program manager for the new ice cream program for your Fortune 500 company, which is so well known around the world for its cereal products. All resources are being provided internally, and everyone on the team is signing a confidentiality agreement so competitors are not aware of this new program. However, already resources are scarce in the organization working on cereal products. You have prepared your schedule and in doing so assumed the needed resources would be available. However, in a meeting with your Governance Board, you now realize you will need to do a lot of negotiating for resources. Fortunately, you have been successful and have three experienced project managers so far assigned who are supporting the three projects thus far in the program. It is important now since these project managers have been assigned that you evaluate their performance according to the—

   a. Project plan
   b. Program management plan
   c. Benefits realization plan
   d. Resource plan

165. You are working to plan your ice cream program for your Fortune 500 company, which is so well known around the world for its cereal products. Because it is venturing into ice cream, all resources are being provided internally, and everyone on the team is signing a confidentiality agreement so competitors are not aware of this new program. However, already resources are scarce in the organization working on cereal products. You have prepared your schedule and in doing so assumed the needed resources would be available. Because of your work in program management, you recognize changes occur on programs, especially given that programs represent a change of some type. Therefore, you and your core team prepared a change management plan. You find it is especially helpful in terms of which of the following types of changes—

   a. Benefits
   b. Stakeholder expectations
   c. Market conditions
   d. Rewards

166. You are working to plan your ice cream program for your Fortune 500 company. All resources are being provided internally, and everyone on the team is signing a confidentiality agreement so competitors are not aware of this new program. However, already resources are scarce in the organization. You have prepared your schedule and in doing so assumed the needed resources would be available. However, in a meeting with your Governance Board, you now realize you will need to do a lot of negotiating for resources. Now you are in year two of your program, and you have four projects. However, now, you have some new members of your Governance Board, and they have been working in different business units of the company. New member E believes the program is too risky, and new member F is also a risk avoidance person. You realize the next meeting of your Board could be quite contentious, and you decided to evaluate the risks of your stakeholders. It is especially important as you perform this evaluation to consider the views of your—

    a. Sponsor
    b. Head of the Governance Board
    c. Enterprise PMO Director
    d. Portfolio Manager

167. You are responsible as the program manager for the development of a new gas transmission pipeline that will span three countries. You are in the early phases, and one of the countries involved has major concerns that the pipeline will impact areas detrimental to the environment. It wants additional information about the program before it will provide the needed permits and approval. Your managers recognize that such approval is paramount for the program to proceed and have asked you to prepare a—

    a. Feasibility study
    b. Roadmap
    c. Mission statement
    d. Vision statement

168. Although your company has been active in project management for many years, it is relatively new to program management. You became certified as a PgMP® and suggested to your supervisor that two of your current projects would be better managed as a program and discussed why program management was more appropriate. One of the executives knew about the usefulness of governance and stage-gate reviews from his previous work in new product development, and he recommended all programs have a governance structure. Such a process now has been implemented. The effectiveness of the governance process is best handled through—

   a. Regularly scheduled reviews
   b. Program performance reports
   c. Formal gate review decision requests
   d. Use of your program management plan

169. You are a program manager in your agency. Your enterprise program management office (EPMO) has a program management information system (PMIS) and a methodology for projects that are undertaken in your agency programs. You will be contributing to the PMIS as you—

   a. Distribute information
   b. Monitor and control risks
   c. Use the lessons learned data base
   d. Perform financial monitoring and control

170. Finally your program to establish the Masters of Science degree in Program Management is complete. You have completed the transition plan to the program director and his staff, and people at the University are pleased with how you managed this program and achieved the benefits in your benefit realization plan. To help future programs at the University, they asked you to identify what you believe is the value of benefits management. As a first step you suggest that—

   a. Each program has an individual on the core team that is responsible for the program's business benefits
   b. Involving as many stakeholders as possible, both internal and external to the program, in the benefits identification process to help secure their buy-in to its goals and objectives
   c. The program be set up with a viable business case that has a list of initial benefits to be achieved
   d. Establish from the start of the program methods to use to measure each identified benefit and ways to track its achievement

Answer Sheet for Practice Test 1

1.	a	b	c	d	20.	a	b	c	d
2.	a	b	c	d	21.	a	b	c	d
3.	a	b	c	d	22.	a	b	c	d
4.	a	b	c	d	23.	a	b	c	d
5.	a	b	c	d	24.	a	b	c	d
6.	a	b	c	d	25.	a	b	c	d
7.	a	b	c	d	26.	a	b	c	d
8.	a	b	c	d	27.	a	b	c	d
9.	a	b	c	d	28.	a	b	c	d
10.	a	b	c	d	29.	a	b	c	d
11.	a	b	c	d	30.	a	b	c	d
12.	a	b	c	d	31.	a	b	c	d
13.	a	b	c	d	32.	a	b	c	d
14.	a	b	c	d	33.	a	b	c	d
15.	a	b	c	d	34.	a	b	c	d
16.	a	b	c	d	35.	a	b	c	d
17.	a	b	c	d	36.	a	b	c	d
18.	a	b	c	d	37.	a	b	c	d
19.	a	b	c	d	38.	a	b	c	d

39.	a	b	c	d
40.	a	b	c	d
41.	a	b	c	d
42.	a	b	c	d
43.	a	b	c	d
44.	a	b	c	d
45.	a	b	c	d
46.	a	b	c	d
47.	a	b	c	d
48.	a	b	c	d
49.	a	b	c	d
50.	a	b	c	d
51.	a	b	c	d
52.	a	b	c	d
53.	a	b	c	d
54.	a	b	c	d
55.	a	b	c	d
56.	a	b	c	d
57.	a	b	c	d
58.	a	b	c	d
59.	a	b	c	d
60.	a	b	c	d

61.	a	b	c	d
62.	a	b	c	d
63.	a	b	c	d
64.	a	b	c	d
65.	a	b	c	d
66.	a	b	c	d
67.	a	b	c	d
68.	a	b	c	d
69.	a	b	c	d
70.	a	b	c	d
71.	a	b	c	d
72.	a	b	c	d
73.	a	b	c	d
74.	a	b	c	d
75.	a	b	c	d
76.	a	b	c	d
77.	a	b	c	d
78.	a	b	c	d
79.	a	b	c	d
80.	a	b	c	d
81.	a	b	c	d
82.	a	b	c	d

83.	a	b	c	d
84.	a	b	c	d
85.	a	b	c	d
86.	a	b	c	d
87.	a	b	c	d
88.	a	b	c	d
89.	a	b	c	d
90.	a	b	c	d
91.	a	b	c	d
92.	a	b	c	d
93.	a	b	c	d
94.	a	b	c	d
95.	a	b	c	d
96.	a	b	c	d
97.	a	b	c	d
98.	a	b	c	d
99.	a	b	c	d
100.	a	b	c	d
101.	a	b	c	d
102.	a	b	c	d
103.	a	b	c	d
104.	a	b	c	d

105.	a	b	c	d
106.	a	b	c	d
107.	a	b	c	d
108.	a	b	c	d
109.	a	b	c	d
110.	a	b	c	d
111.	a	b	c	d
112.	a	b	c	d
113.	a	b	c	d
114.	a	b	c	d
115.	a	b	c	d
116.	a	b	c	d
117.	a	b	c	d
118.	a	b	c	d
119.	a	b	c	d
120.	a	b	c	d
121.	a	b	c	d
122.	a	b	c	d
123.	a	b	c	d
124.	a	b	c	d
125.	a	b	c	d
126.	a	b	c	d

127.	a	b	c	d
128.	a	b	c	d
129.	a	b	c	d
130.	a	b	c	d
131.	a	b	c	d
132.	a	b	c	d
133.	a	b	c	d
134.	a	b	c	d
135.	a	b	c	d
136.	a	b	c	d
137.	a	b	c	d
138.	a	b	c	d
139.	a	b	c	d
140.	a	b	c	d
141.	a	b	c	d
142.	a	b	c	d
143.	a	b	c	d
144.	a	b	c	d
145.	a	b	c	d
146.	a	b	c	d
147.	a	b	c	d
148.	a	b	c	d

149.	a	b	c	d
150.	a	b	c	d
151.	a	b	c	d
152.	a	b	c	d
153.	a	b	c	d
154.	a	b	c	d
155.	a	b	c	d
156.	a	b	c	d
157.	a	b	c	d
158.	a	b	c	d
159.	a	b	c	d
160.	a	b	c	d
161.	a	b	c	d
162.	a	b	c	d
163.	a	b	c	d
164.	a	b	c	d
165.	a	b	c	d
166.	a	b	c	d
167.	a	b	c	d
168.	a	b	c	d
169.	a	b	c	d
170.	a	b	c	d

Answer Key for Practice Test 1

1. b. Portfolio

   The portfolio is where investment decisions are made, resources are allocated, and priorities are identified. Thus, it is one of the truest measures of the organization's intent, direction, risk tolerance, and progress. Program components must be aligned with the organization's strategy to clearly show why they are being undertaken.

   PMI®, *The Standard for Program Management*, 2013, 11

2. c. Have your vendor prepare eLearning modules that team members can access at their convenience

   Considering your team members' various locations and work schedules, the best option is to provide them with training that they can access when time permits. Although MP3 recordings can be accessed on an as-needed basis, audio recordings are much less effective than eLearning modules in helping people to learn a software system.

   PMI®, *Program Management Professional* (PgMP)® *Examination Content Outline*, 2011, 10

3. a. Stakeholder register

   Stakeholder engagement and communications management are closely related. In working to prepare a communications plan for your program, a stakeholder register is another output from Communications Planning to show stakeholder information requirements.

   PMI®, *The Standard for Program Management*, 2013, 74

4. d. Inform the ABS point of contact about the MRA issue

   If you do not pass the MRA, you cannot re-take it for a year. As you are not certified as a PgMP®, and it was a contractual requirement to be certified, you need to inform the client. As part of the PMI® Code of Ethics and Professional Conduct, it is incumbent to act in a truthful matter and under fairness we must disclose any real or potential conflicts of interest to appropriate parties.

   PMI®, PMI Code of Ethics and Professional Conduct. Available from http://www.pmi.org/codeofethicsPDF, 4–5

5. d. Consider her proposed change may be an opportunity to respond adaptively

   The program manager, team members, members of the Governance Board and other stakeholders may initiate change requests for a variety of reasons. Working on programs, the need for change may be viewed as an opportunity. It enables the program manager to respond adaptively to evolving circumstances and ensure the program can deliver its desired benefits and value to the organization. The best approach is for the program manager and the Governance Board to embrace the need for change and work collaboratively to see that needed changes to ensure benefit delivery are pursued.

   PMI®, *The Standard for Program Management*, 2013, 59

6. c. Program goals and objectives

   Goals are clearly defined outcomes as to what the program is to achieve, while objectives are final results, outputs, and deliverables from the individual projects. They are part of the program plan in Program, Strategy Management.

   PMI®, *The Standard for Program Management*, 2013, 28–29

7. d. It will define how and when benefits will be delivered

   The purpose of the benefits realization plan is to document the activities to achieve the program's planned benefits. It thus defines how and when benefits are to be delivered.

   PMI®, *The Standard for Program Management*, 2013, 38

8. a. Served as a baseline for the program with the existing metrics in it

   The benefits realization plan is the baseline document that guides benefit delivery through program performance. When the plan is developed with the measurement criteria in it, it then sets a baseline for the program and it is then communicated to stakeholders, including sponsors.

   PMI®, *Program Management Professional* (PgMP)® *Examination Content Outline*, 2011, 13

   PMI®, *The Standard for Program Management*, 2013, 38

9. d. Determine the optimal supply chain strategy based on a wide variety of factors

   Make-or-buy decisions are business decisions that can have far-reaching impacts on any organization. A decision, for example, to outsource an operation could lead to a lack of core competency in that area. Make-or-buy decisions determine which program elements will be delivered using internal resources as compared to those that will be obtained from outside suppliers.

   PMI®, *The Standard for Program Management*, 2013, 90

10. d. Communications strategy

   Since the program manager communicates to a wide audience at various levels, and is the key communicator for the program, he or she can benefit from a defined and documented strategy for the wide spectrum of communication requirements.

   PMI®, *The Standard for Program Management*, 2013, 75

11. b. Define the high-level requirements.

   Business and high-level requirements need to be developed, documented, and delivered. As the business case Is prepared, the high-level requirements must be determined before moving forward as part of this initial program assessment.

   PMI®, *The Standard for Program Management*, 2013, 28

   PMI®, *Program Management Professional* (PgMP)® *Examination Content Outline*, 2011, 6

   Milosevic, Dragan Z., Martinelli, Russ J., and Waddell, James M. *Program Management for Improved Business Results*. 2007, Hoboken, NJ: John Wiley & Sons, 150

12. b. Program Financial Monitoring and Control

   Environmental changes are critical, because they can affect the program financial management activities. It is necessary for the program's finances and expenditures to be within budget and controlled; these environmental changes could create changes to the budget baseline.

   PMI®, *The Standard for Program Management*, 2013, 81

13. c. Program plan

 A program plan is prepared during Program Strategy Alignment, which is the documented reference by which a program will measure its success and includes metrics for success, a method for measurement, and a definition of success. The program management plan is prepared in Program Preparation and is more detailed based on the various outputs from program formulation.

 PMI®, *The Standard for Program Management*, 2013, 28, 68

14. a. PWBS

 The program work breakdown structure (PWBS) formalizes the program scope in terms of deliverables and the work that must be done. It then is used to build realistic schedules, develop cost estimates, and organize the work.

 PMI®, *The Standard for Program Management*, 2013, 105

15. c. Have her go through a 360-degree feedback analysis

 A 360-degree feedback analysis is an excellent mechanism to look broadly at a person's management, leadership, and interpersonal skills. It can provide an excellent foundation for future development as well as providing key insights by the people that work with her on a daily basis.

 PMI. *Program Management Professional (PgMP)® Examination Content Outline*, 2011, 10

 Levin, Ginger and Ward, J. LeRoy. *Program Management Complexity: A Competency Model*. 2011. Boca Raton, FL: CRC Press, 70

16. b. Update the roadmap

 Planning is an iterative process. As the benefit realization plan is updated, the program roadmap also should be updated especially since among other things the roadmap describes incremental benefit delivery as applicable.

 PMI®, *The Standard for Program Management*, 2013, 38–39

17. c. Enables a focus on changing strategies

 Unlike governance at the project level, which is focused on control to ensure projects are meeting the triple constraint, at the program level, governance is a way in which programs seek authorization and support for dynamically changing program strategies or plans to respond to emerging outcomes.

 PMI®, *The Standard for Program Management*, 2013, 52

18. b. Prepared a roadmap

    This program will last a long time. The roadmap is a chronological representation shown graphically of the program's intended direction and has a set of documented success criteria for each chronological event.

    PMI®, *The Standard for Program Management*, 2013, 29

    PMI®, *Program Management Professional* (PgMP)® *Examination Content Outline*, 2011, 6

19. a. Differentiate between the resources assigned to the program and those at the project level

    An accountability matrix is useful on programs. It can identify and assign program roles and responsibilities in order to build the core team. It is also helpful to differentiate between the program and project resources.

    PMI®, *Program Management Professional (PgMP)® Examination Content Outline,* 2011, 8

20. a. Some projects may need to be integrated with others to provide program benefits

    In a program, some projects may produce benefits that can be realized immediately, and others may deliver capabilities that must be integrated with those of other projects to realize benefits. The program life cycle may be extended as some projects transition and others begin.

    PMI®, *The Standard for Program Management*, 2013, 5, 19

21. b. Identify competency requirements for each role and responsibility

    After the competence requirements are identified, the next step is to negotiate for team members, assess their strengths and weaknesses, and build a training plan. Core team assignments are determined during program infrastructure development.

    PMI®, *The Standard for Program Management*, 2013, 85–86

    Milosevic et al., 2007, 397–400

    Thiry, Michel. *Program Management.* 2010, Surrey, England: Gower Publishing Limited, 93–96

    Levin, Ginger and Ward, J. LeRoy. 2011, *Program Management Complexity: A Competency Model.* Boca Raton, FL: CRC Press

22. a. An assumption

    Assumptions are considered to be true, real, or certain. In this situation, both project managers have assumed that this critical resource will be available as required. The program manager must work to resolve this situation.

    PMI®, *PMI Lexicon of Project Management Terms.* Available from http://pmi.org/lexicomterms

23. c. Hold a status review

    Status reviews are needed throughout the program as part of Program Performance Reporting. Information on status and progress must be communicated to stakeholders. Periodic reports should be prepared, and presentations should be conducted. These reviews should be held regularly to ensure compliance with contracts and with the cost and schedule baselines.

    PMI®, *The Standard for Program Management*, 2013, 77

24. b. The major project life-cycle phases and the activities within them will remain similar

    Although the type of program may influence the life cycle, the primary life-cycle phases and their activities are similar since the purpose of life cycle management is to manage activities regarding program definition, program benefits delivery, and program closure.

    PMI®, *The Standard for Program Management*, 2013, 167

25. a. Positive, because you will be building stronger relationships with your client

    Provided the client's code of ethics does not prohibit such entertainment activities, politicking is a skill and competency that successful program managers practice. In this instance, such activity can be very helpful in uncovering underlying problems.

    PMI®, *Program Management Professional (PgMP)® Examination Content Outline,* 2011, 14

26. a. Demonstrate an understanding of the needs of the customer.

    The business case must demonstrate an understanding of the needs, business benefits, feasibility, and program justification. To do so, skills in feasibility analysis and marketing are required. The business environment and customer requirements information are necessary to build the business case.

    PMI®, *The Standard for Program Management,* 2013, 28

    Milosevic et al., 2007, 281–283

27. c. Determine whether changes are required to components

    The benefits realization plan is used by program governance for a number of reasons. The Governance Board is interested in determining if benefit achievement is occurring as planned or whether changes are needed to the components or to the program.

    PMI®, *The Standard for Program Management*, 2013, 38

28. d. Assigned by the program sponsor

    During Program Initiation, the program sponsor is selected, and he or she assigns a program manager to conduct and manage the initial work for the program.

    PMI®, *The Standard for Program Management*, 2013, 83

29. a. Complete a skill set inventory

    Regardless of the assertions made by the other managers who provided the team members, it is important to fully understand what skill sets each member has. After a skill set inventory is completed, team assignments can be made.

    PMI®, *Program Management Professional (PgMP)® Examination Content Outline*, 2011, 10

30. a. Document the rationale for the decision

    In Program Scope Control, a change management activity is established. As an output, the disposition of the request is determined, and the rationale of the decision is documented.

    PMI®, *The Standard for Program Management*, 2013, 106

31. c. Make them readily accessible for continuous learning

    Lessons learned should be prepared by the program manager and discussed with the team. Then, as part of Knowledge Transition, they should be set up so they are regularly accessible to existing or future programs to facilitate continuous learning and avoid pitfalls that other programs may encounter.

    PMI®, *The Standard for Program Management*, 2013, 88

32. d. Meet with as many end users as is feasible to understand what features they would like in a printer

    In this situation, the program manager has two clients: the retail store that places orders for the printer and the end user who actually uses the product. To ensure that the best product is made that will satisfy the needs of the marketplace, the program manager should meet with as many end users as is feasible.

    Milosevic et al., 2007, 366

33. c. Take corrective action

    Bad debt is money that is not collectible and is therefore worthless. As a result, it is deemed an expense to the business rather than revenue, because the business incurred the expense of providing a service or product for which it was not paid. In response to this problem, you need to take corrective action, which is an output of Program Financial Monitoring and Control.

    PMI®, *The Standard for Program Management*, 2013, 81–82

34. a. What are the assumptions that are part of your analysis?

    Even before programs are authorized, risks must be identified and analyzed. Assumptions analysis is a risk identification tool and technique and also is conducted as part of program strategy analysis in environmental analysis.

    PMI®, *The Standard for Program Management*, 2013, 28, 32

    PMI®, *Program Management Professional* (PgMP)® *Examination Content Outline*, 2011, 6

35. c. Identify tangible and intangible benefits, expressing the intangible benefits in quantifiable terms.

    The business case assesses the program's balance between costs and benefits. The cost/benefit analysis should answer questions such as how much will the program cost to implement, how much work the program will contribute to the bottom line, and is the program worth investing in terms of achievement of specific business objectives. It includes tangible and intangible benefits. The intangible benefits should be expressed in quantifiable terms such as dollars gained or saved, hours saved, and gross margin increase.

    PMI®, *The Standard for Program Management*, 2013, 27–28

    PMI®, *Program Management Professional* (PgMP)® *Examination Content Outline*, 2011, 6

    Milosevic et al., 2007, 282–283

36. c. Public announcements should be prepared

    Distributed information concerning the program should be provided in useful formats and using the appropriate media. Public announcements communicating information useful to the general public should be prepared as appropriate.

    PMI®, *The Standard for Program Management*, 2013, 75

37. b. Stakeholder register

    The stakeholder register is an output of Communications Planning to document information requirements in the register of each stakeholder. It is also prepared in Program Stakeholder Identification and is maintained and updated throughout the program.

    PMI®, *The Standard for Program Management*, 2013, 46, 74

38. b. Requesting a quality assurance audit

    As the products are not passing inspection, a quality assurance audit may be useful to assess the quality control results of the components and to see if overall program quality is being delivered as set forth in the program quality plan.

    PMI®, *The Standard for Program Management*, 2013, 93

39. a. Revisit and update your program documentation as required

Planning is an iterative process. When components are initiated or terminated, all program-level documentation associated with the component needs to be updated to reflect changes.

PMI®, *The Standard for Program Management*, 2013, 61

40. b. Whether the window of opportunity was compromised

Program Benefits and Program Governance are closely linked. The Governance Board, among other things, focuses on benefit delivery and ensuring programs deliver promised benefits. It, along with the program manager and other key stakeholders, may determine the window of opportunity was compromised by actual events in the program, one of which is feature reductions. Investments have time value, and shifts in component schedules may have additional financial impact.

PMI®, *The Standard for Program Management*, 2013, 41

41. c. Revisit the program master schedule

The program master schedule should be reviewed to assess the impact of component changes such as missing a key milestones on the other components and on the program itself, There may be a need to accelerate or decelerate components in the schedule to meet goals. Early identification of slippages such as this one is critical.

PMI®, *The Standard for Program Management*, 2013, 103–104

42. b. Notification of change requests

During the Information Distribution activity, information that is distributed includes notification of change requests to the program and project teams, and eventually, notification of the responses to the change requests.

PMI®, *The Standard for Program Management*, 2013, 75

43. a. Roadmap

The roadmap is an important document that is used throughout the program. In Program Strategy Alignment, it is prepared for a variety of reasons among which is to establish the relationship between the program activities and the expected benefits.

PMI®, *The Standard for Program Management*, 2013, 29

PMI®, *Program Management Professional* (PgMP)® *Examination Content Outline*, 2011, 6

44. b. Resource use

Change requests occur for a variety of reasons. Since most organizations are resource constrained, the most significant requests tend to be ones involving resource use, strategy, or plans.

PMI®, *The Standard for Program Management*, 2013, 59

45. a. Assign program roles and responsibilities

Resource prioritization is a key responsibility for the program manager, and resource use across components must be optimized. A human resource plan is useful to identify, document, and assign program roles and responsibilities to individuals and groups.

PMI®, *The Standard for Program Management*, 2013, 95

46. c. See if residual activities are required

Before closing a program, estimates may be needed to determine costs of sustaining the program's benefits. Residual activities may be required to oversee the ongoing benefits.

PMI®, *The Standard for Program Management*, 2013, 82

47. c. Revisit and update your program plans

Acquisitions and mergers are unplanned events. When they occur, they should trigger a review of existing program plans to see whether updates are required to ensure ongoing usefulness. Planning is an iterative activity as competing priorities must be resolved to address critical factors.

PMI®, *The Standard for Program Management*, 2013, 85

48. d. Stakeholder engagement

In Stakeholder Engagement, the program manager requires negotiation skills. Often, stakeholder groups require facilitated negotiation sessions when expectations conflict.

PMI®, *The Standard for Program Management*, 2013, 50

49. c. Estimate the high-level financial and non-financial benefits

It is essential to estimate the high-level financial and non-financial benefits of the program in order to both obtain funding for it and also to maintain funding authorization for the program. This approach as well drives the prioritization of the projects in the program.

PMI®, *Program Management Professional* (PgMP)® *Examination Content Outline*, 2011, 6

Thiry, 2010, 77

50. a. Are working on a strategic program

There are three typical types of programs; this scenario is an example of a strategic program and is initiated to support the organization's strategic goals and objectives and enable the organization's vision and mission.

PMI®, *The Standard for Program Management*, 2013, 141

51. d. The benefits report

Programs are established to deliver benefits. A defined set of benefit reports or metrics must be prepared and reported to the PMO, Governance Board, sponsors, and other stakeholders to assess the overall health of the program to ensure successful benefit delivery.

PMI®, *The Standard for Program Management*, 2013, 40

52. c. Prepare a stakeholder register

In Program Stakeholder Identification, stakeholders are identified and analyzed to prepare a stakeholder register. The register uses detailed stakeholder analysis as it is prepared to list the stakeholders, their levels of interest and involvement in the program, their degree of support, and other relevant information.

PMI®, *The Standard for Program Management*, 2013, 46

53. d. Release resources when they are no longer needed

In Resource Interdependency Management, the program manager controls the schedule for scarce resources. In all programs, and especially in the one described here, the program manager must ensure resources are released for other programs when they are no longer needed on the current program.

PMI®, *The Standard for Program Management*, 2013, 95

54. d. Develop a program roadmap

During Program Initiation phase, the program roadmap is elaborated. Among other things, it reveals and explains gaps as well as serving as a chronological representation of the program's intended direction.

PMI®, *The Standard for Program Management*, 2013, 84

55. d. Prepare a high-level approach

In organizational strategy and business alignment, since the area to be addressed is understood, the next step is to prepare a high-level approach or plan, often defined In the form of a roadmap.

PMI®, *The Standard for Program Management*, 2013, 27

56. c. Use a program work breakdown structure

Because the PWBS reflects the total scope of the program, it encompasses all benefits (products and services) to be delivered by the program, including the deliverables produced by the components.

PMI®, *The Standard for Program Management*, 2013, 105

57. d. Use open-ended questions

Regardless of the technique used, the best approach is to use open-ended questions to obtain as much information as possible and to solicit stakeholder feedback.

PMI®, *The Standard for Program Management*, 2013, 48

58. c. Program sponsor

The program sponsor is the individual executive, or group of executives, who champions the program initiative, is responsible for providing project resources, and ensures the ultimate delivery of program benefits.

PMI®, *The Standard for Program Management*, 2013, 47

59. c. Approve required changes to the program

Phase-gate reviews serve numerous purposes and should be held throughout the program. They enable the Governance Board to approve or disapprove the passage of the program from one significant phase to the next and to review and approve any required program changes,

PMI®, *The Standard for Program Management*, 2013, 59

60. d. Authorize components

Since the program management plan has been prepared and formally approved, the program now is in the Program Benefits Delivery Phase. During this phase, components are planned, integrated, and managed to facilitate benefit delivery. The components first must be authorized through the governance function.

PMI®, *The Standard for Program Management*, 2013, 68–69

61. b. Meet with stakeholders

After the benefit register is set up, it should be reviewed with key stakeholders to develop the appropriate performance measures for each benefit. These key performance indicators become part of the register for the program.

PMI®, *The Standard for Program Management*, 2013, 36

62 c. Changing culture

The scenario is one in which virtual teams will be used for the first time, and the organization has locations in four continents. This approach is a culture change for the organization, and changing culture takes time.

PMI®, *Program Management Professional (PgMP)® Examination Content Outline,* 2011, 6

Thiry, 2010, 54–56

63. b. Training, coaching, mentoring, and recognizing your team

A high-performing team is critical to success on every program. Leadership Is embedded in the program manager's job throughout the life cycle, The program manager leads human resource functions to improve team engagement and achieve commitment to the program's goals.

PMI®, *Program Management Professional (PgMP)® Examination Content Outline,* 2011, 10

PMI®, *The Standard for Program Management*, 2013, 15

64. a. Root-cause analysis

Stakeholder metrics are included in the stakeholder engagement plan. Program managers need to review metrics regularly to identify potential risks caused by lack of stakeholder participation. Trends and root-cause analysis are used.

PMI®, *The Standard for Program Management*, 2013, 50

65. a. Define the program's scope and benefit strategy

The Initiate Program process helps to define the program's scope and benefits strategy in the charter before the program is officially authorized.

PMI®, *The Standard for Program Management*, 2013, 83–84

66. a. Endorsing or approving recommendations for programs

Program governance covers systems and methods by which programs and its strategy are defined, authorized, monitored, and supported by the organization. It ensures programs are managed effectively and consistency. The Governance Board is charged to endorse or approve recommendations made regarding a program under its authority.

PMI®, *The Standard for Program Management*, 2013, 51

67. b. The benefit register

The benefit register lists the planned benefits and is used to measure and communicate the delivery of the benefits during the program. Among other things, it includes derived key performance indicators and thresholds to evaluate their achievement.

PMI®, *The Standard for Program Management*, 2013, 36

68. c. Upgrading the nation's airspace system

An upgrade to the nation's airspace system would consist of numerous projects as well as ongoing work. If these projects were managed in a coordinated way, then you would have better control over them and would obtain greater benefits.

PMI®, *The Standard for Program Management*, 2013, 4

69. d. 90 days

Establishing a longer period of time to pay your subcontractors than the payment terms you have with the studio ensures that you will have the cash to pay your subcontractors without the need to borrow money or take it from savings.

Milosevic et al., 2007, 358–359

70. d. Conduct a thorough analysis of the situation

It is easy to assume the lack of participation is a problem when it may be that these stakeholders are confident with the program's direction. Through analysis avoids incorrect assumptions about stakeholder behavior that could result in a poor or ineffective decision.

PMI®, *The Standard for Program Management*, 2013, 50

71. a. Obtain needed information to inform the Governance Board

An issue escalation process should be included in the governance plan. There are times when the program manager may need to contact an executive or an external stakeholder, and information obtained should then be provided to the Governance Board. The governance plan defines expectations for issue escalation at all levels including when to engage stakeholders for effective issue resolution.

PMI®, *The Standard for Program Management*, 2013, 56

72. c. Update the business case

As the program manager, you are responsible for guiding the initiating activities and facilitating developments of its outputs. This means you are responsible for business case updates. In this situation, given the budget cuts, it is unlikely the agency will pursue the program or if it does go forward, it will have a lower priority in the portfolio.

PMI®, *The Standard for Program Management*, 2013, 83–84

73. a. Poor performance

Programs may be canceled because of poor performance or changes to the business case that make the program unnecessary. This is a result of poor performance since the competitor's product is on the market.

PMI®, *The Standard for Program Management*, 2013, 89

74. a. It approved the quality plan

The Governance Board approves the quality plan, which establishes mechanisms to ensure program quality by identifying and applying cross-component quality standards.

PMI®, *The Standard for Program Management*, 2013, 58

75. a. Contract management plan

During Program Procurement, the contract management plan is prepared based on the specified items or services within the contract. It is used for contract administration.

PMI®, *The Standard for Program Management*, 2013, 91

76. b. Governance Board

The Program Governance Board is responsible for ensuring program goals are achieved and provides support for addressing risks and issues throughout the organization.

PMI®, *The Standard for Program Management*, 2013, 47

77. b. Resource use

    Program performance reports include summary progress of the program's components, the program's status relative to benefits, and resource use to determine if the program's goals and benefits will be met.

    PMI®, *The Standard for Program Management*, 2013, 87

78. b. Negotiate with stakeholders

    Influence is the ability to affect the beliefs, actions, and attitudes of other people and useful in negotiating with stakeholders in Stakeholder Engagement.

    PMI®, *The Standard for Program Management*, 2013, 50

    Levin and Ward, 2011, 81

79. b. Personally provide a copy of the governance plan to these new members

    Leadership is embedded in the program manager's job, and there is a collaborative relationship between the program manager and the Governance Board. The governance plan set forth the goals, structure, roles, responsibilities, policies, and procedures, and logistics to execute the governance process.

    PMI®, *The Standard for Program Management*, 2013, 15, 55

80. b. Program B

    Program B is quality-driven, as illustrated by its strategy to delay the schedule if necessary in a trade-off situation. Its competitive attribute is superior quality, which aligns with the organization's culture and environment.

    Milosevic et al., 2007, 75–76

    PMI®, Program Management Professional (PgMP)® Examination Content Outline, 2011, 6

81. c. The operational costs

    As part of Program Financial Monitoring and Control, it is necessary to manage the expenditure on the program's infrastructure. These costs cannot be overlooked, and it is necessary to ensure they are within expected parameters.

    PMI®, *The Standard for Program Management*, 2013, 81

82. c. Delivery and transition of benefits

Before the end of benefit delivery phase, when a component is ready for transition and closure, it is reviewed to verify that the benefits were delivered, and the transition is in place for any remaining and sustaining activities. Members of the Governance Board and the sponsor perform this final review.

PMI®, *The Standard for Program Management*, 2013, 70

83. b. Defining quality standards

There are many varieties of PMOs, and they provide support to program managers in different areas, one of which is defining the program's quality standards and the quality standards for the program's components.

PMI®, *The Standard for Program Management*, 2013, 13

84. d. Program performance support

While all are functions performed by the Governance Board, through program performance support, the Governance Board enables the pursuit of programs and optimizes their performance by allocating resources including staff, budget, and facilities.

PMI®, *The Standard for Program Management*, 2013, 57

85. b. Program scope statement

The program scope statement documents, defines, and assesses the context and framework of the program. It establishes the direction to be taken and the essential aspects to be accomplished. Stakeholders should verify and approve the scope statement.

PMI®, *The Standard for Program Management*, 2013, 105

86. d. Program scope statement

The program scope statement is the basis for future program decisions and establishes the expectations of the endeavor. Program stakeholders should verify and approve the scope statement for a common understanding. This is especially important if a stakeholder might erroneously assume that a particular product, service, or result is a program component.

PMI®, *The Standard for Program Management*, 2013, 105

87. b. Program reporting and control

    A best practice followed by many organizations is to define standardized monitoring and control processes applicable to all programs. The Governance Board then assumes compliance with these processes. An example is known program risks, their response plans, and escalation criteria.

    PMI®, *The Standard for Program Management*, 2013, 57

88. d. Program D

    The payback period can be determined by dividing the initial fixed investment in the program by the estimated annual net cash inflows. In this example, the payback period for Program D is 2.5 years, so it should be selected.

    PMI®, *Program Management Professional (PgMP)® Examination Content Outline*, 2011, 6

    Milosevic et al., 2007, 21 and 42

89. d. Have the first draft of the program schedule identify the start and end dates of the components

    The first draft of the program's master schedule often identifies only the order and start and end dates of components. Then, component results can be added as their schedules are developed.

    PMI®, *The Standard for Program Management*, 2013, 102

90. c. Meet with all three project managers and inform them that you will manage any resource redeployment issues

    It is the program manager's responsibility in Resource Prioritization to optimize resource use across program components. The program manager balances the needs of the program with resource availability.

    PMI®, *The Standard for Program Management*, 2013, 95

91. c. Manage a component Governance Board

    While some organizations use the same Governance Board for the program and its components, others have the program manager assume responsibility for the governance function for the program components. Factors to consider if the program manager is to assume this responsibility include the experience of the program manager, the program's level of complexity, and the extent of the coordination effort required to manage the program in the organization.

    PMI®, *The Standard for Program Management*, 2008, 2013, 63–64

92. a. Although the program is over budget, the overrun is insignificant at this time

The cost variance (CV) is calculated by subtracting the actual cost (AC) from the earned value (EV); that is, CV = EV – AC, or €42,000 – €50,000 = –€8,000, which is insignificant compared to the budget at completion (BAC).

PMI®, *The Standard for Program Management*, 2013, 81

PMI® *PMBOK® Guide*—Fifth Edition (2013), 224

93. b. Update your roles and responsibilities matrix

This decision by the Governance Board is a change as much of the work now will be outsourced. The program manager should update the roles and responsibilities matrix.

PMI®, *The Standard for Program Management*, 2013, 59

94. d. Define the objectives

Before moving forward, an initial program assessment should be conducted to ensure the program's alignment with the organization's strategic plan, objectives, priorities, and mission statement. This is done by defining program objectives, requirements, and risks.

PMI®, *The Standard for Program Management*, 2013, 6–7

PMI®, *Program Management Professional (PgMP)® Examination Content Outline*, 2011, 6

95. c. All available financial information and all income and payment schedules are listed in detail as the budget is prepared

In developing the budget it is necessary to compile all available financial information and list all income and payment schedules in sufficient detail. By doing so, the program's costs can be tracked as part of the budget baseline.

PMI®, *The Standard for Program Management*, 2013, 80

96. a. Show "what's in it for me"

All stakeholders should receive timely information about the program. When status information, cost information, risk analysis, and other relevant information are distributed, a best practice is to address the "what's in it for me" question.

PMI®, *The Standard for Program Management*, 2013, 75

97. c. The EPMO provides knowledge management support

Although it is not providing knowledge management support at this time, doing so is an established function of PMOs (or in this case the EPMO) to support program managers.

PMI®, *The Standard for Program Management*, 2013, 13

98. b. Program scope

Program issues such as ones involving human resources, finance, technology, and the schedule need to be identified. Then a course of action is selected consistent with program scope, constraints, and objectives to achieve the program's benefits.

PMI®, *Program Management Professional (PgMP)® Examination Content Outline*, 2011, 6

99. c. Group C

Using net present value (NPV) as a selection criterion, a dollar a year from now is worth less than a dollar today. The more the future is discounted (that is, the higher the discount rate), then the lower the NPV of the program. If the NPV is higher, then the program is rated higher than others. In this example, Group C has the highest NPV and should be selected.

PMI®, *Program Management Professional (PgMP)® Examination Content Outline*, 2011, 6

Milosevic, Dragan, *Project Management ToolBox: Tools and Techniques for the Practicing Project Manager*, 2003, Hoboken, NJ: John Wiley & Sons, 42–44

100. b. Establishing the program's financial framework

The purpose is to assess the overall financial environment for the program and to identify funding sources for the identified milestones. The key output is the program financial framework to coordinate the available funds, constraints, and how payments will be made.

PMI®, *The Standard for Program Management*, 2013, 78–79

101. a. Generate the program schedule

Upon completion of the PWBS, realistic schedules can be built, cost estimates can be developed, and the program's work can be organized.

PMI®, *The Standard for Program Management*, 2013, 105

102. b. Some corrective actions may be required as a result of risk mitigation activities

As a program manager, one must analyze and update the benefit realization and sustainment plans for uncertainty, risk identification, risk mitigation, and risk opportunity in order to determine if corrective actions are necessary and then communicate them to stakeholders.

PMI®, *Program Management Professional (PgMP)® Examination Content Outline*, 2011, 13

103. c. Program Performance Monitoring and Control

These activities are performed throughout the course of the program by the program manager and component management organizations. They include collecting, measuring, and disseminating performance information and assessing program trends.

PMI®, *The Standard for Program Management*, 2013, 87

104. b. Focus groups

Focus used to solicit feedback from stakeholder groups regarding their attitudes to better understand the organization culture, politics, concerns, and the overall impact of the program. Open-ended questions help participants to interact with one another, thus resulting in a deeper understanding of program needs.

PMI®, *The Standard for Program Management*, 2013, 48

105. d. The contractor has the appropriate tools and techniques to safeguard your intellectual property

Intellectual property (IP) is the lifeblood of any company. Outsourcing a project or group of projects to a contractor provides the contractor the opportunity to work with and manipulate your IP. You need to be absolutely certain that the contractor has safeguards in place to protect your IP.

PMI®, *Program Management Professional (PgMP)® Examination Content Outline*, 2011, 9

106. a. Checklists are completed

Program quality control consists of monitoring components and deliverables to determine if they fulfill quality requirements that lead to benefit realization. It is performed throughout the program. An output is a completed quality checklist.

PMI®, *The Standard for Program Management*, 2013, 92–94

107. a. Inform the sponsor in MNO.

As a practitioner in program/project management, we need to make decisions and act in an impartial and objective way. In this situation, it is necessary to take corrective action and avoid a conflict-of-interest situation.

PMI®, *PMI Code of Ethics and Professional Conduct.* Available from: http://www.pmi.org/en/About-Us/Ethics/~/media/PDF/Ethics/ap_pmicodeofethics.ashx

108. a. A program dashboard

A dashboard highlights and briefly describes or illustrates through the use of colors—red (bad), yellow (warning), green (good)—the status of various aspects of the program. It is simple and easy to interpret, making it a useful communication tool at the executive level. Methods to represent status reports are dashboards, memos, and presentations to stakeholders.

Milosevic et al., 2007, 330–336

PMI®, *Program Management Professional (PgMP)® Examination Content Outline*, 2011, 10

109. a. Ensuring legal protection of this valuable asset

It is important not only to capture and document knowledge assets from each project in the program and the overall program and the intellectual property that has been developed, but also to do so in a manner that ensures legal protection of these assets. Ensuring intellectual property is captured for reuse is a performance competency for program managers in closing the program.

Levin and Ward, 2011, 60

110. d. Maintain a benefits register

A benefits register is a best practice and can be easily translated into a benefits report. It is useful to report the benefits and their status to stakeholders following the communications management plan.

PMI®, *Program Management Professional (PgMP)® Examination Content Outline*, 2011, 13

111. a. Identifying high-level risks

Identifying high-level risks is a performance competency in program initiation. It entails preparing a list of such risks, analyzing them with any projects that will be part of the program, and assessing strengths, weaknesses, opportunities, and threats. An initial risk assessment is an activity that is conducted to determine the probability of successful benefit delivery.

PMI®, *The Standard for Program Management*, 2013, 83

Levin and Ward, 2011, 34

112. d. Program Benefit Delivery

This phase is where program components are planned, integrated, and managed to facilitate benefit delivery. It includes component transition and closure.

PMI®, *The Standard for Program Management*, 2013, 68–70

113. d. Update your PWBS

Working in Program Scope Control, there are a number of key activities including establishing an activity to administer scope changes. An output of this process is to update the PWBS.

PMI®, *The Standard for Program Management*, 2013, 105–106

114. b. Aggregate information across projects and non-project activity

Program Performance Reports aggregate all performance information for both project and non-project activity. The reports consolidate performance data to provide stakeholders with information regarding the use of resources to determine if the program's goals and benefits will be met.

PMI®, *The Standard for Program Management*, 2013, 87

115. a. Align the elements of your program more closely with the company's strategy

Programs represent change, and the strategic value of each program should be explicit and driven by the business strategy of the organization. Organizations determine a strategic direction on the basis of competitive attributes that, in turn, focus and define the content of program management elements.

PMI®, *The Standard for Program Management*, 2013, 26–27

PMI®, *Program Management Professional (PgMP)® Examination Content Outline*, 2011, 6

Milosevic et al., 2007, 75–76

116. d. Make sure contractors have comparable acceptance criteria

It is typical on programs to use contractors. The program team needs to bring together the statements of work, legal, and commercial aspects with the program processes so the team can manage in an integrated way using common processes. Acceptance criteria should be comparable and support program processes.

Williams, David and Parr, Tim, 2006, *Enterprise Programme Management*, Hampshire, England: Palgrave MacMillan, 194

Harris, Kurt, "The Influence of Consortiums in Developing and Developed Countries" in Levin, Ginger, 2012, *Program Management A Life Cycle Approach*. Boca Raton, FL: CRC Press, 379–384

117. c. Intangible benefits and tangible benefits

In identifying benefits and preparing a benefits realization plan, categories of benefits are useful. They should be both tangible and intangible, along with risk avoidance.

PMI®, *Program Management Professional (PgMP)® Examination Content Outline*, 2011, 13

Williams and Parr, 2006, 179

118. a. Devise a strategy to collect baseline data such as using questionnaires and interviews

Before setting the baseline, the benefits realization plan and its measurement criteria need to be developed. The baseline then serves as a control tool or mechanism to manage changes to benefits and costs through the implementation of the program. A number of key tasks are recommended including devising a strategy to collect baseline data such as by using questionnaires, interviews, reports, by location, and the organization structure.

PMI®, *Program Management Professional (PgMP)® Examination Content Outline*, 2011, 13

Williams and Parr, 2006,180

119. b. By the program manager, based on his or her scope of authority

During Program Delivery Management, change requests that clearly fall within the program manager's level of authority are approved or rejected.

PMI®, *The Standard for Program Management*, 2013, 87

120. b. Communicate personnel performance to each team member's line manager

Line managers typically assign resources to programs and projects. It is important for the program manager to communicate personnel performance to line managers so that it can be used as input for salary reviews, future development, and so on.

PMI®, *Program Management Professional (PgMP)® Examination Content Outline*, 2011, 10

121. d. It will be difficult to recover from this performance, and a decision now is needed to terminate the program.

The SPI is EV/PV. In this case, it is 0.86, which means you are 14 percent behind schedule. It will be difficult to recover. The Governance Board now should implement closure procedures as it realizes it is impossible to recover and terminate the program.

PMI®, *The Standard for Program Management*, 2013, 61–62

PMI®, *PMBOK® Guide*, 2013, 224

122. d. Leadership

A successful program manager must have a special blend of knowledge, skills, and competencies. Leadership is required in working with the program management team and functional managers; it is embedded in the job of the program manager and occurs throughout the program.

PMI®, *The Standard for Program Management*, 2013, 15

123. b. The benefits are aligned with the University's strategic objectives

It is important to prioritize benefit delivery especially on those programs in which benefits are delivered incrementally. Proof of early benefits also assists in securing funding to continue the program. In prioritizing benefits, items to consider include alignment with strategy, short-and long-term expected results, expertise of the resources available, and the probability of success.

Williams and Parr, 2006, 181

124. b. Risk opportunity

Benefits realization requires analysis throughout the program. This scenario is an example of a risk opportunity, which if accepted by the Governance Board, then will lead to the need to update the benefit realization plan and also the sustainment plan.

PMI®, *Program Management Professional (PgMP)® Examination Content Outline*, 2011, 11

125. c. Are expressed in policy statements

Risk profiles are used to construct the most suitable approach to managing program risks, adjusting risk severity, and monitoring risk criticality. Risk profiles may be expressed in policy statements or revealed in actions.

PMI®, *The Standard for Program Management*, 2013, 97

126. a. Organize program knowledge as a reference

Program management supporting activities may include work and resources required to address knowledge management on programs. During the program, applying knowledge management will include activities associated with timely identification, storage, and delivery of key program knowledge to aid in decision making and for a reference.

PMI®, *The Standard for Program Management*, 2013, 65

127. d. Component initiation requests

A number of activities are required to verify the component supports the program's outcomes before it is authorized; each component requires an initiation request.

PMI®, *The Standard for Program Management*, 2013, 60–61, 69

128. b. Update your program resource plan

Changes in the assignment of program staff are reflected in an update to the program resource plan prepared first as an output of the Resource Planning activities.

PMI®, *The Standard for Program Management*, 2013, 94–95

129. d. Program charter

The program charter contains a section on stakeholder considerations. It should be complemented with a draft of the program's communication plan.

PMI®, *The Standard for Program Management*, 2013, 84

130. b. Program work breakdown structure (PWBS)

The PWBS, among other things, provides a framework for performance reporting and tracking.

PMI®, *The Standard for Program Management*, 2013, 105

131. b. Program B

Programs should have a strategic fit with the organization's long-term goals. In selecting a program to pursue, this is one area to consider. In this example, Program B fully supports four of the five goals.

PMI®, *The Standard for Program Management*, 2013, 23

Milosevic et al., 2007, 286

132. d. Determine minimal acceptance criteria

The Governance Board establishes the minimal acceptance criteria for a successful program and the methods to use to monitor these criteria.

PMI®, *The Standard for Program Management*, 2013, 57

133. c. Stakeholder Engagement

Stakeholder engagement requires the program manager to be an excellent communicator. He or she strives to ensure all stakeholder communications are adequately logged, including action items that may require resolution.

PMI®, *The Standard for Program Management*, 2013, 50

134. a. Identifying impacts to the components from overruns or under-runs

In Program Financial Monitoring and Control, the program manager must be proactive in identifying factors that create changes to the budget baseline Another example of being proactive is to identify impacts from components from overruns or under-runs. If a component is under-running its budget, the program manager may be able to reallocate some funding elsewhere in the program. If the program is overrunning, the program manager needs to determine the root cause and impact on both the component and the overall program.

PMI®, *The Standard for Program Management*, 2013, 81

135. a. The program sponsor

Governance structures differ based on numerous factors with the purpose to monitor and review the progress of the program and delivery of the benefits from the project and non-project work. The program sponsor typically is an executive with a senior role in the organization. In many organizations, the program sponsor is the chairperson of the Governance Board.

PMI®, *The Standard for Program Management*, 2013, 62

PMI®, *Program Management Professional (PgMP)® Examination Content Outline*, 2011, 15

136. a. Have a thorough understanding of the financial environment

Programs using public money are often complex, expensive, and of long duration. The program manager needs to have a thorough understanding of the financial environment.

PMI®, *The Standard for Program Management*, 2013, 78–79

137. b. Determine actions that could affect other components

Program management should support the risk activities of the program components. The program component's risk response plans should be reviewed to assess proposed actions that could affect the program risk responses for better or for worse. This enables response mechanisms that could benefit more than one component to be suggested and implemented as managing the interdependencies among the component risks and those at the program level provide both program and project benefits.

PMI®, *The Standard for Program Management*, 2013, 98–99

138. c. Prepare a quality assurance change request

Audits take time, and results must be documented. The program management team is responsible for implementing required quality changes. As a result of the audit, a quality assurance change request should be issued to implement the auditor's findings.

PMI®, *The Standard for Program Management*, 2013, 93

139. b. Assess strategic alignment of the program

Gate reviews serve a number of different purposes. In addition to ensuring that criteria to fulfill the requirements for exiting a phase and moving on to the next phase are met, they also can focus on strategic alignment of the program and its components with the intended goals of the program and the organization.

PMI®, *The Standard for Program Management*, 2013, 59–60

140. a. Brainstorming

A brainstorming session with the core team is useful in identifying potential stakeholders, their roles, and significance to the program.

PMI®, *The Standard for Program Management*, 2013, 48

141. c. Program sponsor

The program sponsor is the individual responsible for providing program resources and ensuring program success; typically the program sponsor is a senior manager responsible for defining the direction of the organization and investment decisions.

PMI®, *The Standard for Program Management,* 2013, 62

142. d. Competitive analysis

Competitive analysis or market analysis is useful to help identify organizational benefits for the potential program. A well-developed business case will include a certain level of analysis and comparison against real or imagined alternative efforts. Such comparisons generate substantive debate with respect to the best solution.

PMI®, *The Standard for Program Management,* 2013, 31

PMI®, *Program Management Professional (PgMP)® Examination Content Outline,* 2011, 6

143. a. The availability of key staff members

Resource requirements and the program's resource plan are used in Resource Prioritization. As the program manager conducts resource planning, availability is a key consideration in order that during Resource Prioritization, critical resources can be optimized for use across components.

PMI®, *The Standard for Program Management,* 2013, 94–95

144. b. Encourages ownership of the solution

A regularly scheduled benefit report is essential in stakeholder communication in terms of achieving the planned benefits. It also is helpful to ensure ownership of the solution and benefits within the relevant business area, reduces the risk of "optimistic" reporting from the program team, and enables benefits reports to be available within regular management reports.

Williams and Parr, 2006, 181–182

145. a. Quality management

Quality management permeates program management. As noted in Program Quality Planning it should be considered when defining all program management activity and for every deliverable and service. It is recommended that a program quality manager participate in planning activities such as resource management to verify that quality activities and controls are applied and flow down to the component subprograms and projects even if they are performed by contractors.

PMI®, *The Standard for Program Management*, 2013, 93

146. c. Communications plan

The communications plan should consider cultural and language differences; therefore, it is where you would specify use of the 4,000-word common English vocabulary.

PMI®, *The Standard for Program Management*, 2013, 74

147. c. Root cause identification

Root causes are the fundamental conditions or events that may give rise to a risk. Program-specific risk activities include determining the primary causes of a program's risks, which can be done by sharpening the definition of each risk and grouping risks by cause. More effective risk responses can be prepared after the root causes are identified.

Shimizu, Motoh. 2012. *Fundamentals of Program Management Strategic Program Bootstrapping for Business Innovation and Change*. Newtown Square, PA: Project Management Institute, 122

Williams and Parr, 2006, 156–159

148. a. Risk trigger

A risk trigger is a sign that a particular risk may occur.

PMI®, *The Standard for Program Management*, 2013, 100

149. d. Program charter

The charter authorizes the program manager to use organizational resources to perform the program and links the program to the business case and the organization's strategic priorities. It also contains a section on program governance.

PMI®, *The Standard for Program Management*, 2013, 54, 85

150. c. Determine stakeholder issues that may lead to risks

Stakeholder issues and concerns are likely to affect aspects of the program. Impact analysis techniques should be used to understand the urgency and probability of stakeholder issues and determine which issues may become risks to the program.

PMI®, *The Standard for Program Management*, 2013, 50

151. b. Ethical concerns

In evaluating program objectives ethical concerns are a key consideration. In this example, student privacy is an example of an ethical concern to satisfy.

PMI®, *Program Management Professional (PgMP)® Examination Content Outline*, 2011, 6

PMI®, *PMI Code of Ethics and Professional Conduct*. Available from: http://www.pmi.orgcodeofethicsPDF

152. a. Have a program management information system

An effective program management information system is essential in program management and program governance. It provides tools and mechanisms to store information about the program and a quick way to retrieve needed information. It provides a mix of manual and automated tools, techniques, processes, and procedures relevant to the management of programs and priorities in the portfolio.

PMI®, *The Standard for Program Management*, 2013, 64–65

PMI®, *Program Management Professional (PgMP)® Examination Content Outline*, 2011, 15

153. b. Ensure the new director understands the benefits of this program and how they will be sustained

A benefits sustainment plan is required for programs. In this case, it is essential to then transition the benefits to the new program director. One approach to help sustain the benefits is to involve the new director in preparing this plan and making sure the director understands the benefit realization plan and reports prepared to date.

PMI®, *Program Management Professional (PgMP)® Examination Content Outline*, 2011, 13

154. c. Governance Board

The Governance Board approves recommendations for program closure confirming that conditions that warrant closure are satisfied, and recommendations for closure are consistent with the current organizational vision and strategy.

PMI®, *The Standard for Program Management*, 2013, 61–62

155. a. Are the champion for change

The program manager must be familiar with organizational change management. He or she is the champion for change and must be the key communicator of program changes, both positive and negative.

PMI®, *The Standard for Program Management*, 2013, 46

156. a. Increase the benefits to be realized by the product

The purpose of programs is to attain more benefits than if the projects were managed in a standalone fashion. This scenario shows the program manager is exploiting the strategic opportunities for change with the merger in order to maximize benefit realization for the company.

PMI®, *The Standard for Program Management*, 2013, 4

PMI®, *Program Management Professional (PgMP)® Examination Content Outline*, 2011, 7

157. d. Prepare a contract closeout report

Program Procurement Closure involves closing out each contract on the program after ensuring deliverables have been completed satisfactorily. A contract closeout report should be prepared.

PMI®, *The Standard for Program Management*, 2013, 91

158. b. Update the lessons learned data base

Lessons learned represent a compilation of the program knowledge assets. This data base should be updated regularly as components close and at the end of the program.

PMI®, *The Standard for Program Management*, 2013, 76

159. a. Update the governance plan based on decisions made

Requests for approval of proposed program changes require a variety of updates to program documentation. One of these is to update the program's governance plan.

PMI®, *The Standard for Program Management*, 2013, 59

160. d. Review the benefits realization plan and implement improvements based on lessons learned to date

Benefit reviews can be conducted throughout the program. They enable the program team among other things to review the effectiveness of the benefits strategy and make changes to it based on lessons learned, inform stakeholders of progress, identify further benefits to the program, assess overall performance to date, and provide an opportunity to publicize the program and its success thus far.

Williams and Parr, 2006, 182

PMI®, *The Standard for Program Management*, 2013, 41

161. b. Readiness

In it important to evaluate the organization's capability for new products by consulting with its leaders to develop, validate, and assess the program's objectives. Readiness analysis can help to establish new benefits from the program, ensure resources are available, and evaluate the current state to prioritize requirements.

PMI®, *Program Management Professional (PgMP)® Examination Content Outline*, 2011, 6

162. c. Determining constraints

The financial framework serves as the high-level initial; plan for coordinating available funding, determining constraints, and determining how money is paid out as it describes the program funding flows.

PMI®, *The Standard for Program Management*, 2013, 78–79

163. c. Resource leveling

Resource leveling is a useful approach to show the impact on the schedule if the resources are not available as planned. It is also a way to optimize the program management plan and the resource plan by leveling the resource requirements in order to gain efficiencies and maximize productivity/synergies among constituent projects.

PMI®, *Program Management Professional (PgMP)® Examination Content Outline*, 2011, 9

164. a. Project plan

Project managers' performance is evaluated according to their ability to execute the project according to the project plan. This approach is used to then maximize their contribution to achieving program goals.

PMI®, *Program Management Professional (PgMP)® Examination Content Outline*, 2011, 10

165. d. Rewards

Each program should manage changes in accordance with the change management plan. The purpose is to control scope, quality, schedule, cost, contracts, risks, and rewards.

PMI®, *Program Management Professional (PgMP)® Examination Content Outline*, 2011, 11

166. a. Sponsor

In stakeholder management, it is important to evaluate any risks to the program identified by stakeholders, and it is especially important to evaluate those of the sponsor, since the sponsor is the champion for the program and is providing its resources and funding. As necessary, this evaluation should be part of the risk management plan.

PMI®, *Program Management Professional (PgMP)® Examination Content Outline*, 2011, 14

167. c. Mission statement

The purpose of the mission statement is to describe why the program is important and why it exists. It is prepared by evaluating stakeholders' concerns and expectations in order to establish program direction.

PMI®, *The Standard for Program Management*, 2013, 28

PMI®, *Program Management Professional (PgMP)® Examination Content Outline*, 2011, 6

168. a. Regularly scheduled reviews

Governance Board meetings are the most common method used to perform governance oversight activities. Regularly scheduled review meetings with well-planned agendas and documented decision records enhance the effectiveness of the governance process.

PMI®, *The Standard for Program Management*, 2013, 55–57

169. c. Use the lessons learned data base

As the lessons learned data base is updated, an output of this activity is the PMIS, if applicable, since it contains among other things document, data, and knowledge repositories.

PMI®, *The Standard for Program Management*, 2013, 76

170. c. The program be set up with a viable business case that has a list of initial benefits to be achieved

A business case is required for each program, and as part of it, benefits are identified for the program. This business case should be reviewed and updated throughout the program and be realistic so people will commit to it to help achieve overall program success.

Williams and Parr, 2006, 185

PMI®, *The Standard for Program Management*, 2013, 36

Practice Test 2

1. Finally both the Boeing 787 and the Airbus 380 are operational. Assume you are the Program Manager now for the Boeing 797. You have reviewed all the lessons learned from the work done on the 787 as you are determined this time that the 797 will be in service before the scheduled date. However, the 797 uses new technology, and you have different subcontractors than those of the 787. Your executive managers recently returned from the Paris Air Show and already have some orders, and you and your team are just identifying the various projects that will comprise this important program. You have been asked since you are the program manager to provide your sponsor and your Governance Board with regular updates on the status of the program's benefits, and you need to be able to measure the benefits that have accrued during each reporting period. You decided to track the benefits in a—

   a. Benefits register
   b. Benefits realization report
   c. Benefits control system
   d. Benefits monitoring system

2. You are working to establish program management in your organization. You recognize since you are working in the Portfolio Management Office that there are many benefits to be attained if projects that are somehow related can be part of a program structure so through the program, more benefits can be attained than if they were managed separately. You recognize the importance to aligning program goals and benefits with long-term organizational goals. Therefore, you realize as the company embraces program management, you will need to hire people as program managers, or appoint people from within the organization, who have skills in—

   a. Leadership
   b. Organizational awareness
   c. Political awareness
   d. Strategic visioning

3. Your organization has a defined career path in project and program management and you are now a program manager. Since you have your PMP®, when PMI announced the PgMP® certification, you asked if you could move into a program management position so you could gain the hours needed to qualify for this credential. This is your first program management job. Your program management plan now has been approved. Your emphasis now should be on—

   a. Holding a kickoff meeting with your team
   b. Delivering intended benefits
   c. Chartering projects and appointing project managers
   d. Determining needed knowledge, skills, and competencies for potential team members

4. You are working for pharmaceutical company, GenBioform, as program manager for the development of a breakthrough drug to inhibit the growth of cancer tumors and eliminate the need for chemotherapy or radiation treatments. Your CEO is determined that your company will be the first to get approval from the Food and Drug Administration (FDA) for this new drug. You have performed an in-depth analysis of stakeholders in your company and have identified the following key external stakeholders: consumer groups, oncologists, the FDA, and cancer patients. Your next step is to—

   a. Finalize the results of your stakeholder identification and analysis by preparing a transition plan
   b. Note stakeholder considerations in your program charter
   c. Rank the stakeholders by importance and assign key team members to work with the top two
   d. Ask your Marketing Department to perform an analysis of the competition

5. You are a newly hired program manager in your company and plan to use a number of contractors and serve as the system integrator on your program. Your Procurement Department suggested that the qualified vendor list be used to simplify the procurement process and pointed out one vendor that had performed well on a similar program in the past. The problem is that this vendor's company is owned by your cousin. You should—

   a. Use the vendor since the Procurement Director suggested the company based on past performance
   b. Disclose this relationship to the Procurement Director and to your sponsor immediately
   c. Suggest that since this vendor's firm is owned by your cousin that it is more appropriate to have a competitive process with a RFP
   d. Use a competitive process with a RFP and do not include past performance work with your company as an evaluation criterion

6. You are working for pharmaceutical company, GenBioform, as program manager for the development of a breakthrough drug to inhibit the growth of cancer tumors and eliminate the need for chemotherapy or radiation treatments. Your CEO is determined that your company will be the first to get approval from the Food and Drug Administration (FDA) for this new drug. So far on your program, with its six projects, you have had a number of change requests, which is not surprising given the complexity of the program. At the program level, analysis of change requests involves identifying, documenting, and estimating the work the change would entail. As program manager, you also need to—

   a. Determine which components are affected
   b. Meet with the program Governance Board for approval, rejection, or deferral of the request
   c. Convene a meeting of the configuration control board
   d. Maintain a change log for status

7. The emphasis at your logistics company has always been to 'do projects right'. Therefore, your management established a Project Management Office, with the responsibility to develop a methodology that project managers would follow that was consistent across the organization. This has proven to be effective. Now the organization is doing the same for program management. Since it has been successful in 'doing projects right' and is 'doing programs right', the organization now has implemented portfolio management to ensure it is 'doing the right programs and projects'. The relationship between portfolio management to program management thus is—

    a. One comparable to a child-parent
    b. Influenced by requirements
    c. Focused on achieving planned outcomes
    d. One that emphasizes management of issues and risks with an escalation process

8. You are managing a systems integration program for your company, Globus Enterprises, which is under contract to the government of Moldova. This program includes a hardware systems project and an information systems project; other projects are expected to be added as the program progresses. Because this program will include numerous projects, you have decided to—

    a. Have each project use a distinct life cycle as defined by the program management office (PMO)
    b. Define a common life-cycle model for the various projects
    c. Deploy the program organization
    d. Prepare the project management plans

9. You have been appointed program manager for the closing phase of the systems integration program for Globus Enterprises, under contact to the government of Moldova. As the closing program manager, you must ensure that all administrative activities are complete. One best practice is to review the—

    a. Program work breakdown structure (PWBS)
    b. Business case
    c. Program management plan
    d. Benefits management plan

10. You are pleased to finally move into a program management position in your city, and as the program manager for the new wastewater treatment initiative, you have now completed your program management plan. You have selected project managers and also a core team and have defined criteria to help you evaluate the various candidates. You are fortunate that you have worked with two of the people before on specific projects, but the others are new to you, and the team has not worked together previously as a team. As a program manager, you must be an effective leader. A key area of focus is—

    a. Ensuring task delivery
    b. Adding value to decision making
    c. Setting directives and procedures
    d. Establishing program direction

11. You are managing a program that comprises new systems application development and maintenance activities. These applications are critical to your company, CDE, as they involve access to proprietary data. The systems must be available to your clients on a 24/7/365 basis. Much of the work on you program will be outsourced as you have an aggressive schedule to meet; fortunately CDE has a qualified vendor list to simplify the acquisition process. This program has high visibility in CDE. You and your core team realize the high level of interest and have worked hard to identify the key stakeholders and determine their position toward your program. You have prepared your stakeholder engagement plan, and it has been approved by your sponsor and Governance Board. Now, the next step for you and your team is to—

    a. Provide guidelines for project-level stakeholder engagement
    b. Prepare a stakeholder inventory
    c. Ensure the stakeholder management plan supports CDE's strategic plan
    d. Communicate to all stakeholders a need for change to the new systems applications

12. On your new 797 program, you have a larger number of stakeholders than did your counterpart program manager on the 787. You are working actively to identify early all the key stakeholders and prepare and follow a stakeholder engagement plan. To date, you find the stakeholder's major interests are in the program's benefits. However, the program is progressing as planned. In your plans, you have decided to conduct an overall review of the program's benefits with the Governance Board during the—

    a. Execution phase
    b. Delivery of Program Benefits phase
    c. Program Closing phase
    d. Program Setup phase

13. As the manager of your company's natural gas distribution program, you are pleased to have this program as it is ranked number one in the company's portfolio. So far, you have five separate projects, and the program is scheduled to last four years. In order to gauge program quality, a powerful metric is—

    a. End user satisfaction
    b. Benefit sustainment
    c. Effectiveness of adherence to the program's quality policy
    d. Cross-program inter-project quality relationships

14. Now that you have moved into this program management role in your manufacturing company, you realize your work really involves active involvement with stakeholders at a variety of levels. It is also compounded because on your program you have external stakeholders involved and need to spend time communicating with this group. Additionally, your Governance Board is extremely interested in your program and wants to meet more regularly than solely at phase-gate review sessions. They have requested these other meetings in order to—

    a. Ensure expected benefits are in line with the original business plan
    b. Focus on alignment of the program and your projects in it with the organization's strategic plan
    c. Determine if the level of risk still remains acceptable to your organization
    d. Focus on ongoing performance and progress

15. As a program manager in an aerospace organization, you are managing the next fighter plan. It is considered to be one that is high risk. It is going to require new technology, different types of scientific experts, a different manufacturing line, and new suppliers and subcontractors. Some members of the executive team, although they did approve the business case, are skeptical and believe that if the program does move ahead, and if it does not prove to be financially beneficial, it can jeopardize the reputation of the company in such a detrimental way that the company may not remain dominant in its field. This is why it is important in the early stages to—

    a. Prepare a program charter
    b. Prepare a high-level scope statement
    c. Develop a roadmap
    d. Define standard measurement criteria

16. As you work to propose a program to your Portfolio Review Board to develop a new colon cancer detecting approach that does not involve any pre-preparation work or after effects to patients, you want to also to identify high-level financial and non-financial benefits for this program. You also want to make sure the benefits are congruent with the funding goals for the program as the financial organization will not be a passive stakeholder. One business case driver for financial management that often is overlooked is—

    a. Mission statements
    b. Reducing risks
    c. Increasing efficiency
    d. Streamlining administration

17. As the program manager for the landfill program for your county, you have assembled your program team. It consists of civil engineers, regulatory specialists, project managers, and environmental engineers. This program is considered to be a very large one that will take a number of years to complete to deliver the societal benefits as planned. You plan to add some key subject matter experts as required. You also will have contractors on your team. With the various contractors, you are considering—

    a. Using your PMO
    b. Adding a specialist in contract management to the core team
    c. Using blanket purchase agreements
    d. Using fixed-price contracts with incentives for early completion

18. Now that you have moved into this program management role in your manufacturing company, you realize your work really involves active involvement with stakeholders at a variety of levels. It is also compounded because on your program you have external stakeholders involved and need to spend time communicating with this group. Additionally, your Governance Board is extremely interested in your program and wants to meet more regularly than solely at phase-gate review sessions. While you have two projects in your program, the Manufacturing Director at your company, CCC, has requested that you add another project to your program. Criteria for initiating a project is contained in the—

    a. Program management plan
    b. Program business case
    c. Program charter
    d. Governance plan

19. As the program manager working to upgrade and integrate the back office components of your organization's systems, you have five projects in your program. You realize all programs, and projects, have risks associated with them, and some of the high-level risks are in your program charter. As you prepare a risk management plan, it is essential to define—
    a. Risk profiles
    b. Market conditions
    c. Risk management consolidation
    d. How the risk may affect program success

20. You are a program manager and are responsible for a major project to integrate the back office components of your organization's systems. You have five projects in your program. Quality is important to your company. A quality control measurement you plan to use is—
    a. Number of defects
    b. Number of workarounds
    c. Customer satisfaction surveys
    d. Cost of quality

21. You are the program manager to restructure your department within your government agency. The head of the agency informed your sponsor that she wants to change the scope of the program so you will be working to restructure the entire agency instead of just one department. The Agency Administrator felt this change would be beneficial as the Agency also has to undergo some funding cuts in the next three fiscal years. This represents a major change to your program. You decided before moving forward that your best course of action was to—
    a. Inform your team and involve them in planning the next steps
    b. Meet with your program sponsor
    c. Convene a meeting of your Governance Board
    d. Meet with the Director of the Enterprise Program Management Office as obviously you now need additional resources for your program

22. As the program manager for the systems integration program for Globus Enterprises, which is under contract to the government of Moldova, you have a number of projects in your program. First, your program includes a hardware systems project. Second, you have an information systems project. Now, you recently added a software engineering project, and you plan to add a verification and validation project in the fourth quarter. Other projects also are on your roadmap. Your overall program success is measured in terms of—

    a. Benefits delivery
    b. Earned value
    c. Each project's adherence to its schedule
    d. Products delivered according to specification

23. The roadmap is an important document used in program management. One key purpose of it is to—

    a. Use it as part of the program's business case
    b. Evaluate through it your program's alignment to the strategic plan
    c. Summarize the supporting infrastructure
    d. Show internal details of components

24. You met with the organizational leaders for your colon cancer detection program that does not involve any pre-preparation work or after effects to patients, and its business case was approved. You then were asked to take over sponsorship for a program for a long-time customer, which would be awarded to your company under contract, to develop drugs for use by people before undergoing a colon cancer detection program. Your company has never developed these types of drugs before, but your customer is convinced it will not be an issue. You do not wish to disappoint this customer. In this situation—

    a. You should proceed with the colon cancer detection program as its business case has been approved
    b. Tell your customer you cannot take on this opportunity now because you are committed to another program
    c. Meet with your organizational leaders
    d. Diversify the portfolio and sponsor both programs

25. At the last strategic planning meeting, the CEO set forth a three-year plan with a major goal to be the leading provider of portfolio, program, and project management training in your country; it still will offer general managerial and business analyst training. You are the program manager for this new initiative, and your program management plan has been approved. Resources are limited. To provide guidance to component managers, you decide to—

    a. Prepare a program resource plan
    b. Set up a resource pool that is managed at the program level for the components
    c. Prepare a staffing management plan
    d. Set up a process so component managers can escalate any resource issues to you for prioritization

26. You are the program manager to restructure your department within your government agency. The head of the agency informed your sponsor that she wants to change the scope of the program so you will be working to restructure the entire agency instead of just one department. The Agency Administrator felt this change would be beneficial as the Agency also has to undergo some funding cuts in the next three fiscal years. You now have acquired additional resources for this major change and have re-structured your program. You realize, however, that with this change, you should have—

    a. Followed appropriate procedures and guidelines
    b. An appropriate governance structure in place
    c. Updated all your plans
    d. Communicated with every stakeholder

27. You are managing a landfill program for your county. Your program team consists of civil engineers, regulatory specialists, project managers, and environmental engineers. You also have a number of internal and external stakeholders. Your client, the county executive, has informed you that your program must be completed no later than September 15, 2015, to comply with a regulatory mandate. You have prepared the program's master schedule, and the program dates for each component have been identified, which are—

    a. Constraints
    b. Assumptions
    c. Dependencies
    d. Schedule risks

28. When you were a project manager, you found the risk register to be an extremely useful tool. Now that you are a program manager, you ask your project managers to use a risk register, and you assign a member of your core program team to identify, analyze, and track program-level risks. You also need to—

    a. Conduct risk audits
    b. Review residual risks
    c. Track schedule risks
    d. Track scope risks

29. You have been appointed program manager for the closing phase of Program CCC. As closing program manager, you must ensure that all administrative activities are complete. Sixty-two contracts were awarded during the life of this program. You contact the Contracts Department and a contracts specialist assists you. You need to—

    a. Review the contracts management plan
    b. Make sure the contractors completed performance reports as stated in their contracts
    c. Ensure payments were made
    d. Review contract closure procedures

30. Assume you are managing the reward loyalty operational activity for your airline. Members have been complaining about the difficulty of actually using an award, especially your elite members who tend to fly on your airline at least one million miles per year. You feel you will lose elite members to other airlines unless the program changes dramatically, and you believe it needs to offer more possible rewards in conjunction with free stays at leading hotels of the world and also free car rentals. You have received authority from your Portfolio Review Board to establish a new program to emphasize improvements in how rewards are to be handled. You now are in the Initiating process. The key output of it is—

    a. Identification of the program manager
    b. The program charter
    c. The benefits analysis plan
    d. Feasibility studies

31. Assume you are the program manager to redesign the reward loyalty operational activity for your airline. Members have been complaining about the difficulty of actually using an award, especially your elite members who tend to fly on your airline at least one million miles per year. You feel you will lose elite members to other airlines unless the program changes dramatically, and you believe it needs to offer more possible rewards in conjunction with free stays at leading hotels of the world and also free car rentals. Therefore, you want to plan for success from the beginning of the program. This need means that the program manager requires which one of the following skills?
    a. Facilitation
    b. Political
    c. Emotional intelligence
    d. Conflict resolution

32. Assume that you have completed your program to re-design your organization's approach to how it works with other companies. Now that the process is in place and has been followed, it is time to close this program. You must transition the benefits of your program. This is demonstrated—
    a. According to strategic alignment
    b. Through value delivery
    c. By implementing required change efforts
    d. By providing operational support as requested

33. You are responsible for business development in your division, which is a subsidiary of a large defense contractor. Recently, you attended a conference and learned that many of your competitors are focusing on continuous improvement in the area of sales strategies and techniques and are conducting maturity assessments. When you returned to your office, you prepared a business case and recommended that such a program be initiated. One of the criteria you used was—
    a. Representatives from each business unit in the organization would participate in the program
    b. The program duration would be short because a maturity assessment typically can be conducted in three months
    c. It would be necessary to set up some specific projects as a result of the improvement plan from the maturity assessment, but these projects would be unique to each business unit
    d. The benefits that would accrue from the program would be independent of specific deliverables of the various associated projects

34. Your company has established a program to manage the development of new pet food products, and you have been appointed manager of this program. One of your five projects has completed its deliverables successfully, and a transition request has been processed. As the program manager, you should—

    a. Reallocate the resources to the other four projects
    b. Update the resource plan
    c. Update the program roadmap
    d. Send the transition request to the program sponsor for approval

35. You are the program manager for a program that is using multiple suppliers. Even though you have signed partnering agreements with each supplier, you know performance problems will surface, especially with this program because more than 75 percent of the work is being done by third-party suppliers. Also, your company has not worked with five of these suppliers in the past, and two are start-up companies. You have identified the various stakeholders on this program and classified them. As part of stakeholder analysis and planning you should document—

    a. The organizational culture and readiness for change
    b. Affected individuals and organizations
    c. Perceptions of program outcomes
    d. Attitudes about the program and its sponsors

36. Because of extreme droughts in Haddad, Jordan, water restrictions have been imposed. Your company is awarded a contract to eliminate the need for these restrictions. The program includes a project to formulate and implement policies and procedures that ensure continuity of operations and performance of associated equipment. Another project will oversee improvements and modifications to existing treatment methods and facilities. A third project will design modifications to increase productivity and effectiveness. As program manager, you will manage, contract, and provide oversight for capital improvement projects. You will need various types of resources and a variety of office supplies. To assist in managing contracts, you should—

    a. Conduct inspections and audits
    b. Use performance/earned value reports
    c. Follow your procurement management plan
    d. Use written deviations

37. You are the program manager for a program that is using multiple suppliers. Even though you have signed partnering agreements with each supplier, you know performance problems will surface, especially with this program because more than 75 percent of the work is being done by third-party suppliers. Also, your company has not worked with five of these suppliers in the past, and two are start-up companies. Many in your organization are interested in this program and especially how the integration efforts will be accomplished given the large number of suppliers involved. It is important in this situation to ensure—

    a. A contact change control system is in place
    b. A contract administrator is a member of your core team
    c. There is compliance with legal policies
    d. Key stakeholders have active involvement in the program at all times

38. As a program manager in the Department of the Interior, you are working on ways to ensure continued availability of water resources. You have a number of projects in your program, but you are particularly interested in the effect of earthquakes on water resources. You have appointed a manager for this project, and he has assembled an outstanding team that does impressive work. You have already determined your program's budget requirements for the next fiscal year; your Governance Board concurs with your financial analysis and includes your requirements in the budget submitted to the Office of the Secretary. However, the Office makes 30 percent cuts across the board, thus forcing you to eliminate the earthquake analysis project. Your next step is to—

    a. Disband your team
    b. Assign the project manager to another project so that he does not lose his job
    c. Update your program plans as required
    d. Make another attempt to secure funding for this project

39. Your program in the Department of Interior to ensure continued availability of water resources to the citizens of your country has a number of projects, now seven are under way, and unless there are no other budget cuts, you expect at least three more to be added. In most programs, there is a core infrastructure which is the—

    a. Governance Board
    b. Program management team
    c. Program management office (PMO)
    d. Program office

40. As the manager of a major program in your company, you have access to various supporting resources. Your organization uses a balanced matrix organizational structure, and supporting resources come from a variety of functional departments. One member of your program team regularly prepares resource deviation reports. These reports are—
   a. Part of Resource Interdependency Management
   b. Described in the resource plan
   c. Helpful to determine if the program's benefits will be met
   d. Used as part of Risk Monitoring and Control

41. You have been appointed program manager to develop digital yo-yos. You are excited by this challenge, and when you learned of this possible opportunity, you decided to attain your PgMP® and also take a course on managing programs for best practices. This is your first time as a program manager, and this program is ranked number three in your organization. You are preparing a high-level program plan, which has a number of key purposes one of which is to—
   a. Demonstrate the value the program is to deliver
   b. Justify the required resources
   c. Serve as a reference to measure program success
   d. Establish the relationship between program activities and expected benefits

42. As the program manager on the digital yo-yo program, you realize for success on this program, you need an outstanding team, and you have been negotiating for the best and the brightest people to manage the seven identified projects that will comprise the program and will be in your Program Management Office. It has been a difficult process working with the company's department managers to obtain needed resources. You know for success you also need—
   a. A determination of contractor resources for your use
   b. Agreement among the team as to the program values
   c. Standard measurement criteria
   d. Risks identified by stakeholders

43. You are a program manager in a global software company that uses virtual teams. Work is passed 24/7 from team members on one continent to those on another continent. Since this is a complex program with a significant amount of associated uncertainty, changes in program direction may be needed. Recognizing this can occur on your program, you should—
    a. Use adaptive change
    b. Provide consistent messages about changes to stakeholders
    c. Set up an approach to facilitate timely decision making about needed changes
    d. Follow your communications management plan

44. As the program manager for a new wastewater treatment initiative in your city, you must deliver both tangible and intangible benefits. You must also identify the interdependencies of the benefits delivered in various projects in your program. This means that you must map benefits to program outcomes. In terms of the benefits management life cycle, this is done during—
    a. Benefits identification
    b. Benefits setup
    c. Benefits analysis and planning
    d. Benefits delivery

45. You and your core team realize the high level of interest in your program and have worked hard to identify the key stakeholders and determine their position toward your program. You decided to use mapping to help develop a stakeholder matrix to put stakeholders into certain categories. One of the advantages of the mapping approach is that it—
    a. Can be done easily through brainstorming sessions
    b. Shows the stakeholder's attitude toward the program
    c. If done correctly, can promote stakeholder engagement
    d. Visually shows the stakeholders' current and desired support and influence

46. Before preparing your stakeholder engagement plan, you decided to conduct stakeholder analysis and planning. Your first step is to—
    a. Brainstorm the possible stakeholders to get a complete list of them
    b. Evaluate the degree of support or opposition each stakeholder has regarding the program
    c. Gain an understanding of expectations of program benefit delivery
    d. Perform a detailed review of the Statement of Work and other key documents already completed

47. Your company is noted for its maturity and excellence in program management. It has received awards for program and project delivery. People seem dedicated to the success of the company and in its management of programs and their projects, which is due to—

    a. Awareness of the influence of environmental enterprise factors
    b. Use of a common program approach
    c. A portal for sharing information
    d. An up-to-date program management information system

48. You are the program manager for a global Fortune 100 software company. The company has determined that it must pursue Cloud Computing, and it wants to use agile methods as it enters this market to speed the time to complete the Cloud Computing program and to develop a marketing campaign for it. You also know you will need to do extensive testing before the program is complete. One tool you should develop to help execute the program is a—

    a. Work authorization system
    b. Issue and risk escalation process
    c. Roadmap
    d. Decision log

49. You are the program manager for a global Fortune 100 software company. It has determined that it must pursue Cloud Computing, and it wants to use agile methods as it enters this market to speed the time to complete the Cloud Computing program and to develop a marketing campaign for it. You are responsible for ongoing management of program benefits. You must ensure that the program transition activities provide for continued management of benefits through the framework of—

    a. Ongoing operations
    b. Transfer of the benefits to the customer
    c. Program closure
    d. Consolidation of the benefits

50. You are the legacy system conversion program manager in your company. You need to upgrade the company's business development/sales tracking system, which was developed in C++. You now have projects in your program to also upgrade the accounting/financial management system, interface them to the program management information system, and add a knowledge management system. You have a complex program. With these additional projects, you and your core team realize you need to prepare your stakeholder engagement plan. In developing this plan, you should—

    a. Analyze the stakeholder register
    b. Determine how receptive the stakeholder is to communications from the program
    c. Prioritize stakeholders in a matrix according to their ability to influence the program outcomes, either positively or negatively
    d. Determine the degree of support or opposition the stakeholder has for the program's objectives

51. You are the program manager for a program that is using multiple suppliers. Even though you have signed partnering agreements with each supplier, you know performance problems will surface, especially with this program because more than 75 percent of the work is being done by third-party suppliers. Also, your company has not worked with five of these suppliers in the past, and two are start-up companies. Today, one of the suppliers responsible for Project D informed you that it did not have sufficient financial capacity and resources to continue on the program and was going to declare Chapter 11 and file then for bankruptcy. Obviously, this change involves other projects on your program and the entire program's ability to deliver its benefits on time. You have decided that the best course of action is to first—

    a. Call an immediate meeting with your program team
    b. Contact the Procurement Department to obtain their services in obtaining another qualified supplier
    c. Contact the suppliers with whom you have had positive working relationships in the past to see if they can take on this company's work
    d. Follow the issue escalation process

52. As the manager for a water-gasification program that will provide potable sparkling mineral water from public water fountains in Garvey, England, you have leased some of the needed equipment. Unfortunately, you have found that on two of your projects, some of these leased resources did not meet specifications. The project managers on Projects A and D advised you of their concerns because they were concerned that overall program progress might be affected. You need to identify a course of action to best achieve program benefits, which means you need to—

    a. Perform an issues analysis
    b. Assess stakeholder risk tolerance
    c. Conduct a risk audit
    d. Manage program level issues

53. Assume you are managing the next generation SMART car so it runs entirely on ethanol rather than gasoline now that your country has ethanol stations in all major cities and on interstate highway systems. Your executives believe this type of SMART car will increase in popularity. Since there are a number of benefits associated with this new line of SMART cars, you decided to use a benefit register to track the benefits accrued by each of the projects in your program so your organization can realize them and then through its dealers be able to sustain them. As the program manager, you develop this benefits register during—

    a. Benefits identification
    b. Benefits analysis and planning
    c. Benefits transition
    d. Benefits delivery

54. You have successfully finished your new line of SMART cars, and they have been well received. In all, you have four different models, all using ethanol and all with advanced safety measures. They also are environmentally efficient. Now that the cars are being purchased, to derive the optimal value from the work you and your team accomplished, as the program manager, you should—

    a. Conduct team satisfaction surveys
    b. Plan the transition from program management to operations
    c. Ask an independent party to contact end users to ensure the effectiveness of customer relationship management
    d. Provide support to end users throughout the product life cycle

55. As the key member of your company's Program Selection Committee, you are responsible for deciding which programs to undertake. Your Committee meets on a quarterly basis and then selects new programs and projects as appropriate and also then rebalances the company's portfolio accordingly. As you consider the proposed business case for a new program and assess the suggestions of the other committee members, a key factor is—
   a. Constituent component identification and definition
   b. Total available resources
   c. Overall stakeholder interest
   d. The project's feasibility study

56. You are the program manager for a program that is using multiple suppliers. Even though you have signed partnering agreements with each supplier, you know performance problems will surface, especially with this program because more than 75 percent of the work is being done by third-party suppliers. Also, your company has not worked with five of these suppliers in the past, and two are start-up companies. Many in your organization are interested in this program and especially how the integration efforts will be accomplished given the large number of suppliers involved. Given the extensive work being done by suppliers, you expect you will have more internal audits than usual on your program. Their specific timing should be—
   a. In your program's roadmap
   b. Set forth in an audit plan
   c. Set forth in your program plan
   d. In your program schedule

57. You are the program manager to restructure your department within your business unit. The head of the company informed your sponsor that she wants to change the scope of the program so you will be working to restructure the entire company instead of just one department. You prepared a stakeholder register as part of your planning efforts for the restructured program and then worked to—
   a. Assess the stakeholders' ability to influence strategic goals
   b. Determine metrics to evaluate stakeholder participation in the program
   c. Prioritize a list of stakeholders
   d. Outline how stakeholders will be engaged in the program

58. You are managing a program in your company, and you are following the phases articulated in the Project Management Institute's *The Standard for Program Management*. Assume you have prepared your benefit realization plan, and It was approved. Now, you must concentrate on—

    a. Linking component activities to planned outcomes
    b. Delivering benefits
    c. Mapping the benefits to the program components
    d. Establishing a program architecture

59. You are the program manager for a program that is using multiple suppliers. Even though you have signed partnering agreements with each supplier, you know performance problems will surface, especially with this program because more than 75 percent of the work is being done by third-party suppliers. Also, your company has not worked with five of these suppliers in the past, and two are start-up companies. Many in your organization are interested in this program and especially how the integration efforts will be accomplished given the large number of suppliers involved. Recently, your organization made a major change in its financial management policies and now is requiring a 10% retainage as part of each supplier's contract. This means that—

    a. You require a person specializing in contracts and procurement management to be a member of your core team
    b. Suppliers are now a major stakeholder
    c. You need to actively work to rewrite each contract and then submit it to your Contracts Department
    d. A supplier engagement plan should be prepared

60. Assume that you are the program manager for a product to be delivered to an external customer, and you are now planning your program. This new product is to be completed in two years. So far, you have three projects in your program and plan to add several more as the program continues. You believe you have an excellent team with the key competencies to assist you in the program. You also are glad to have a Governance Board. Conflicts, though, are program challenges, which means you should—

    a. Actively listen
    b. Use a variety of approaches to lead the team
    c. Assume program ownership and take responsibility
    d. Leverage political dynamics to promote program goals

61. You are managing a program to produce the next generation of hurricane-, tornado-, and typhoon-resistant glass. Technical specialists in your company will support each of the projects in this program. Four projects are in process. Project A is fully staffed; Project B has about 75 percent of the staff members it needs; and Projects C and D are about to begin, but these two projects will require the services of several key specialists now working on Projects A and B. You tell Project Manager A that he must release two staff members to support Project C and three to support Project D. He uses resource leveling to analyze this change and tells you that the end date for Project A will need to be extended, as he will be understaffed. The program Governance Board and the executive sponsor agree to extend the schedule for Project A. The five specialists are released to the other projects. Your next step is to—

    a. Commend Project Manager A for his willingness to release these resources
    b. Meet with the five people involved and tell them they must move to the new projects
    c. Update the program-level documentation and records
    d. Continue to prioritize resources as needed

62. You are managing a program to produce the next generation of hurricane-, tornado-, and typhoon-resistant glass. Four projects are in process. Project A is fully staffed; Project B has about 75 percent of the staff members it needs; and Projects C and D are about to begin. Your program team identifies several issues that force you to modify program requirements. Some changes are minor, but one issue requires a program scope change. Your next step is to—

    a. Involve the program's Governance Board in its resolution
    b. Prepare a change request
    c. Update the program management plan
    d. Update the scope statement

63. You are the legacy system conversion program manager in your company. You need to upgrade the company's business development/sales tracking system, which was developed in C++. You now have projects in your program to also upgrade the accounting/financial management system, interface them to the program management information system, and add a knowledge management system. You have a complex program, and it now has increased risks with the variety of systems involved and the stakeholders who are used to these legacy systems and do not see the need to change. You also have three sponsors on this program. You should therefore update a number of the plans you have prepared with the first one to—

    a. Update your quality management plan
    b. Update your schedule management plan
    c. Update your financial management plan
    d. Update your risk management plan

64. You are the developing your communications plan for your legacy system conversion program manager in your company. Compared to projects, this program is far more complex. It has a greater degree of uncertainty, and it will take longer to complete. Plus multiple vendors will be used. As you develop this plan another concern is—

    a. You lack needed resources now for some of the new projects
    b. New stakeholders will become known and addressed
    c. You will be spending more time communicating with more groups
    d. You realize you will require strong leadership skills to deal with the complexity of this program

65. Assume you have just been named program manager to develop and manufacture a new drug designed to have fewer side effects than the existing ones on the marketplace to strengthen bones and help to minimize bone cancer. A number of benefits therefore will be associated with this program. You want to establish a program architecture in order to—

    a. Provide a process to determine the extent each benefit is achieved before the program closes
    b. Describe how each benefit will be measured
    c. Establish a performance baseline for the program
    d. Map how the components will deliver outcomes to achieve the program's benefits

66. Your company is a leader in the pharmaceutical industry. It has received approval from the Food and Drug Administration (FDA) for a new drug that will cure all glaucoma conditions. You are managing a process to upgrade the manufacturing process, and your CEO has given you an aggressive schedule, especially so the glaucoma drug can reach its numerous possible patients. You have five projects in this program, and you are getting ready for your second gate review on it. Although it is cumbersome assembling all the required materials for these reviews, you know they are useful as they ensure—

    a. Expected benefits are in line with the benefits realization plan
    b. Lessons learned are collected in order to prevent any future problems and improve overall processes
    c. Alternatives can be uncovered when problems are identified
    d. Processes and procedures are being used as designed

67. You are the program manager to restructure your department within your government agency. The head of the agency informed your sponsor that she wants to change the scope of the program so you will be working to restructure the entire agency instead of just one department. The entire agency basically is a stakeholder as everyone is concerned about the impact of the reorganization and the funding cuts that have been proposed. As the program manager, you need to—

    a. Use expert judgment
    b. Bridge the gap between the current state and the to-be state
    c. Demonstrate how the reorganization supports strategic goals
    d. Hold meetings with affected groups to listen to their concerns and obtain their buy in to the program

68. As a program manager for Destruct, AB, a leading defense contractor, you must determine which components should be part of your program. Your program involves the development of the next generation parachute. It is to be completely safe, easy to deploy, and available in one year at a reasonable price. Your executives want it to be completed at the time of the next Paris Air Show. When you do this, you are working in the—

    a. Benefits planning
    b. Pre-program preparations
    c. Program initiation
    d. Component identification

69. It is easy to focus primarily on the benefits programs will deliver to the organization and the deliverables the projects in each program will produce. Many organizations though do not have a clear understanding of all of the programs and projects that are under way, and many people do not want to disclose some 'pet' program they are working on as they believe they are breakthrough initiatives for the company. However, assume you are in an organization that lacks such a list of all the work in progress, and your company needs such a list as the executives have mandated that a portfolio management process be followed. The executives plan to meet monthly to review the existing portfolio and determine whether or not new programs and projects should be added and others deferred or terminated. The overall objective is to ensure the—

    a. Programs and projects in the portfolio are focused on alignment to strategic objectives
    b. The portfolio's strategy is one in which it focuses on preventing poor return on investments in the programs and projects that are pursued
    c. Program and project inputs are emphasized along with direct program deliverables and metrics
    d. The emphasis continues on the triple constraint as programs and projects to pursue are considered

70. Assume you are working toward your doctoral degree in program management part-time as you work in your City government office that oversees all existing regulations and standards. You have suggested based on your studies that many of the existing projects to overhaul and review these regulations and standards might be better handled as a program since through a program the benefits from proposed projects can be coordinated more effectively especially if the benefits are interdependent. Intended interdependencies of benefits are stated in the—

    a. Program management plan
    b. Benefits management plan
    c. Benefits realization plan
    d. Project management plan

71. Assume your suggestion to your City government to combine projects into programs in the regulations and standards area has been well received. After a meeting of the City's Commissioners, they appointed you as the program manager to oversee this work. You have decided as one of your first tasks to prepare a benefits register and will base it on the expected benefits as defined in the—

    a. Program charter
    b. Program business case
    c. Program management plan
    d. Organization's strategic plan

72. You are the program manager for a new product development program for Company AAA. This product will serve to make sure that consumers will be able to wash all types of clothing through use of your product, and therefore, they no longer will need to spend money at dry cleaning establishments. To complete your program successfully, you have identified five projects. You also will require some specialized resources that are always in demand in your organization; therefore, you meet with members of your core team and subject matter experts to—

    a. Assign roles and responsibilities
    b. Determine reporting relationships
    c. Prepare a staffing management plan
    d. Prepare a program resource plan

73. You are the program manager for a new product development program for Company AAA. This product will serve to make sure that consumers will be able to wash all types of clothing through use of your product, and therefore, they no longer will need to spend money at dry cleaning establishments. To complete your program successfully, you have identified five projects. You want to assess the likelihood of achieving these planned outcomes so you decide to—

    a. Use trend analysis
    b. Prepare a forecast
    c. Conduct a benefit audit
    d. Conduct a risk review

74. Your organization is embarking on an international program to update all processes now used in portfolio, program, and project management to ensure they are useful and are not responsible for bureaucratic overhead. It this situation, it is useful to—

    a. Appoint the program manager from outside of headquarters given its global nature
    b. Ensure each location is represented on the Governance Board
    c. State that the vision for the program is standardized processes in the three areas to promote common understanding
    d. Recognize the need to address cultural, socioeconomic, and political differences

75. As the program manager in your company responsible for establishing a culture of portfolio management, you were fortunate to be assigned early so you could participate in the development of the program's charter. Your program management plan and the other key subsidiary plans have been approved. As you are working to provide oversight on the program and its four components, you realize a new component is needed to integrate the efforts of the existing components. This is needed because—

    a. There are resource prioritization issues that are causing existing components to miss scheduled milestones
    b. You are using earned value and now are at 15% into your program and forecasts show your schedule and budget targets will not be met
    c. You must continually escalate issues and risks to the Governance Board for resolution
    d. The components are producing deliverables as planned, but their benefits are not being realized successfully

76. Working with a small core team, you completed your program management plan and the other key subsidiary plans and also prepared a master schedule. As your company follows the PMI® *Program Management Standard* for guidance, you know lessons learned are useful but should be organized effectively in order that they—

    a. Assist in preparing the final program report and in overall program transition
    b. Serve as a useful reference for other program and project managers
    c. Provide data for use in quickly responding to stakeholder requests for additional program information
    d. Serve as a reference for the program manager for program information and documentation accessibility

77. You are the program manager for a program that is using multiple suppliers. Even though you have signed partnering agreements with each supplier, you know performance problems will surface, especially with this program because more than 75 percent of the work is being done by third-party suppliers. You also have a large number of internal stakeholders who are actively involved or interested in your program. To help your stakeholders have a common understanding of the high-level expectations for the program, you should provide stakeholders with information contained in the—

   a. Stakeholder engagement strategy
   b. Business case
   c. Benefits transition plan
   d. Program management plan

78. You are sponsoring a new program to be implemented at the beginning of the corporation's fiscal year. This program is to design the next generation refrigerator that also can serve as a dishwasher and a stove with an oven so there is only one large appliance in one's home. It will use state-of-the-art technology but will be offered at an affordable price. The new appliance is to be designed to be attractive and also not to require much space. As the validity of the business case was assessed to also help develop the charter, you prepared—

   a. An analysis of the expected benefits from the program
   b. A feasibility study
   c. An analysis of competing efforts under way in the corporation
   d. A SWOT analysis

79. You are the contract program manager to restructure a department in a government agency. The head of the agency informed your sponsor that she wants to change the scope of the program so you will be working to restructure the entire agency instead of just one department. The Agency Administrator felt this change would be beneficial as the Agency also has to undergo some funding cuts in the next three fiscal years. Since most everyone is involved to some extent, there is extreme resistance to change, and many key stakeholders have been going directly to the Administrator and not to you since your firm has never worked with this agency before as to why their department should not be part of the reorganization. You and your team are striving to gain the support of all stakeholders, both positive and negative. You decide to—

   a. Actively use your stakeholder register
   b. Use a questionnaire to get everyone in the agency involved in the process
   c. Conduct interviews with the heads of each of the departments and support offices
   d. Re-evaluate your stakeholder engagement plan

80. Your company is a leader in the pharmaceutical industry. It has received approval from the Food and Drug Administration (FDA) for a new drug that will cure all glaucoma conditions. You are managing a process to upgrade the manufacturing process, and your CEO has given you an aggressive schedule, especially so the glaucoma drug can reach its numerous possible patients. You have five projects in this program, and you are getting ready for your second gate review on it. Your Governance Board is one that is extremely proactive, and it also holds a number of periodic health checks on your program in between these gate reviews. This is because—

   a. They want further involvement than just a possible four meetings during the life cycle
   b. They want to determine if the level of risk associated with this program remains acceptable especially given the lengthy regulatory process
   c. They want to assess performance against the strategic direction of the organization
   d. They want to assess performance against expected benefits and sustainment

81. Your stakeholder engagement plan now is complete. As you prepared this plan, you recognized that some stakeholders' interests needed special consideration. However, with this plan you now have—

    a. An in-depth understanding of the organization's environment
    b. A detailed strategy for effective stakeholder engagement
    c. A method to communicate program benefits to affected stakeholders
    d. A way to balance the impact of negative or resistant stakeholders with those who view the program positively

82. You are the program manager to set up one integrated system in your company that provides a single point of entry that is easy to use rather than the numerous legacy systems that now exist. You have people who are actively interested and strong supporters of this program, and others are resistors as no one really likes change. You have prepared a stakeholder register. This register—

    a. Shows information distribution methods
    b. May require access restrictions
    c. Becomes the basic document used to prepare the communications plan
    d. Sets forth a stakeholder engagement strategy

83. You are responsible for a major systems integration program that involves converting customer relationship management software, supplier management software, human resources software, and telecom systems from legacy systems to an integrated platform. Your program management plan has been approved. Because of poor performance on two of the projects and by associated vendors, you needed to implement a number of preventive actions and workarounds. You have had to implement a number of change requests. A best practice to follow is to—

    a. Ensure they are ones you can approve or reject
    b. Consult the Governance Board for assistance because the performance of these projects may be such they should be terminated
    c. Establish an integrated change control process
    d. Set up Change Control Boards for each project and at the program level

84. You are responsible for a major systems integration program that involves converting customer relationship management software, supplier management software, human resources software, and telecom systems from legacy systems to an integrated platform. You prepared a program risk response plan. Because of poor performance on two of the projects and by associated vendors, you needed to implement a number of preventive actions and workarounds. However, this program is long and complex, and changes are inevitable. You have described the scope, limitations, expectations, and business impact of the program along with a description of each project and its resources, but now you need to—

    a. Set up a scope change control system
    b. Update the scope statement
    c. Focus on preparing and following a change management plan
    d. Establish metrics to track adherence to the scope management plan

85. You are the program manager for a new accounting system that will affect more than 500 accounting professionals in 10 locations. You have a core team of five people, and your preliminary schedule shows that in month 13, the transition of your system to the users will begin. This aggressive schedule recently was made even more difficult as every program in your company will have a five percent budget cut; this means it will be even harder for you to get the key subject matter experts you need when you need them. You have a Governance Board for your program. It is important before you submit a recommendation to formally close the program to the Board that you—

    a. Ensure the members of the operations group are actively involved in the program from the start
    b. Provide extensive job aids to the people who will be responsible for running the program once it is completed
    c. Document your final lessons learned after you submit a performance report
    d. Ensure conditions for closure are satisfied

86. You have numerous stakeholders, both internal and external as your program involves members of the public. You also are using five different vendors. Different stakeholders have different areas of interest at different times and may be positive toward the program or negative. You have decided you should—

    a. Use a stakeholder impact and issue tracking and prioritization tool
    b. Work with a mentor to update your own negotiation and influencing skills as you work with negative stakeholders on this program
    c. Conduct another stakeholder analysis to make sure you have a greater understanding of the culture of the organization
    d. Set up specific channels of communications

87. You have been appointed as manager for a new program in your organization. This program will receive $250,000 as an initial investment; $175,000 at the beginning of year 2; $150,000 at the beginning of year 3; and $125,000 at the beginning of year 4. The program will start with a core team of seven senior managers; three project managers will be added during year 2, and two more project managers during year 3. While you work on this program, it is essential to ensure you can—

    a. Identify and evaluate integration opportunities and needs
    b. Set up a PMO for overall support, especially in administrative requirements
    c. Focus in your planning first on a bottom-up approach and then integrate it with a top-down approach
    d. First address the program's vision and justification

88. Wanting to make sure that existing lessons learned from every project and program undertaken in your organization are actually captured and used, you have received approval from your Portfolio Selection Committee to establish a program in knowledge management for your services company. The purpose is not only to record these lessons learned in an easily accessible fashion but to also make sure they are used by future program and project managers. You have identified four projects so far that will be part of this program. You recognize for this program to have visibility among the executives of your company that the mission, vision, and strategic fit of the program must be aligned with the organization's objectives. This is done as part of the—

    a. Pre-Program Preparations
    b. Program Initiation
    c. Program Strategy Alignment
    d. Benefits Identification

89. You are the program manager for a new accounting system that will affect more than 500 accounting professionals in 10 locations. You have a core team of five people, and your preliminary schedule shows that in month 13, the transition of your system to the users will begin. You have a Governance Board for your program. Possible members of your Governance Board were first identified—

   a. As a section in the governance plan
   b. At the time the business case was developed
   c. As part of the program management plan
   d. At the end of the program formulation

90. Rarely have hurricanes reached the northern states of the United States until the past two years. People were not equipped to deal with them. You are the program manager to help ensure people are prepared. Your company won a government contract and developed a business case for the program that was approved quickly. You have a Governance Board set up, but in the last three meetings, the Chief Information Officer or a substitute from IT did not attend. You have defined metrics to monitor performance of stakeholders in your program in the—

   a. Communications plan
   b. Stakeholder engagement strategy
   c. Stakeholder engagement plan
   d. Stakeholder register

91. As you plan your program, so far you have identified three projects, and you are to complete it in six months. It is especially important to identify the program's resource requirements and prepare a resource plan. A useful tool and technique to use is—

   a. Capacity planning
   b. Resource assignment matrix
   c. Resource breakdown structure
   d. Program management information system

92. Working on an internal program to restructure your company so it is more customer facing is a major challenge. No one ever likes reorganizations, and many people fear they will lose their jobs as a result of your program. However, it has relied on its existing customer base for its 20 year life, and a new focus is part of the company's strategic plan to attract new customers and enter new markets. As you plan your program, so far you have identified three projects, and you are to complete the reorganization in six months. You are determined to control expenditures to stay within your budget. Therefore. you are focusing on the need to—

    a. Identify opportunities to return funds back to the company
    b. Completing the program ahead of schedule
    c. Avoid use of contingency and management reserves
    d. Monitor costs reallocation impact and results between components

93. Your company is a leader in the pharmaceutical industry. It has received approval from the Food and Drug Administration (FDA) for a new drug that will cure all glaucoma conditions. Although demand for the product is high, your company has many other drugs to manufacture. You are managing a process to upgrade the manufacturing process, and your CEO has given you an aggressive schedule. Many people who have responsibility for other drugs in your company are concerned that once your manufacturing upgrade program is complete, the production of the glaucoma drug will be given preferential treatment, and their products will not be produced in sufficient quantities. You and your team realize you have a large number of stakeholders, and many of them are negative toward your program. This means you need to foster use of—

    a. Leadership skills
    b. Management skills
    c. Strategic visioning skills
    d. Political skills

94. On your program, you and your team realize you have a large number of stakeholders. Of course you require a number of interpersonal skills, but the most important one is—

    a. Leadership skills
    b. Communications skills
    c. Strategic visioning skills
    d. Political skills

95. Working on your glaucoma program, you have received approval from the Food and Drug Administration (FDA) for a new drug that will cure all glaucoma conditions. Although demand for the product is high, your company has many other drugs to manufacture. You are managing a process to upgrade the manufacturing process, and your CEO has given you an aggressive schedule Many people who have responsibility for other drugs in your company are concerned that once your manufacturing upgrade program is complete, the production of the glaucoma drug will be given preferential treatment, and their products will not be produced in sufficient quantities. You and your team realize you have a large number of stakeholders; many seem to be negative toward your program. Given this situation, your best course of action should be to—

    a. Focus on customer expectations
    b. Proceed according to your program management plan
    c. Establish buy-in from stakeholders to ensure program success
    d. Escalate this issue to your Governance Board to seek assistance in dealing with these stakeholders

96. You have three projects that comprise your program. Your aggressive schedule recently was made even more difficult as every program in your company will have a five percent budget cut; this means it will be even harder for you to get the key subject matter experts (SME) you need when you need them. You have a Governance Board for your program. Today, you had your regularly scheduled status meeting with Project Manager A. He told you he needed a key SME earlier than anticipated because of a new technological risk that had occurred. You were able to negotiate for this SME by meeting later with Project Manager C and getting the SME reassigned for two months to Project A. This was handled appropriately by Project Manager A as he—

    a. Immediately reported the problem to you
    b. Followed the issue escalation process
    c. Realized that the SME was on Project Manager C's team and notified you accordingly
    d. Asked Human Resources where he might locate a SME before contacting you

97. You were appointed program manager early in your program's life cycle, and you are leading the development of the benefits realization plan. You are working in benefits analysis and planning, which is important in that you are—

    a. Establishing the program's performance baseline
    b. Establishing processes to measure progress against the benefits plan
    c. Creating tracking and communications processes
    d. Defining the program's critical success factors

98. You are meeting with your company's Program Selection Committee. Because your company has limited resources, you are selecting one of two programs to undertake. The return on investment (ROI) and payback periods for the programs are basically identical, so the major factor in making your decision is—

    a. The balance between cost and benefit
    b. The ability to realize benefits before the program is complete
    c. Whether the business benefits are easily quantifiable
    d. Extrinsic versus intrinsic benefits

99. As you work as the program manager to establish Centers of Excellence in your global company on every continent except Antarctica, you have a large number of stakeholders who are interested in your program. You also have 12 different projects and know others will be added as the program continues. Your team, therefore, is a large virtual one, and you hold conference calls regularly, rotating the times in which they are held so no one is always inconvenienced. You also do a lot of traveling to the various sites. You realize you as well as your project managers must be excellent in—

    a. Communicating
    b. Understanding cultural differences
    c. Distributing consistent messages
    d. Actively engaging stakeholders

100. You are the legacy system conversion program manager in your company. Your Governance Board recognizes the importance of improving other projects in this upgrade so there is an integrated system for all applications in your company. You now have projects in your program to also upgrade the accounting/financial management system, interface them to the program management information system, and add a knowledge management system. You have a proactive Governance Board, which can assist in—

    a. Managing quality across the life cycle
    b. Ensuring you have the most competent people assigned to your program
    c. Enabling you to use a benchmarking forum with other organizations that have done similar programs
    d. Providing you with direct access to the senior executives in your company as needed.

101. Assume that your organization specializes in programs to handle conferences for government agencies. Each conference tends to attract about 800 to 1,000 people throughout the country in different locations. Each conference is a separate program as it involves different agencies, subject matter, themes, and speakers. Your company handles all the logistical requirements and basically is transparent to the agencies for which it works. Most of your programs, therefore, are initiated as a result of—

    a. Alignment with the company's mission statement
    b. The business case
    c. A decision to bid on a contract
    d. The desire to remain competitive in the field

102. In each of these conferences, the program sponsor has important responsibilities as this person has primary responsibility for securing finances and ensuring the program delivers its intended benefits. The sponsor is identified—

    a. When the business case for the program is presented
    b. Before program initiation
    c. In the program initiation
    d. In the pre-program preparations process

103. Assume that your organization specializes in programs to handle conferences for government agencies. You are the program manager for an upcoming conference on portfolio management for government agency representatives. This conference is expected to attract about 200 people as each agency will send at least five people to it, many of whom will be political appointees. You realize as you plan this program, with your five identified projects in it thus far, that changes are inevitable. In your program planning, you want to include an approach to communicate scope changes. This should be included as part of your—

    a. Integrated Change Control Plan
    b. Scope Management Plan
    c. Communications Management Plan
    d. Scope Control Plan

104. Program governance covers systems and methods by which program and its strategy are defined, authorized, and monitored. It conducts periodic reviews of the program in delivering its benefits enabling the organization to assess the viability of the program and the organization's strategic plan and the level of support needed to achieve program goals. The structure for your Governance Board and its meeting schedules are part of the—

    a. Overall governance framework
    b. Gate review requirements established by the Enterprise Program Management Office
    c. Governance plan
    d. Program management plan

105. Assume you are working for a dry foods company. For the past five years, every one of your projects in this company has met its goals in terms of being on schedule, within budget, and meeting its specifications. However, your company finds that even though its projects are meeting its goals, overall the company is not meeting its strategic goals and objectives. You were asked to meet with the executive team to discuss your opinions as to what is occurring in the company as you are an experienced and successful project manager. You pointed out that you felt the basic problem was:

    a. The projects should be managed as a program
    b. The projects were defined in too narrow a fashion
    c. The organization's strategic goals would change, but the project managers were not aware of the changes
    d. The organization requires a Program Management Office

106. You are managing a complex training program in your company. It has a number of component projects plus some ongoing work especially in logistical areas. Your team consists of instructional system design specialists who support the program on a full-time basis. For each training project, you need the services of subject-matter experts (SMEs) to complement the instructional designers. Assume that you met today with the manager of Functional Unit C in your company, and she agreed to release two chemists to support Project D in your program. You now need to—

    a. Meet with Project Manager D and inform him that you have acquired the needed SMEs
    b. Transition the SMEs to the program position
    c. Determine how this assignment can benefit the SMEs in their career path
    d. Update the program resource plan

107. You have a complex program. Thus far, you have passed gate 3 and are executing your program. Because the executing phase in the life cycle will last over a year, your Governance Board is holding periodic performance reviews with you and your team on a bi-monthly basis. The Governance Board has assumed responsibility for compliance with organizational reporting and control functions. An example is—

    a. Benefit transition
    b. Strategic and operational assumptions
    c. Quality criteria and standards
    d. Code of conduct compliance

108. In managing a program, you terminated three contracts that supported your projects. One of the contractors went bankrupt, and the other two were unable to deliver as promised. You now are preparing your final report as your program is ready for closure. In it these problems show—

    a. The need to conduct contractor performance reviews
    b. The importance of following documented contract closure procedures
    c. A major area of improvement
    d. Why contractual terms and conditions need to be revised

109. Assume that you just finished a meeting with your Program's Governance Board. It was not a stage gate review but was a more informal health check as several of the key stakeholders were concerned that a key milestone had been missed, and an incremental benefit from the program now would be delayed. They also were concerned that missing this milestone may lead to missing future milestones. Unfortunately, you are not using earned value on your program, but when you prepared your benefits realization plan, you did include a number of metrics that you and your core team have been tracking. To ensure continual realization of the intended benefits and to reassure your stakeholders and the Governance Board members that the program is not in trouble, you and your team have used which of the following techniques before taking corrective action—

   a. Delphi technique
   b. Decision trees
   c. Brainstorming
   d. Causal analysis

110. You are the program manager for a new accounting system that will affect more than 500 accounting professionals in 10 locations. You have a core team of five people and your preliminary schedule shows that in month 13, the transition of your system to the users will begin. This aggressive schedule recently was made even more difficult as every program in your company will have a five percent budget cut; this means it will be even harder for you to get the key subject matter experts you need when you need them. You have set up a stakeholder register and are using it to—

   a. Provide an inventory of how each type of stakeholder will be impacted the program
   b. Provide a way to make sure the key stakeholders remain engaged in the program
   c. Show how best to manage the impacts of the program on stakeholders
   d. Report and distribute program deliverables and formal and informal communications

111. You and your team have prepared your stakeholder register for your organizational change program. In preparing it, you and your team found which of the following techniques to be the most useful—

   a. Nominal group technique
   b. Organizational analysis
   c. Interviews
   d. Open-ended questions

112. Programs need to be funded to the degree noted in the approved program plan for success in realizing their benefits. Funding should be provided consistently with program needs and organizational priorities, which may be defined in the organization's portfolio management process. This responsibility is one that is handled by the—

   a. Portfolio manager
   b. Program sponsor
   c. Governance Board
   d. Finance Department

113. You are the program manager to restructure your entire government agency. Since no one likes change, you are holding meetings every two weeks that are recorded and made available to everyone in the Agency as to your progress. You are requesting comments from people throughout the Agency after each meeting. You feel these meetings can better help you understand the urgency and probability of stakeholder-related risks so basically you are—

   a. Updating your stakeholder register
   b. Updating your communications log
   c. Striving to focus on risks as opportunities
   d. Conducting a program impact analysis

114. Working in portfolio management and helping program sponsors prepare the business case for new programs in your chemical company, you want to make sure each program supports at least one of the objectives in your company's five year strategic plan. You encourage one program sponsor to meet with the strategic planners to make sure there is alignment and also to make sure the strategic planners do not expect any major changes in the next three years, the proposed length of the sponsor's program. One best practice is to prepare a high-level roadmap and continue to use it during the program. However, a disadvantage of the roadmap is—

   a. People believe it is the program's schedule
   b. It is difficult to keep its information current and relevant
   c. It typically is not possible to balance the timing of program demands with resource availability
   d. It is hard to use it to provide senior and program managers with a view of the programs in the portfolio over time

115. Working as the program manager for Guenther, Germany's water-alleviation program, you have an outstanding core team of five subject matter experts and a Program Management Office to support you. So far, you have three projects in your program. As you create your program work breakdown structure (PWBS), decomposition is useful to identify program deliverables and related work. The decomposition process is complete when—

    a. Each phase of the program life cycle has been detailed
    b. The program manager has the desired level of control
    c. The work packages of the various projects in the program have been identified
    d. Verifiable products, services, or results from each project have been determined

116. Continuing to work on your water-alleviation program in Guenther, Germany, you and your team now have prepared your program's work breakdown structure. This turned out to be a far more difficult process than you imagined because in the past, you had templates you could use to assist you in preparing the PWBS. However, you and your team completed it. The next step is to—

    a. Organize the work
    b. Prepare the program schedule
    c. Develop cost estimates
    d. Prepare a scope management plan

117. You are pleased to be the program manager for Guenther, Germany's water alleviation program. So far, you have three projects in your program. Six months after your plan was approved, Guenther issued some new regulations, and you requested approval and received it to add a new project to address regulatory compliance. However, this project is consuming extensive time, and it affects other initiatives under way in the organization. Your best approach is to—

    a. Request additional resources and reprioritize some that now support the other projects
    b. Suggest to the Governance Board that this project be moved from your program to be a distinct program
    c. Conduct a quality assurance audit to determine the extent of compliance with the new regulations
    d. Reprioritize resources to the regulatory project and acquire the services of a qualified vendor to support the other projects

118. As the program manager for Guenther, Germany's water alleviation program, you have many challenges. So far, you have three projects in your program. One challenge of course is the aggressive schedule you must meet and the high priority of this program in your company's portfolio. You also have a number of technical SMEs on your program, who seem to want to really work on technical topics in a functional environment. Also, as program manager you must work with stakeholders at all levels as well as with your team and your Governance Board. Your flexibility in managing this program is limited by—

    a. Communication channels
    b. Constraints
    c. Assumptions
    d. Benefits analysis

119. For Guenther, Germany's water-alleviation program, you have many challenges. Fortunately, you have assembled your core team and have a PMO. You also have met individually with your key stakeholders. You regularly communicate with your program sponsor. So far, you have three projects in your program. Your core team uses earned value at the program package level. Your cost performance index (CPI) is at 0.67, although the schedule performance index (SPI) is at 0.88. Your team recognizes the cost overrun and the fact that you are only 15 percent into the program. The team revises the Estimate at Completion, and you present the revision to your Governance Board. The Estimate at Completion is—

    a. A forecast
    b. A trend
    c. Atypical
    d. An inappropriate technique at this time

120. You have been managing Guenther, Germany's water alleviation program for three years. Fortunately, you have had an outstanding core team and have a PMO. Your project managers have diligently completed their projects, and their deliverables have been accepted by the City. Now, the program is officially complete, as all deliverables have been accepted by the City. Your next step is to—

    a. Prepare your closure report
    b. Archive your program records
    c. Meet with the sponsor for a closure review
    d. Obtain a signed final acceptance from the customer

121. You are the director of your telecommunications company's enterprise project management office (PMO). Your company has more than 200 projects under way, and you are considering managing some of them as a program. It took about six months to even determine how many projects were in process as many people felt if they described every project they worked on, their "pet" project that they felt would really benefit the company might be canceled. Obtaining the trust of the project professionals was a major challenge, but you believe you have an inventory now of all the project work. As you move into program management, which of the following is best suited to manage as a program?

    a. Conducting a training class in program management
    b. Providing product support to a recently introduced cellular phone
    c. Developing the next-generation cellular phone and related products
    d. Preparing a marketing campaign to introduce the next phone when it is developed

122. Leading organizations in diverse fields have noted the importance of governance for effective programs and to ensure programs are completed successfully as defined by their business case. To begin to establish governance processes, the first step is to—

    a. Prepare a governance plan
    b. Follow processes established by the Enterprise PMO
    c. Define governance goals for each program
    d. Have a sponsor organization

123. You are managing a program to develop a new source of energy to use in the tropics when solar power is not available. Working with your core program team and your Governance Board, you identify a number of component projects. However, several other key projects are under way in your company, and resources will be difficult to acquire for a new program. In determining whether you will use internal or external resources, you should consider—

    a. When the resources will be needed
    b. Your ability to negotiate with functional managers for the needed staff
    c. Previous work by the staff as a successful team
    d. The need to advertise for the open positions

124. You are managing a program to develop a new source of energy to use in the tropics when solar power is not available. Working with your core program team and your Governance Board, you identify a number of component projects. You also have identified some non-project activities. Analysis of program costs must be performed, although some overlook the need to consider the non-program/non-project cost activities. You are, however, analyzing them on your program as you believe doing so is a best practice for program and project managers. Accordingly, they—

   a. Should be tracked outside the program's budget
   b. Ensure costs are within expected parameters
   c. Are part of earned value
   d. Are an expense to be consumed by the program

125. Assume you have sponsored a program to develop a new stent for coronary patients that is based on new laser technology and that will only take 30 minutes from the time the patient actually enters the hospital. Then, the patient will be able to be discharged and resume normal activities as if nothing happened. The patient will not experience any side effects from this new approach. You have obtained approval from your Executive Committee to develop this program in more detail so you are now in the initiating process. Once the charter is approved—

   a. The program's financial framework is prepared
   b. A draft communications management plan is prepared
   c. The program is linked to the ongoing work and strategic priorities
   d. A high-level plan for components is prepared

126. Assume your company has a new program to develop a new stent for coronary patients that is based on new laser technology and that will only take 30 minutes from the time the patient actually enters the hospital. Then, the patient will be able to be discharged and resume normal activities as if nothing happened. The patient will not experience any side effects from this new approach. As a project manager, when you prepared your schedule, you focused on identifying activities on your critical path and managing them aggressively. Now you are the program manager. Your focus now is on—

   a. Estimating program activity duration
   b. Using a critical chain to incorporate buffers and manage drum resources that affect your component projects
   c. Identifying interdependences among the constituent projects
   d. Performing "what if" analyses to ensure that the key stakeholders' expectations for program deliverables are met

127. Recently, a member of your core team on your program for the next generation air traffic control system in your country obtained his Risk Management Professional credential from the Project Management Institute. While you and your core team spent time early in the program preparing a risk management plan, which was approved by your Governance Board, and you have been maintaining a program risk register, this core team member felt you and the other team members needed to perform another in depth session identifying risks given that the program had slightly changed direction during the past year and had added one more project than planned. Also, the Administrator of your government agency resigned to take a position in industry, and the new Administrator is more risk adverse, especially where new technology is involved. You have a choice of different technologies to employ. As you considered each one in terms of possible risks, you and your team used which of the following techniques to best make a recommendation to the Administrator and the core team in terms of overall program benefits—

   a. Sensitivity analysis
   b. Modeling through Monte Carlo simulation
   c. Decision-tree analysis
   d. Risk urgency analysis

128. In developing your benefit realization plan for this air traffic control upgrade system, you and your core team set it up in order that you would have specific metrics in place to help monitor the actual realization of the benefits throughout the program. The plan includes both tangible and intangible benefits of this major program. While the tangible benefits are easy to monitor, you now are finding the intangible benefits to be a challenge. One approach that has been useful to you so far is to use—

   a. Business value measurement
   b. Total cost of ownership
   c. Cost of quality
   d. Trend analysis

129. In your role as program manager for your country's food safety department to ensure the safety of imported food in your country, you are facing a number of challenges. It seems as if more imported food is arriving rather than producing the food domestically. Many of the food products are totally new to your country. You lack the needed number of inspectors who have expertise in some of the exotic food that now is being imported, and you are implementing a Hazard Analysis Critical Control Program approach as part of this important program. You realized you needed a Governance Board to assist in ensuring your program continued to meet the Department's strategic objectives. Your sponsor agreed and assisted you in preparing a governance plan and also obtained commitments from senior level executives in the Department to be Board members. As you worked on your plan, you realized a key activity that occurs within governance is—

   a. Resource prioritization
   b. Issue management
   c. Risk response planning
   d. Transition planning

130. You are a member of your company's Program Selection Committee, which is deciding which program to pursue in consideration of the company's limited resources. Your company prides itself on time to market as an attribute that distinguishes it from its competitors in the automobile parts field. Each program has prepared a business case addressing its strategy, organization, process, metrics and tools, and culture. Proposed Program A will eliminate features if necessary in a trade-off situation; Proposed Program B will delay its schedule if necessary; Proposed Program C has a flexible structure to ensure innovative features at a minimum cost; and Proposed Program D will focus on technical, cost, and schedule in its metrics. Which program should be selected?

   a. Program A
   b. Program B
   c. Program C
   d. Program D

131. No one likes to prepare cost estimates since almost every estimate turns out not to be accurate even if you have outstanding historical information to help you in this process and organizational templates. However you have prepared your estimate and financial management plan. Your next step is to—

   a. Publish this cost estimate
   b. Prepare the budget baseline
   c. Determine program financial metrics
   d. Have component managers prepare component cost estimates

132. You realize since your company recently merged with a competitor, and there is a revised strategic plan that for your program to continue to be in alignment, you need to add a new project. To do so, you require approval from your Governance Board, and the Board 's approval generally requires—

a. Highlighting any possible risks
b. Ensuring compliance with existing program processes and procedures
c. Ensuring communication of critical component-related information to stakeholders
d. Confirming the business case for the new project

133. You are managing a program to build your country's new embassy, consulate, residences, and other facilities in the Republic of Sarsmania. It will be the largest construction project on the Isthmus of Rak, requiring more than 50 subcontractors working on 20 projects. To have ownership of subcontractor selection, the selection process criteria must be defined—

a. At the program level
b. At the project level
c. By professionals in the construction business working with the program manager
d. By local Sarsmanian officials working with the program team

134. Managing a program to improve the services of your city government to elderly people, you have six projects in progress. Your program is to be completed in two years. Project Manager B met with you today and requested a change to the scope of her project. She noted that this scope change also affected Projects A and E, which is why she is escalating it to you. The next step should be to—

a. Convene a meeting of all six project managers to discuss the ramifications of this change
b. Analyze the change request
c. Ask a member of your core team to analyze the change request and determine its impact in terms of overall program benefits
d. Meet with your Governance Board to inform them of this change and receive their authorization to implement it

135. Rarely have hurricanes reached northern states in the United States until the past two years. You are a contractor to the government to manage a program to help people prepare should a hurricane occur. As you are the program manager, you want to keep all of your stakeholders apprised of your process on this program and want to obtain information from them to better understand their concerns relative to your program so you used—

   a. Interviews
   b. Focus groups
   c. Questionnaires
   d. Organizational analysis

136. On your program you and your team prepared a detailed stakeholder register. You also used a variety of methods to better understand stakeholder concerns about your program. However as the program manager, a best practice to follow is to—

   a. Establish a balance between people who have negative views about the program and those who are advocates
   b. Work diligently with stakeholders that have been identified as program resistors to better understand there issues
   c. Prepare a stakeholder inventory to help classify stakeholder groups who are affected positively and negatively
   d. Prepare a stakeholder management strategy

137. You are a member of your insurance company's Program Selection Committee, which is considering a number of possible programs to pursue. Each one has identified benefits that will support your company's overall strategic plan. Program A is estimated to cost $100,000 to implement and will have annual net cash inflows of $25,000; Program B is estimated to cost $250,000 to implement, with annual net cash inflows of $75,000; Program C is estimated to cost $300,000 to implement, with annual net cash inflows of $80,000; and Program D is estimated to cost $500,000 to implement, with annual net cash inflows of $225,000. You should recommend that your company select—

   a. Program A
   b. Program B
   c. Program C
   d. Program D

138. You are managing a program, BBB, for your manufacturing firm. You have five projects in your program (three were under way before the program officially began). While some contracts will be ones at the program level, some have been awarded already at the project level on the existing projects. The best approach to follow for these existing contracts is to—

a. Conduct regular supplier performance reviews
b. Have one provider that supports several projects
c. Have service level agreements
d. Have the project managers report procurement results to the program manager

139. You have just received approval from your Executive Team to begin to develop the next generation of stealth shield aircraft. You prepared a business case, which the Executive Team accepted, and it showed you could achieve a payback on your investment in this new program within three years. You received approval to begin to initiate this program. Now, you are preparing estimates of cost and—

a. Schedule
b. Scope
c. Risk
d. Benefits

140. You have been the program manager for an aerospace company on its stealth shield aircraft program now for five years and officially closed the program. However, your product support team monitors the product from a reliability and availability-for-use perspective and compares it with the expected performance, which was predicted when the product was developed. The team cites a need to improve reliability and uncovers various anomalies in the software system. Your best approach in this situation is to—

a. Use project management to perform the upgrade
b. Contact the client and all stakeholders immediately
c. Support this new problem independently of the program through an operations function in the company
d. Relinquish the product support function to the client

141. You are the manager for a wind-energy program that will last for eight years. You identify a number of component projects and expect to add others as the program proceeds, especially since this program will last such a long time. Although you have fully staffed your program team, you realize that some of your core team members and project managers will leave the organization or your program for other opportunities. You have decided to facilitate the development of your team members and in doing so perhaps turnover will be minimal. A best practice to follow is—

    a. Set up a succession program for career advancement
    b. Support coaching
    c. Support mentoring
    d. Set up a 360 degree performance evaluation system

142. On your program you have a large number of stakeholders, many of whom are not supporters. To listen to their concerns as you work with these stakeholders over this large and complex program, you should—

    a. Follow your stakeholder engagement strategy
    b. Update your stakeholder register
    c. Use an issue log
    d. Update your communications plan

143. You are a member of your energy services company's Program Selection Committee, which is considering a number of possible programs to pursue. Each one has identified benefits that will support your company's overall strategic plan. You have the following data on four possible programs. You may select only one because of resource limitations.

Program A NPV at	*Program B NPV at*	*Program C NPV at*	*Program D NPV at*
5% = 3,524	5% = 2,201	5% = 6,400	5% = 3,055
10% = 2,901	10% = 2,254	10% = 3,275	10% = 2,857
15% = 1,563	15% = 1,632	15% = 1,679	15% = 1,125

Note: NPV = net present value.

You should recommend that your company select—

    a. Program A
    b. Program B
    c. Program C
    d. Program D

144. Assume you are the program manager to implement enterprise resource planning software in all the agencies in your province. This program would be difficult if it were limited to only one agency, but it is especially hard because you have 17 agencies in the province, and each one has its own legacy system that it uses. You will have to have a separate project for each agency as well as projects for training, implementation, and maintenance. This program thus will span several years and budget cycles. Before the budget is baselined, you must—

  a. Add program overhead costs
  b. List income and payment schedules
  c. Determine component payment schedules
  d. Update the program management plan

145. Quality is essential in IT projects especially in complex ones such as enterprise resource planning software development and implementation. A quality management plan contains—

  a. Standard templates
  b. A schedule for planned quality assurance audits
  c. Checklists
  d. A method to handle change requests from quality assurance and control results

146. Assume you are the program manager to implement enterprise resource planning software in all the agencies in your province. This program would be difficult if it were limited to only one agency, but it is especially hard because you have 17 agencies in the province, and each one has its own legacy system that it uses. The executive director of your program Governance Board suggests that you explore local consulting firms for additional resource support. The best document to use to identify potential sellers is the—

  a. Request for information
  b. Invitation to bid
  c. Contract terms and conditions
  d. Contract statement of work

147. Introducing program management to your electric company has been a challenge but is finally being embraced as executives to team members now are seeing that using programs can produce more benefits to the company and its customers than if projects were managed in a standalone way. One approach that has been useful to you in your role of leading this culture change in the electric company has been to prepare a benefits realization plan and to get it signed off by your sponsor, members of the Governance Board, and other key stakeholders. Your company also uses the balanced scorecard approach, and your benefits realization plan considered it when you developed it so the benefits are aligned to the scorecard. One benefit that is often overlooked is—

a. Cost of quality
b. New income
c. Competitive advantage
d. Risk avoidance

148. One of the first programs you managed at your electric company, DDD, was for a city in Draeger, New York. The purpose was to reduce the numerous power outages so that if a power outage occurred, residents in Draeger would only lose power momentarily until a backup system could be deployed to provide time for on-site personnel to arrive at the location and diagnose the problem and provide corrective action. When you prepared your benefits realization plan for this program early on, one of the items you included in it was—

a. Review sessions to be held on a periodic basis by citizens of Draeger
b. Methods to maximize citizen satisfaction in the program delivery
c. Ways to ensure all stages of the program are managed in a way to satisfy the use of the program's outputs
d. Overall business requirements, including scope and limitations

149. Researchers have noted the emergence of corporate program management and note that its processes must be structured to coordinate and manage the multiple components that together contribute to business value and organizational structure. It therefore is clear that being a program manager is different from being a project manager as required competencies as a program manager are significantly different. As the business case for a program is being prepared, a performance competency for the program manager is—

a. Marketing
b. Political awareness
c. Aligning program objectives with strategic goals
d. Preparing a benefits realization plan

150. Your organization receives an award for the construction of a new courthouse complex in the state capital of State A. Your company is located in State B, approximately 1,000 miles away, and has never worked in State A. You plan to use a number of contractors and to hire local people to support the program team. From time to time, you will need cranes. To facilitate acquiring these cranes, you should—

    a. Purchase the cranes
    b. Develop a qualified seller list
    c. Issue an Invitation for Bid
    d. Issue a Request for Proposals

151. Your organization receives an award for the construction of a new courthouse complex in the state capital of State A. Your company is located in State B, approximately 1,000 miles away, and has never worked in State A. You plan to use a number of contractors and to hire local people to support the program team. From time to time, you will need cranes. However, you always have some type of risks whenever you use contactors. Therefore, it is important as a best practice to—

    a. Only use contractors on the qualified seller list
    b. Perform a site visit to each contractor's headquarters to demonstrate to its leaders the importance of your program
    c. Have each contractor prepare a monthly performance report
    d. Manage risk in accordance with the risk management plan

152. Assume this is the first time you are managing a program. You have had success in your company in project management, and you are on a career path that now leads to program management. On your program, you want to apply some of the successful best practices you used on your projects, recognizing the differences between programs and projects and their greater complexity. However, since you have been in project management for so long now in this company (17 years), you also know that—

    a. You need to prepare a comprehensive WBS for the program that includes the work of the projects
    b. You want to build your program schedule only after all the project schedules are complete
    c. You recognize the importance of qualifying and quantifying all possible risks
    d. You realize project stakeholders are also program stakeholders

153. You are managing a program that comprises new systems application development and maintenance activities. The program has been under way for three years. One of the projects has completed its deliverables, and its benefits have been realized. However approval by your Governance Board is required, and their review generally includes—

   a. Ensuring communications of closure to stakeholders
   b. Reviewing your program issues register
   c. Verifying customer acceptance of deliverables
   d. Reviewing compliance with quality assurance plans

154. In your organization, the program Governance Board has assumed organizational responsibilities that its programs are prepared for audits that may be required or desired. These audits—

   a. Are part of the quality assurance function
   b. Should be documented in the master schedule
   c. Should be included in the roadmap
   d. Focus on management processes

155. In determining whether it is better to use program management or project management, the culture of the organization should be considered. Your organization is considering implementation of program management, and you are leading a team to recommend this approach to your CEO and other members of the executive team. One of your arguments for the change is that the organization's culture has transitioned so that it is now characterized by—

   a. A specialist level of business expertise
   b. A strong connection between execution output and strategic objectives
   c. A lower dependency between cross-discipline specialties in the organization
   d. Less need for a time-to-money improvement

156. You are managing a program that comprises new systems application development and maintenance activities. These applications are critical to your company, CDE, as they involve access to proprietary data. The systems must be available to your clients on a 24/7/365 basis. Much of the work on you program will be outsourced as you have an aggressive schedule to meet; fortunately CDE has a qualified vendor list to simplify the acquisition process. This program has high visibility in CDE and is a major change to the organization. Therefore, CDE's CEO decided to serve as the executive director of the program and chairs each meeting of your program's Governance Board. Before Board meetings are held to review program performance, your Board members have asked you to submit—

    a. Benefit realization reports
    b. Estimate to complete data
    c. To-complete performance index data
    d. Financial reports

157. Now that you have moved into this program management role in your manufacturing company, you realize your work really involves active involvement with stakeholders at a variety of levels. It is also compounded because on your program you have external stakeholders involved and need to spend time communicating with them. It seems as if each time you pass a stage gate review, the number of stakeholders increase, or people who lacked interest in the program now are interested. Therefore, the primary skill to best engage stakeholders—

    a. Negotiation
    b. Conflict management
    c. Communications
    d. Influencing

158. One of the project managers in your program has told you that although he did a thorough job of risk management planning, a new risk has emerged that has major negative ramifications for the project. This risk could also affect another project in the program, as it involves a lack of critical resources. Another project manager tells you that he will need this same resource on his project, although he did not consider it during resource planning. In this situation, you should—

    a. Implement your contingency reserve to hire needed resources to support these projects
    b. Propose a solution to these risks escalated by the project managers
    c. Ask each project manager to revise the risk register to add these risks and to use a workaround
    d. Revise your program work breakdown structure (PWBS) accordingly, because this risk shows that a key planning package is missing

159. You are a member of your organization's Program Selection Committee. The company's strategic plan includes five major goals, which are all weighted equally. Goal 1 is to fall within the time-to-market window; goal 2 is to reduce operational costs; goal 3 is to differentiate the products from others on the market; goal 4 is to deliver the highest-quality product; and goal 5 is to promote economic sustainability. At the next committee meeting, you will consider four programs and recommend one. Program A partially supports goal 1, fully supports goals 2–4, and does not support goal 5. Program B fully supports goals 1, 3, 4, and 5, but does not support goal 2. Program C fully supports goals 1 and 2, partially supports goals 3 and 4, but does not support goal 5. Program D partially supports goals 1, 2, and 5, and fully supports goals 3 and 4. With this information, which program will you recommend?

    a. Program A
    b. Program B
    c. Program C
    d. Program D

160. You are managing a complex program to develop the next-generation submarine. It is planned to replace the existing non-nuclear submarines in your country with nuclear weapons. It is estimated to take about nine years to complete as you will be using new technology now not available in your country. The program includes a number of projects, and you plan to use subcontractors extensively. You also plan contracts for services or for insurance to protect the program. For these contracts, you need to—

   a. Use qualified seller lists
   b. Document the relevant parties' responsibilities regarding risk
   c. Prepare a contract administration plan
   d. Prepare component cost estimates

161. It is a challenge to effectively exchange information among all program stakeholders. This is one reason why the program manager must have excellent communications skills. Managing information on programs may become a formidable task in itself. To assist in this key area, the Governance Board may—

   a. Establish a standard reporting process
   b. Set up a knowledge management system
   c. Set up a program management information system
   d. Protect intellectual property

162. Your organization recently conducted an Organizational Project Management Maturity Assessment (*OPM3®*). The assessment results and the improvement plan showed much work needed to be done in the area of portfolio management. It was especially apparent that many projects, and almost every program, lacked a defined business case that had been prepared by the sponsor and then approved and authorized by leadership. After receiving the reports from the *OPM3®* assessor, you held a focus group of program sponsors to determine why business cases were not regularly prepared. It turned out many of the people in the focus group lacked an understanding of the benefits of preparing one. You explained that the primary benefit is to—

   a. Establish alignment with strategic goals
   b. Provide a perspective on how best to execute the program
   c. Determine how the program will help the organization meet its business and strategic goals
   d. Make the portfolio process more effective

163. Your organization announces that funds in all areas will be cut by 10 percent. Even though you are still in the planning stages and your program is a high priority for your company, your program is not exempt from the budget cuts. Management has also mandated certain delivery dates that will be hard to meet with the budget cuts. As you decide which program components should be handled internally and which should be outsourced, you consider the—

   a. PWBS
   b. Program scope statement
   c. Make-or-buy analysis
   d. Qualified seller lists

164. Assume that your program for Draeger, New York is in its final stages. The purpose was to reduce the numerous power outages so that if a power outage occurred, residents in Draeger would only lose power momentarily until a backup system could be deployed to provide time for on-site personnel to arrive at the location and diagnose the problem and provide corrective action. Recently, there was a power outage in one part of the City. The new power station's backup capability was available in less than two minutes. It is now time to close this program and transition it to ongoing operations. Before doing so, a best practice is to—

   a. Review the program's scope statement
   b. Conduct a customer satisfaction survey
   c. Review the quality assurance plan
   d. Review the benefits realization plan

165. In determining whether to pursue a program, it is important to assess goals and objectives. In your new product development organization, of the triple constraint, quality and scope are the dominant. This does not imply the schedule and budget are not important, but given that the programs must achieve regulatory approval, quality dominates in the company. Quality goals that are too low may lead to customer and end-user dissatisfaction, whereas goals that are too high may result in a high cost to the business. Therefore, it is important to consider—

   a. Market needs and expectations
   b. The value proposition
   c. Cash-flow management
   d. Risk analysis and assessment

166. As part of your procurement management plan for this new product development program, you have explicitly stated the actions that you and your program team can take on its own and those that require involvement by or should be deferred to the Procurement or Contracting Department. As you prepare your procurement management plan, the best practice is to optimize procurements to meet program objectives and deliver benefits. To do so you need to—

   a. Address commonalities and differences across components
   b. Review your resource management plan
   c. Use pre-negotiated contracts and blanket purchase agreements
   d. Direct procurements to be centralized at the program level

167. You are Company A's program manager for the development of an online banking system for your community bank. One of its objectives is to make sure all transactions are secure. You have a large team supporting you as program manager, and you have four projects thus far. Two of the project managers are new to your company and lack familiarity with the company's standard program management procedures. Because time and quality are of the essence in this program, you are need to make sure these two project managers understand what must be done to comply with the various procedures. Your best approach to do so is through—

   a. One-on-one meetings each day
   b. Developing an on-line training system to show all the various procedures to follow
   c. Using mentoring
   d. Using skills in creative thinking

168. You are Company A's program manager for the development of an online banking system for your community bank. One of its objectives is to make sure all transactions are secure. You have a large team supporting you as program manager, and you have four projects thus far. Two of the project managers are new to your company and lack familiarity with the company's standard program management procedures. You have set up a change management plan as you know programs involve change and with this program and its four projects, changes will occur. You especially want to use it to help control—

   a. Benefits
   b. Issues
   c. Quality
   d. Human resources

169. Assume you are sponsoring a proposed program. You have identified tangible benefits such as a one year payback period, a high return on investment, and an increase in productivity by 25 percent. Some of the intangible benefits that you have identified include an increase in employee morale with retention of intellectual property. You also believe it will contribute to knowledge sharing. You are getting ready to present your business case to the Portfolio Review Board. Before doing so, you want to make sure it has been completed properly so you first should—

    a. Present a cost/benefit analysis
    b. Describe the business opportunity and product, service, or result that you are proposing
    c. Identify the Key Performance Indicators
    d. Describe the high-level risks if the program is approved

170. The organization is new to program management but has been a leader in program management. A new CEO was appointed, who used program management extensively in his previous organization. He has set up programs and Governance Boards. The Governance Board is a first step and it should—

    a. Establish policies and procedures
    b. Provide training in program management
    c. Determine the knowledge, skills, and competencies of existing project managers to manage programs
    d. Provide the link to portfolio management

Answer Sheet for Practice Test 2

1.	a	b	c	d	20.	a	b	c	d
2.	a	b	c	d	21.	a	b	c	d
3.	a	b	c	d	22.	a	b	c	d
4.	a	b	c	d	23.	a	b	c	d
5.	a	b	c	d	24.	a	b	c	d
6.	a	b	c	d	25.	a	b	c	d
7.	a	b	c	d	26.	a	b	c	d
8.	a	b	c	d	27.	a	b	c	d
9.	a	b	c	d	28.	a	b	c	d
10.	a	b	c	d	29.	a	b	c	d
11.	a	b	c	d	30.	a	b	c	d
12.	a	b	c	d	31.	a	b	c	d
13.	a	b	c	d	32.	a	b	c	d
14.	a	b	c	d	33.	a	b	c	d
15.	a	b	c	d	34.	a	b	c	d
16.	a	b	c	d	35.	a	b	c	d
17.	a	b	c	d	36.	a	b	c	d
18.	a	b	c	d	37.	a	b	c	d
19.	a	b	c	d	38.	a	b	c	d

39.	a	b	c	d
40.	a	b	c	d
41.	a	b	c	d
42.	a	b	c	d
43.	a	b	c	d
44.	a	b	c	d
45.	a	b	c	d
46.	a	b	c	d
47.	a	b	c	d
48.	a	b	c	d
49.	a	b	c	d
50.	a	b	c	d
51.	a	b	c	d
52.	a	b	c	d
53.	a	b	c	d
54.	a	b	c	d
55.	a	b	c	d
56.	a	b	c	d
57.	a	b	c	d
58.	a	b	c	d
59.	a	b	c	d
60.	a	b	c	d

61.	a	b	c	d
62.	a	b	c	d
63.	a	b	c	d
64.	a	b	c	d
65.	a	b	c	d
66.	a	b	c	d
67.	a	b	c	d
68.	a	b	c	d
69.	a	b	c	d
70.	a	b	c	d
71.	a	b	c	d
72.	a	b	c	d
73.	a	b	c	d
74.	a	b	c	d
75.	a	b	c	d
76.	a	b	c	d
77.	a	b	c	d
78.	a	b	c	d
79.	a	b	c	d
80.	a	b	c	d
81.	a	b	c	d
82.	a	b	c	d

83.	a	b	c	d
84.	a	b	c	d
85.	a	b	c	d
86.	a	b	c	d
87.	a	b	c	d
88.	a	b	c	d
89.	a	b	c	d
90.	a	b	c	d
91.	a	b	c	d
92.	a	b	c	d
93.	a	b	c	d
94.	a	b	c	d
95.	a	b	c	d
96.	a	b	c	d
97.	a	b	c	d
98.	a	b	c	d
99.	a	b	c	d
100.	a	b	c	d
101.	a	b	c	d
102.	a	b	c	d
103.	a	b	c	d
104.	a	b	c	d
105.	a	b	c	d
106.	a	b	c	d
107.	a	b	c	d
108.	a	b	c	d
109.	a	b	c	d
110.	a	b	c	d
111.	a	b	c	d
112.	a	b	c	d
113.	a	b	c	d
114.	a	b	c	d
115.	a	b	c	d
116.	a	b	c	d
117.	a	b	c	d
118.	a	b	c	d
119.	a	b	c	d
120.	a	b	c	d
121.	a	b	c	d
122.	a	b	c	d
123.	a	b	c	d
124.	a	b	c	d
125.	a	b	c	d
126.	a	b	c	d

127.	a	b	c	d
128.	a	b	c	d
129.	a	b	c	d
130.	a	b	c	d
131.	a	b	c	d
132.	a	b	c	d
133.	a	b	c	d
134.	a	b	c	d
135.	a	b	c	d
136.	a	b	c	d
137.	a	b	c	d
138.	a	b	c	d
139.	a	b	c	d
140.	a	b	c	d
141.	a	b	c	d
142.	a	b	c	d
143.	a	b	c	d
144.	a	b	c	d
145.	a	b	c	d
146.	a	b	c	d
147.	a	b	c	d
148.	a	b	c	d

149.	a	b	c	d
150.	a	b	c	d
151.	a	b	c	d
152.	a	b	c	d
153.	a	b	c	d
154.	a	b	c	d
155.	a	b	c	d
156.	a	b	c	d
157.	a	b	c	d
158.	a	b	c	d
159.	a	b	c	d
160.	a	b	c	d
161.	a	b	c	d
162.	a	b	c	d
163.	a	b	c	d
164.	a	b	c	d
165.	a	b	c	d
166.	a	b	c	d
167.	a	b	c	d
168.	a	b	c	d
169.	a	b	c	d
170.	a	b	c	d

Answer Key for Practice Test 2

1. a. Benefits register

   The benefits register is set up as benefits are identified and is maintained throughout the program. It Is used to measure and communicate the delivery of benefits and contains, among other things, target dates and milestones for benefit achievement.

   PMI®, *The Standard for Program Management*, 2013, 36

2. d. Strategic visioning

   Program managers require a combination of knowledge, skills, and competencies. Strategic visioning and planning are two critical skills that are required to align program goals and benefits with the organization's long-term goals. The program manager also must align individual project plans with the program goals and benefits.

   PMI®, *The Standard for Program Management*, 2013, 15

3. b. Delivering intended benefits

   After the program management plan has been approved, the Program Benefit Delivery Phase begins. During this phase, the purpose is to plan, manage, and integrate components to facilitate delivery of intended benefits.

   PMI®, *The Standard for Program Management*, 2013, 68

4. b. Note stakeholder considerations in your program charter

   It is highly appropriate to perform market research to identify any potential stakeholders who may have an interest in or influence over your program and its component projects. The program charter should describe stakeholder considerations, including an initial strategy to effectively engage them.

   PMI®, *The Standard for Program Management*, 2013, 84

5. b. Disclose this relationship to the Procurement Director and to your sponsor immediately

   Under PMI's "Code of Ethics and Professional Conduct", fairness is a mandatory standard. This situation can easily be perceived as a conflict of interest as under 4.3.3 in the Code, contracts are not to be awarded based on personal considerations, one of which is nepotism.

   PMI®, *PMI Code of Ethics and Professional Conduct*. Available from http://www.pmi.org/codeofethics/PDF, 4

6. a. Determine which components are affected

   In Program Scope Management, the program manager must determine the components that are affected by the requested scope change and update the PWBS accordingly.

   PMI®, *The Standard for Program Management*, 2013, 106

7. b. Influenced by requirements

   As an organization manages its portfolio, programs are influenced by a number of portfolio needs, one of which is requirements; they are then translated into the program scope, deliverables, budget, and schedule.

   PMI®, *The Standard for Program Management*, 2013, 10–11

8. c. Deploy the program organization

   In Program Preparation, which ends when the program management plan is reviewed and approved, the program organization is deployed, and an initial team is established to develop the program management plan.

   PMI®, *The Standard for Program Management*, 2013, 68

9. b. Business case

   The business case and current goals of the organization are used to judge successful program completion.

   PMI®, *The Standard for Program Management*, 2013, 89

10. d. Establishing program direction

    Substantive leadership skills are required to manage multiple project teams in the program life cycle. Program leadership entails establishing program direction, identifying interdependencies, communicating requirements, tracking progress, making decisions, and resolving conflicts and issues, among other important tasks.

    PMI®, *The Standard for Program Management*, 2013, 15

11. a. Provide guidelines for project-level stakeholder engagement

    While the stakeholder engagement plan documents how stakeholders will be engaged throughout the life of the program, the program manager also provides guidelines for component stakeholder engagement to the individual projects and non-project work that are part of the program.

    PMI®, *The Standard for Program Management*, 2013, 49

12. c. Program Closing phase

    During the Program Closing phase, all program work has been completed and program benefits are accruing. A key activity in this phase is for the program manager to review the status of the benefits with the Governance Board as the program transitions.

    PMI®, *The Standard for Program Management*, 2013, 70

13. a. End user satisfaction

    Quality control is performed throughout the program. It is important to ensure components and the program fulfill quality requirements for adequate benefit realization. End user satisfaction is considered a key metric to gauge program quality.

    PMI®, *The Standard for Program Management*, 2013, 93–94

14. d. Focus on ongoing performance and progress

    In addition to phase-gate reviews, Governance Boards tend to have less formal 'periodic health check' sessions to assess ongoing performance and progress especially toward the realization and sustainment of benefits.

    PMI®, *The Standard for Program Management*, 2013, 56

15. d. Define standard measurement criteria

    While all of the answers relate to the initiating activities, given the high level of risk associated with the program and the skepticism of some key stakeholders, standard measurement criteria are required for success to monitor and control the program.

    PMI®, *Program Management Professional (PgMP)® Examination Content Outline*, 2011, 8

    Miller, L. Trae, "Program Initiation", in Levin, Ginger. 2012. *Program Management A Life Cycle Approach*. Boca Raton, FL: CRC Press, 69–71

16. b. Reducing risks

    Reducing risk is essential as a business case driver for financial control and compliance with external requirements such as corporate reporting and mandatory audits.

    PMI®, *The Standard for Program Management*, 2013, 28

    PMI®, *Program Management Professional (PgMP)® Examination Content Outline*, 2011, 6

    Williams, David and Parr, Tim. 2006. *Enterprise Program Management Delivering Value*, Hampshire, England: Palgrave MacMillan, 124

17. a. Using your PMO

While the PMO performs many functions in support of programs, it is not uncommon for it on large and intricate programs to provide support for contracts and procurements.

PMI®, *The Standard for Program Management*, 2013, 13

18. d. Governance plan

Component initiation criteria are part of the program's governance plan, and the initial gate review for a component is at its initiation. The Governance Board typically approves the initiation of components based on their business plans.

PMI®, *The Standard for Program Management*, 2013, 56

19. a. Risk profiles

In preparing the program risk management plan, it is essential to define risk profiles of the organizations involved in the program to construct the most suitable approach to manage program risk, adjust risk sensitivity, and monitor risk criticality.

PMI®, *The Standard for Program Management*, 2013, 97

20. c. Customer satisfaction surveys

During Program Quality Control, it is essential to determine fitness for use of the benefits, products, or services delivered by the program by the end users. Programs therefore often use customer satisfaction surveys as a quality control measurement.

PMI®, *The Standard for Program Management*, 2013, 94

21. c. Convene a meeting of your Governance Board

Program governance activities are conducted throughout the program life cycle. One purpose is to establish and enforce policies addressing managing program change. The Governance Board should be consulted about this major change and how best to handle it.

PMI®, *The Standard for Program Management*, 2013, 58–59

22. a. Benefits delivery

Success on programs is measured by the degree to which programs realize the needs and benefits for which they are undertaken.

PMI®, *The Standard for Program Management*, 2013, 8

23. c. Summarize the supporting infrastructure

    The roadmap serves numerous functions in program management. Among other things, it provides a high-level snapshot of the supporting infrastructure and component plans.

    PMI®, *The Standard for Program Management, Second Edition,* 2013, 30

    PMI®, *Program Management Professional (PgMP)® Examination Content Outline,* 2011, 6

24. c. Meet with your organizational leaders

    You have a conflict as these are competing programs. It is incumbent on you to meet with the organization's leaders as the customer's request also is one in which is not consistent with the organization's background or the core background, experience, skills, and qualifications of its staff.

    PMI®, *The Code of Ethics and Professional Conduct.* Available from wwwpmi.org/codeofethicsPDF, p. 2

    PMI®, *Program Management Professional (PgMP)® Examination Content Outline,* 2011, 6

25. a. Prepare a program resource plan

    While a program resource plan is prepared in Resource Planning, it is one for the entire program as resource requirements are identified. Now that the program management plan has been approved, you are working to prioritize resource use. A program resource plan then often is prepared that describes the use of scarce resources and the priority for which component can plan for that resource.

    PMI®, *The Standard for Program Management,* 2013, 95

26. b. An appropriate governance structure in place

    The governance structure ensures the program's goals and objectives are aligned with the strategic goals. This program's original governance structure may no longer be appropriate given the dramatic change to the program. Different people may now be needed as members of the Governance Board, including that of the program sponsor.

    PMI®, *The Standard for Program Management,* 2013, 55

27. a. Constraints

Constraints limit the options of the program management team. Once the high-level program master schedule is determined, the dates for each component are identified. These dates are used to develop the component's schedule and are constraints for each component team.

PMI®, *The Standard for Program Management*, 2013, 102

28. c. Track schedule risks

In Program Schedule Control, slippages and opportunities should be identified and used in risk management. This means program schedule risks should be tracked as part of the risk management activity.

PMI®, *The Standard for Program Management*, 2013, 103

29. c. Ensure payments were made

In Program Procurement Closure, it is necessary to close out all contracts. This is done after determining all deliverables were completed satisfactorily, all payments have been made, and there are no outstanding contractual issues.

PMI®, *The Standard for Program Management*, 2013, 91

30. b. The program charter

Approval of the program charter is critical as it formally authorizes the commencement of the program.

PMI®, *The Standard for Program Management*, 2013, 85

31. a. Facilitation

Program managers require a number of interpersonal skills. With facilitating, one key element is to plan for success from the start of the program. Milestones can be set in the high-level program plan that can be easily met in order that early successes can lead to an atmosphere of later successes among the team.

Levin, Ginger and Ward, J. LeRoy. 2011. *Program Complexity A Competency Model*, Boca Raton, FL: CRC Press, 87–89

32. b. Through value delivery

Value is delivered when the organization, community, or other program beneficiaries are able to use the program's benefits.

PMI®, *The Standard for Program Management*, 2013, 41

33. a. Representatives from each business unit in the organization would participate in the program

Such internal programs serve as a catalyst for change. Participation across the various business units is desirable so that resources can be shared. Furthermore, while the maturity assessment itself is typically conducted rather quickly, it takes time to implement the various recommendations, each of which is a specific project that depends on other projects to create a set of benefits.

PMI®, *The Standard for Program Management*, 2013, 27

PMI®, *Program Management Professional (PgMP)® Examination Content Outline*, 2011, 7

34. c. Update the program roadmap

The processing of the transition request is complete with updates to the roadmap. These updates reflect go/no-go decisions and approved change requests affecting major milestones, scope, or timing of major stages or blocks of the program.

PMI®, *The Standard for Program Management*, 2013, 87

35. d. Attitudes about the program and its sponsors

Stakeholder analysis and planning is performed before the stakeholder engagement plan is prepared. Among other items to consider is the attitudes the stakeholders that have been identified have toward the program and is sponsors.

PMI®, *The Standard for Program Management*, 2013, 49

36. b. Use performance/earned value reports

The program manager maintains visibility in Program Procurement Administration to ensure the program budget is being spent properly to deliver benefits. An output is the use of performance/earned value reports to assist in this role.

PMI®, *The Standard for Program Management*, 2013, 91

37. c. There is compliance with legal policies

The Governance Board often assumes responsibility for program reporting and control. An example of one of its many functions is compliance with corporate and legal policies appropriate since this example includes so many suppliers.

PMI®, *The Standard for Program Management*, 2013, 57

38. c. Update your program plans as required

    Budget cuts, the organization's fiscal year, and the budget planning cycle may affect programs and projects. If they affect your program, as program manager, you have the responsibility to revisit and update program plans as necessary. Planning is an iterative activity as competing priorities assumptions, and constraints are resolved.

    PMI®, *The Standard for Program Management*, 2013, 85

39. c. Program management office (PMO)

    For most programs, the program management office (PMO) is the core of the program infrastructure. Program Infrastructure Development includes the PMO to support the management and coordination of the program's work and that of the components.

    PMI®, *The Standard for Program Management*, 2013, 86

40. c. Helpful to determine if the program's benefits will be met

    Program performance reports include identification of resource use to determine if the program's goals and benefits will be met and summarize the components' progress and the program's status relative to benefits.

    PMI®, *The Standard for Program Management*, 2013, 87

41. c. Serve as a reference to measure program success

    The program plan has many purposes, and it is the documented reference by which the program will measure its success during the program; it includes metrics for success, a method for measurement, and a definition of success.

    PMI®, *The Standard for Program Management*, 2013, 28

42. c. Standard measurement criteria

    On each program, standard measurement criteria for success must be defined for all consistent projects. This is done by analysis of stakeholder expectations and requirements across the projects in order to manage and control the program.

    PMI®, *Program Management Professional (PgMP)® Examination Content Outline*, 2011, 8

43. a. Use adaptive change

Although the program management plan and roadmap will show the intended program direction and its benefits, the entire suite of components may not be known The program manager should provide oversight during the benefit delivery phase and if necessary replan for proper integration or changes in program direction through adaptive change.

PMI®, *The Standard for Program Management*, 2013, 69

44. c. Benefits analysis and planning

Benefits are mapped into the program plan during benefits analysis and planning along with deriving and prioritizing components, deriving benefit metrics, and establishing the benefit realization plan.

PMI®, *The Standard for Program Management*, 2013, 35

45. d. Visually shows the stakeholders' current and desired support and influence

Mapping is a useful stakeholder identification technique to analyze stakeholders and map them into various categories. It visually represents the interaction of all stakeholders' current and desired level of support and influence regarding the program.

PMI®, *The Standard for Program Management*, 2013, 46

46. c. Gain an understanding of expectations of program benefit delivery

One purpose of stakeholder analysis and planning is to understand the stakeholders' expectations of program benefits delivery. After stakeholder analysis and planning is complete, the result is the stakeholder engagement plan.

PMI®, *The Standard for Program Management*, 2013, 49

47 b. Use of a common program approach

The program approach defines how the program will deliver its goals and benefits; a common approach can lead to repeatable program success.

PMI®, *The Standard for Program Management*, 2013, 153

48. c. Roadmap

The roadmap has many purposes one of which is that it is a valuable tool to help manage the execution of the program and to assess its progress toward achieving specific benefits.

PMI®, *The Standard for Program Management*, 2013, 30

49. a. Ongoing operations

Even after the program life cycle ends, benefits management allows the organization to realize and sustain the benefits from its investment. The program manager ensures that this is accomplished within the framework of ongoing operations in the organization.

PMI®, *The Standard for Program Management*, 2013, 41–42

50. a. Analyze the stakeholder register

Stakeholder engagement planning is done to outline how program stakeholders will be engaged In the program. The stakeholder register should be analyzed to help understand the environment in which the program will operate.

PMI®, *The Standard for Program Management*, 2013, 49

51. d. Follow the issue escalation process

The issue escalation process should be used in this situation to escalate this issue to your Governance Board and involve them in the decision-making process as stated in your governance plan.

PMI®, *The Standard for Program Management*, 2013, 56

52. d. Manage program level issues

Issues are concerns that may affect the program. It is necessary to manage program level issues, such as ones involving human resource management, finance, technology, and the schedule, by defining and selecting a course of action consistent with program scope, constraints, and objectives to achieve program benefits.

PMI®, *Program Management Professional (PgMP)® Examination Content Outline*, 2011, 11

53. a. Benefits identification

The benefits register is prepared during benefits identification and is maintained and updated until it is time to transition the benefits or if the program ends prematurely.

PMI®, *The Standard for Program Management*, 2013, 35–36

54. b. Plan the transition from program management to operations

Through benefit sustainment the ongoing sustainment activities are transferred to operations or subsequent programs. The program and component managers plan for ongoing sustainment during the program. One aspect is to plan the transition of product or capability support from program management to operations.

PMI®, *The Standard for Program Management*, 2013, 43–44

55. b. Total available resources

Resources—funding, equipment, and people—are limited in all organizations. In selecting a program, it is necessary to consider the total available resources that will be required to successfully implement it. The estimated resources should be included in the preliminary business case.

Thiry, Michel. *Program Management.* 2010. Surrey, England: Gower Publishing Limited, 119

56. b. Set forth in an audit plan

The Governance Board may assume responsibility for creating organizational or program-specific plans for audits to be used on programs. Audit plans provide details on audit expectations, audit processes, anticipated schedules, roles and responsibilities and policies to communicate audit results.

PMI®, *The Standard for Program Management*, 2013, 65

57. c. Prioritize a list of stakeholders

After the stakeholder register is prepared, information is obtained to better understand the organizational culture, politics, and concerns about the program and its overall impact. From this information, a prioritized list of stakeholders is prepared to help focus the engagement effort on the people and organizations that are most important to the program.

PMI®, *The Standard for Program Management*, 2013, 48

58. b. Delivering benefits

After the benefit realization plan is prepared, the focus shifts to delivering the expected benefits as defined in the plan.

PMI®, *The Standard for Program Management*, 2013, 39, 67

59. b. Suppliers are now a major stakeholder

In this situation, suppliers are a major stakeholder especially because of the changing policies and procedures in your organization. They require communications about this change and will need interaction with the program manager and his or her team so they do not become negative stakeholders.

PMI®, *The Standard for Program Management*, 2013, 48

60. a. Actively listen

Program managers require strong communications skills. A key part of communications is to actively listen, understand, and respond to stakeholders. It is essential to pay close attention to the speaker and make sure there is an understanding of the speaker's concerns, showing empathy for the points of view of others.

PMI®, *The Standard for Program Management*, 2013, 15

Levin and Ward, 2011, 61

61. a. Commend Project Manager A for his willingness to release these resources

The program manager manages the individual component managers and members of the core team. The program manager, therefore, reviews the performance of these individuals. In this situation, Project Manager A should be commended as his releasing these resources will improve team engagement and help achieve greater commitment to the program's goals.

PMI®, *Program Management Professional (PgMP)® Examination Content Outline*, 2011, 10

62. b. Prepare a change request

A key activity in Program Scope Control is to set up a change management activity. The first step in it is to capture requested scope changes following policies and procedures that are part of this change management activity.

PMI®, *The Standard for Program Management*, 2013, 106

63. d. Update your risk management plan

It is important to evaluate the risks stakeholders identify, including sponsors, and then incorporate them in the risk management plan.

PMI®, *Program Management Professional (PgMP)® Examination Content Outline*, 2011, 14

64. b. New stakeholders will become known and addressed

Preparing a communications plan at the program level is far more difficult than at the project level. New stakeholders will become known and addressed, and new components will be added. Since programs take longer to complete, many stakeholders will leave during the program as new stakeholders are added. Using multiple vendors adds to the number of stakeholders to consider.

PMI®, *The Standard for Program Management*, 2013, 74

65. d. Map how the components will deliver outcomes to achieve the program's benefits

The program architecture defines the structure of the components by identifying the relationships between them and the rules that govern their inclusion in the program.

PMI®, *The Standard for Program Management*, 2013, 39

66. a. Expected benefits are in line with the benefit realization plan

The gate review assesses the program with respect to a number of quality and strategic-related criteria including whether the expected benefits are in line with the benefit realization plan.

PMI®, *The Standard for Program Management*, 2013, 56

67. b. Bridge the gap between the current state and the to-be state

The program manager is the champion for change. He or she needs to bridge the gap between the "as-is" state and the desired vision of the "to-be" state to show an understanding of the current state and be able to describe the benefits that will accrue as the organization moves to the "to-be" state.

PMI®, *The Standard for Program Management*, 2013, 46

68. c. Program initiation

During the Program Initiation phase, the program components are defined and configured to deliver the program. This phase may also include a high-level plan for all components.

PMI®, *The Standard for Program Management*, 2013, 84

69. a. Programs and projects in the portfolio are focused on alignment to strategic objectives

Portfolio management involves the process of creating, managing, and evaluating a portfolio of strategic initiatives focused on delivering lasting results and benefits. The objective is to align the portfolio to strategic objectives, approving only those components that support business objectives. If the strategic direction changes, the portfolio is reexamined.

PMI®, *Program Management Professional (PgMP)® Examination Content Outline*, 2011, 6

PMI®. *The Standard for Program Management*, 2013, 10–11

Williams and Parr, 2006, 19

70. c. Benefits realization plan

The benefits realization plan identifies the business benefits and documents the plan to realize them. It includes intended interdependencies of benefits being delivered by the various projects in the program. It identifies organizational processes and systems required, changes to these processes and systems, and how and when the transition to the new arrangements will occur.

PMI®, *The Standard for Program Management*, 2013, 38

71. b. Program business case

The benefits register is established during benefits realization and uses the program's business case since the business case is the formal declaration of the value the program is expected to deliver and the resources required to do so.

PMI®, *The Standard for Program Management*, 2013, 36

72. d. Prepare a program resource plan

A program resource plan is prepared as an output of Resource Planning. In order to execute the program and its components, it is necessary to determine the needed resources, when they will be needed, and in what quantities.

PMI®, *The Standard for Program Management*, 2013, 94–95

73. b. Prepare a forecast

Forecasts are part of Program Performance Monitoring and Control. They enable the program manager and stakeholders to assess the likelihood of achieving planned outcomes.

PMI®, *The Standard for Program Management*, 2013, 87

74. d. Recognize the need to address cultural, socioeconomic, and political differences

Although the program manager must determine the optimal approach for overall program management, this is a global program. It is necessary to therefore tailor program management activities, processes, and interfaces to address effectively cultural, socio-economic, political, and environmental differences.

PMI®, *The Standard for Program Management*, 2013, 142–143

75. d. The components are producing deliverables as planned, but their benefits are not being realized successfully.

During Component Oversight and Integration, different components produce benefits at different times. The program manager receives status information and uses it to integrate components into the program activities. In many cases the program manager may initiate a new component to conduct integration efforts especially if components are producing deliverables, but benefits are not being realized without coordinated delivery.

PMI®, *The Standard for Program Management*, 2013, 69–70

76. d. Serve as a reference for the program manager for program information and documentation accessibility

Program management supporting activities may include work addressing knowledge management on programs. By organizing program management information for use as a reference, this enables the program manager to ensure that important program information and documentation are easily accessible and available to those who need it, and it can help support decision making.

PMI®, *The Standard for Program Management*, 2013, 65

77. b. Business case

To help stakeholders establish common expectations of the program's benefits, the program manager provides stakeholders with information from the program charter and the business case to summarize the details of the dependencies, risks, and benefits.

PMI®, *The Standard for Program Management*, 2013, 50

78. d. A SWOT analysis

Environmental analyses are used to assess the validity of the business case and the program plan. A SWOT analysis is one type of analysis to conduct and it then provides information to develop the charter and the program plan.

PMI®, *The Standard for Program Management*, 2013, 31

79. b. Use a questionnaire to get everyone in the agency involved in the process

Given the magnitude of this program in that it affects almost everyone in the agency to some extent, the questionnaire is a key approach to solicit feedback from stakeholders to have a better understanding of the organization's culture.

PMI®, *The Standard for Program Management*, 2013, 48

80. d. They want to assess performance against benefit realization and sustainment

Phase-gate reviews are not a substitute to periodic performance reviews, which are used to asses performance against expected outcomes and against the need to realize and sustain program benefits into the long term.

PMI®, *The Standard for Program Management*, 2013, 56

81. b. A detailed strategy for effective stakeholder engagement

Stakeholder engagement planning shows how the stakeholders will be engaged during the program. When the plan is complete, the program manager has a detailed strategy for effective stakeholder engagement for the program.

PMI®, *The Standard for Program Management*, 2013, 49

82. b. May require access restrictions

The stakeholder register should be easy to access by the program team, but it may contain political ad sensitive information. Therefore, access and review restrictions may be needed that the program manager establishes.

PMI®, *The Standard for Program Management*, 2013, 47

83. a. Ensure they are ones you can approve or reject

Change requests are common on programs and their components. The program manager must ensure that the ones he or she are able to approve or reject change are within one's scope of authority as part of Program Delivery Management.

PMI®, *The Standard for Program Management*, 2013, 87

84. b. Update the scope statement

Program Scope Control is necessary as the program develops to ensure successful completion, and scope changes can originate from many sources. As a result, an output is an updated program scope statement.

PMI®, *The Standard for Program Management*, 2013, 105–106

85. d. Ensure conditions for closure are satisfied

Before submitting the closure recommendation, conditions warranting closure must be satisfied and recommendations for closure must be consistent with the organization's vision and strategy.

PMI®, *The Standard for Program Management*, 2013, 61–62

86. a. Use a stakeholder impact and issue tracking and prioritization tool

Stakeholder issues and concerns should be tracked to closure. Using a tool to document, prioritize, and track these issue and stakeholder interests can help ensure the stakeholder concerns are properly addressed.

PMI®, *The Standard for Program Management*, 2013, 50

87. a. Identify and evaluate integration opportunities and needs

In strategic program management, once organizational leadership for the program has been obtained, and the authorization to initiate the program is received, it then is necessary to identify and evaluate integration opportunities and needs. These range from human capital, human resource requirements and skills sets, to facilities, finance, assets, processes, and systems within the program and its operational activities to align and integrate benefits across the organization.

PMI®, *Program Management Professional (PgMP)® Examination Content Outline*, 2011, 6

88. b. Program Initiation

A statement of the program's justification, vision, and strategic fit is included as part of the program charter, which is developed in the Program Initiation phase. The charter provides the authority to move forward to commence the program or to Planning in the life cycle from the *Examination Content Outline.*

PMI®, *The Standard for Program Management*, 2013, 84–85

89. d. At the end of the program formulation

Among other things, at the end of the program formulation, the governance structure is described as well as stakeholder considerations as the charter is prepared. The program project sponsor and program manager are assigned.

PMI®, *The Standard for Program Management*, 2013, 68, 84–85

90. c. Stakeholder engagement plan

Working to actively engage stakeholders, metrics are needed to measure performance of stakeholder engagement activities, such as meeting attendance and communication plan delivery. These metrics are part of the stakeholder engagement plan as it describes among other things how to effectively engage stakeholders in the program.

PMI®, *The Standard for Program Management*, 2013, 49

91. d. Program management information system

A common way to measure resource availability is to consult the PMIS. It can assist in early identification of resource issues as well as in resource allocation activity. The program manager analyzes resource availability and allocation to ensure the resource is not overcommitted. Limitations in resources must be addressed if the program is to be successful.

PMI®, *The Standard for Program Management*, 2013, 94

Levin and Ward, 2011, 45

92. d. Monitor cost reallocation impact and results between components

A number of activities are performed in Program Financial Monitoring and Control. By monitoring cost reallocation impact and results between the program's components, the program manager is being proactive and is striving to control costs and stay within the budget baseline.

PMI®, *The Standard for Program Management*, 2013, 81

93. d. Political skills

While a number of key interpersonal skills are needed in program management, the program manager must recognize the dynamic human aspects of each program stakeholder's expectations and manage accordingly. He or she must leverage the organization's political dynamics to promote program goals in building relationships with stakeholders.

PMI®, *The Standard for Program Management*, 2013, 15

Levin and Ward, 2011, 73–75

94. b. Communications skills

Although program management requires a special blend of technical skills, time management, and a sound foundation of people skills, communications is the most important competence. The program manager requires strong communications skills to deal with all the stakeholders—team members, sponsors, executives, functional managers, customers, vendors, the public, and other stakeholders.

PMI®, *The Standard for Program Management*, 2013, 15, 145–147

95. c. Establish buy-in from stakeholders to ensure program success

All the interests of stakeholders are important ones. As the program manager it is important to initiate, engage, and maintain effective stakeholder relationships to manage the program and achieve desired benefits. Active stakeholder engagement is needed to build and maintain ongoing program support.

PMI®, *The Standard for Program Management*, 2013, 15

96. b. Followed the issue escalation process

The issue escalation process described in the governance plan operates at two levels, one of which is between component teams and the program management team.

PMI®, *The Standard for Program Management*, 2013, 56

97 a. Establishing the program's performance baseline

A number of key activities are performed in benefits analysis and planning in addition to preparing the benefit realization plan. One is to establish the performance baseline for the program and communicate program performance metrics to key stakeholders.

PMI®, *The Standard for Program Management*, 2013, 37

98. a. The balance between cost and benefit

The program's business case is developed to assess the program's balance between cost and benefit. It can be high level or detailed and includes parameters used to assess the program's objectives and constraints.

PMI®, *The Standard for Program Management*, 2013, 27–28

99. a. Communicating

Communication skills are part of overall general management skills and are required by program and project managers. Program managers require strong communications skills to interact effectively with stakeholders at all levels.

PMI®, *The Standard for Program Management*, 2013, 15

100. a. Managing quality across the life cycle

In many programs, it is important that program quality is ensured at the program level. Program managers prepare quality plans, which the Governance Board approves. The quality plan establishes mechanisms for ensuring program quality by identifying and applying cross-component quality standards.

PMI®, *The Standard for Program Management*, 2013, 58

101. b. The business case

The program's business case along with a program mandate are the key inputs organizational leaders consider to charter and authorize programs.

PMI®, *The Standard for Program Management*, 2013, 28

102. c. In program initiation

The sponsor is selected to oversee the program in program initiation and secures funding and ensures the program delivers its intended benefits.

PMI®, *The Standard for Program Management*, 2013, 83

103. b. Scope Management Plan

In Program Scope Planning, once the scope is determined, then a scope management plan to manage, document, and communicate scope changes is prepared.

PMI®, *The Standard for Program Management*, 2013, 105

104. c. Governance plan

The governance plan contains several sections, which include its structure and meeting schedules. This plan may become a section in the program management plan. It describes the goals, structure, roles and responsibilities, policies, procedures and logistics for executing the governance polices.

PMI®, *The Standard for Program Management*, 2013, 55

105. c. The organization's strategic goals would change, but the project managers were not aware of the changes

Organizations face numerous complexities and challenges, which lead to changes in its strategic goals and objectives, but typically a project manager is too far removed from the process to know about these changes or lacks the experience, competencies, and skills to understand why the goals have changed and the impact on the project.

Shuler, Kai. "Achieving Business Advantages through Program Management". in Levin, Ginger. 2012. *Program Management A Life Cycle Approach*. Boca Raton, FL: CRC Press, 7–8

PMI®, *Program Management Professional (PgMP)® Examination Content Outline*, 2011, 6

106. d. Update the program resource plan

Staffing internally involves identifying existing personnel qualified for the positions, negotiating for their services with their management, and then transitioning them to the program position. Changes in assignment of program staff are expected during Resource Prioritization reflected in updates to the program resource plan.

PMI®, *The Standard for Program Management*, 2013, 95

107. b. Strategic and operational assumptions

The Governance Board assumes responsibility to ensure programs comply with standardized reporting and control processes applicable to all programs in many cases. One example is compliance with strategic and operational assumptions. Often assumptions turn out to be false. They require review as they can turn into risks at either the strategic or operational areas.

PMI®, *The Standard for Program Management*, 2013, 57–58

108. c. A major area of improvement

The problems with these contractors show a major area of improvement is needed to prevent future, similar problems. Areas of improvement are items to discuss in the program's final report.

PMI®, *The Standard for Program Management*, 2013, 88

109. d. Causal analysis

Causal analysis is a technique that is used to provide the real reason why something has happened in order to then take corrective action for focused change activity. It emphasizes the root cause, and often cause-and-effect diagrams are used.

PMI®, *Program Management Professional (PgMP)® Examination Content Outline*, 2011, 13

110. d. Report and distribute program deliverables and formal and informal communications

The stakeholder register is used throughout the program as it lists all the stakeholders and is used for reporting, distributing program deliverables, and formal and informal communications. It is the primary output of the Program Stakeholder Identification.

PMI®, *The Standard for Program Management*, 2013, 46–47

111. a. Nominal group technique

Brainstorming sessions with the program team and other stakeholders is useful in preparing the stakeholder register. The nominal group technique is a form of brainstorming that allows everyone present to discuss ideas without interruption, enabling active participation from all participants.

PMI®, *The Standard for Program Management*, 2013, 48

112 c. Governance Board

Often program funding is provided through a budget process that is controlled by a Governance Board responsible for overseeing several programs. The purpose is to ensure funds are provided in a manner consistent with both program and organizational priorities that may be defined by portfolio management.

PMI®, *The Standard for Program Management*, 2013, 54

113. c. Updating your stakeholder register

Stakeholder Engagement is a continuous activity on programs as the list of stakeholders and their attitudes to the program will change. After each of these meetings, the stakeholder register should be updated. It should be referenced often and evaluated by the program manager and the team and updated as needed.

PMI®, *The Standard for Program Management*, 2013, 49

114. b. It is difficult to keep its information current and relevant

A high-level program roadmap or framework can set a baseline for program definition, planning, and execution. It is dynamic and is prepared or updated along with the portfolio management process. A disadvantage to it is that developing and updating the roadmap requires discipline that many organizations lack to keep its information current and relevant.

PMI®, *The Standard for Program Management,* 2013, 29–30

Milosevic, Dragan Z., Martinelli, Russ J., and Waddell, James M. 2007. *Program Management for Improved Business Results*. Hoboken, New Jersey: John Wiley & Sons, 295–296

PMI®, *Program Management Professional (PgMP)® Examination Content Outline*, 2011, 6

115. b. The program manager has the desired level of control

The program work breakdown structure (PWBS) does not replace the work breakdown structure (WBS) on each of the program's projects. From a program perspective, the PWBS should be decomposed to the level of control that the program manager requires, which typically corresponds to the first one or two levels of the WBS of the component projects.

PMI®, *The Standard for Program Management*, 2013, 105

116. d. Prepare a scope management plan

Once the program scope is determined and has been described, a scope statement has been prepared, and a PWBS has been prepared, the next step is to prepare the scope management plan. It serves to manage, document, and communicate scope changes.

PMI®, *The Standard for Program Management*, 2013, 105

117. b. Suggest to the Governance Board that this project be moved from your program to be a distinct program

Compliance programs are initiated because of legislation, regulations, or contractual obligations. This situation is an example of the need to establish a new program because of the new regulations as even though it is not a strategic initiative, it is one that must be performed by the organization.

PMI®, *The Standard for Program Management*, 2013, 141

118. b. Constraints

Constraints are factors that limit the program team's options; typically, they affect schedule, cost, resources, or program deliverables. They are common throughout parts of a program may restrict action.

PMI®, *The Standard for Program Management*, 2013, 165

119. a. A forecast

The Estimate at Completion is a forecasting technique; it is an estimate to complete the remaining work for an activity, program package, or control account. It is an output from Program Financial Monitoring and Control.

PMI®, *The Standard for Program Management*, 2013, 81–82

120. c. Meet with the sponsor for a closure review

It is important to obtain formal acceptance of the program through a review with the sponsor. The program is formally closed after receiving closure acceptance from the Governance Board or the sponsor that the program has achieved its objectives.

PMI®, *The Standard for Program Management*, 2013, 89

121. c. Developing the next-generation cellular phone and related products

The development of the next-generation cellular phone and related products is best suited to be managed as a program. It will include numerous projects that should be managed in a coordinated way to obtain greater benefits and control than would be possible if they were managed individually.

PMI®, *The Standard for Program Management*, 2013, 4

122. d. Have a sponsor organization

Establishing governance in organizations requires a sponsoring organization to implement governance processes that then enable the organization to monitor the program's goals and objectives to ensure they remain in compliance with organizational needs.

PMI®, *The Standard for Program Management*, 2013, 54

123. a. When the resources will be needed

Resource availability should be part of the program resource plan. Among other things, it indicates availability of the personnel, assets, materials, or capital resources that are required to accomplish program goals and deliverables and is a key factor in determining whether or not to conduct procurements.

PMI®, *The Standard for Program Management*, 2013, 94–95

124. b. Ensure costs are within expected parameters

It is necessary to manage the expenditures on the program infrastructure to ensure these costs are within their expected parameters and do not have an impact on the budget baseline and need corrective actions.

PMI®, *The Standard for Program Management*, 2013, 81

125. c. The program is linked to the ongoing work and strategic priorities

When the charter is approved, the program has formal authority to start. Approval of the charter also links the program to the organization's ongoing work and strategic priorities.

PMI®, *The Standard for Program Management*, 2013, 85

126. c. Identifying interdependences among the constituent projects

As a program manager, you must ensure that the independencies among the constituent projects are reflected and managed in the program schedule, whereas the project manager concentrates on detailed activities in the project schedule. Internal and external dependencies are a key input to this process. The program schedule includes component milestones that represent an output to the program or share an interdependency with other components.

PMI®, *The Standard for Program Management*, 2013, 101

127. c. Decision-tree analysis

Decision-tree analysis is used to assist in choosing available alternatives when some future scenarios or outcomes are uncertain. It helps organizations identify the relative values of alternate actions. In program management it is a technique that is helpful in analyzing and updating the benefit realization plan and sustainment plans for uncertainty, risk identification, risk mitigation, and risk opportunity.

PMI®, *Program Management Professional (PgMP)® Examination Content Outline*, 2011, 13

128. a. Business value measurement

Business value measurement is useful in overall benefit measurement but especially in measuring intangible benefits. This approach tests the intangible benefits against business strategies and objectives continually to ensure they are robust, relevant, and in some way measureable even if against an artificial scale aligned to a business objective.

PMI®, *Program Management Professional (PgMP)® Examination Content Outline*, 2011, 13

Williams and Parr, 2006, 179

129. b. Issue management

Issue escalation is an activity that occurs within governance. Skillfully tracking, managing, and resolving program-level and inter-component issues helps enable effective governance.

PMI®, *The Standard for Program Management*, 2013, 56–57

130. a. Program A

Program A will drop features if necessary in a trade-off situation. It is schedule-driven and supports the time-to-market attribute of the company, thus aligning itself with the organization's culture and environment.

Milosevic et al., 2007, 75–76

PMI®, *Program Management Professional (PgMP)® Examination Content Outline*, 2011, 6

131. c. Determine program financial metrics

In Program Financial Management Plan Development, the program's financial management plan is a key output. However, other outputs are program funding schedules, component payment schedules, program operational costs, and program financial metrics. These metrics are necessary as they are used to measure the program's benefits.

PMI®, *The Standard for Program Management*, 2013, 79–80

132. c. Ensuing communication of critical component-related information to stakeholders

In most organizations, the Governance Board approves the initiation of individual components. Governance approval includes several key activities, one of which is to communicate critical component-related information to key stakeholders. Such communication is essential for stakeholder engagement and support.

PMI®, *The Standard for Program Management*, 2013, 60–61

133. a. At the program level

To achieve consistency at the program level across all construction activities, responsibilities regarding subcontractors and their selection and performance should be defined at the program level as the buyer or owner.

Shimizu, Motoh. 2012. *Fundamentals of Program Management Strategic Program Bootstrapping for Business Innovation and Change.* Newtown Square, PA: Project Management Institute, 89

134. b. Analyze the change request

As part of Program Scope Control, a change management activity should be established to handle scope changes. After the change request is accepted, the next step is to evaluate or analyze it.

PMI®, *The Standard for Program Management*, 2013, 106

135. b. Focus groups

Focus groups are useful to provide a deeper understanding of the program impacts than can be done through individual interviews or a questionnaire; they provide feedback from groups of stakeholders regarding their attitude toward the program and approaches for communications and impact mitigation.

PMI®, *The Standard for Program Management*, 2013, 48

136. a. Establish a balance between people who have negative views about the program and those who are advocates

After the stakeholder register has been prepared and the stakeholder concerns are better understood, it is up to the program manager to establish a balance to mitigate the effects of stakeholders who have negative views about the program and encourage the active support of positive proponents for it.

PMI®, *The Standard for Program Management*, 2013, 48–49

137. d. Program D

The payback period can be determined by dividing the initial fixed investment in the program by the estimated annual net cash inflows. In this example, the payback period for Program D is 2.2 years, and it should be selected.

PMI®, *Program Management Professional* (PgMP)® *Examination Content Outline*, April 2011, 6

Milosevic et al., 2007, 21 and 42

138. d. Have the project managers report procurement results to the program manager

In Program Procurement Administration, administration and closeout of many contracts is handled by the components. The details of contract deliverables, requirements, deadlines, costs, and quality are handled at the component level.

PMI®, *The Standard for Program Management*, 2013, 91

139. b. Scope

Estimates of scope, resources, and scope are prepared in program initiation. These studies are determined early to assess the organization's ability to execute the program, as the program is being compared with other initiatives to determine its priority.

PMI®, *The Standard for Program Management*, 2013, 83

140. a. Use project management to perform the upgrade

Delivered benefits must be sustained when the program is over. It may be necessary to assure that ongoing product support adds value by managing the post-production life cycle. Project management is often used to deliver upgrades to the product during its life cycle.

PMI®, *The Standard for Program Management*, 2013, 43–44

141. c. Support mentoring

Mentoring is a key personal competency for the program manager and encourages and facilitates team member professional development. It differs from coaching and among other things encourages the program manager to display a genuine interest in team member performance as well as in team development.

PMI®, *Program Management Professional (PgMP)® Examination Content Outline*, 2011, 10

Levin and Ward, 2011, 90–93

142. c. Use an issue log

Stakeholder meetings serve two main purposes: communicating program status and hearing issues and concerns of the stakeholders. These issues and concerns then are captured in an issue log to document, prioritize, and track them to help understand the feedback that is provided.

PMI®, *The Standard for Program Management*, 2013, 50

143. c. Program C

In using net present value (NPV) as a selection criterion, the time value of money is considered based on the fact that a dollar one year from now is worth less than a dollar today. The more the future is discounted (that is, the higher the discount rate), then the less the NPV of the program. If the NPV is higher, then the program is rated higher. In this situation, you would select Program C.

Milosevic, Dragan. 2003. *Project Management ToolBox: Tools and Techniques for the Practicing Project Manager*. Hoboken, NJ: John Wiley & Sons, 43–44

PMI®, *Program Management Professional (PgMP)® Examination Content Outline*, 2011, 6

144. a. Add program overhead costs

Although the majority of the program's cost is attributable to the components and to work done by contractors, the budget cannot be baselined until program overhead is added to the initial budget figure.

PMI®, *The Standard for Program Management*, 2013, 80

145. c. Checklists

Checklists are contained in the program quality plan. Checklists can be very helpful in ensuring that items are not missed and also for use in quality assurance and quality control.

PMI®, *The Standard for Program Management*, 2013, 93

146. a. Request for information

The request for information is used to help the organization to formulate its requirements and identify qualified sellers to support program procurement in a timely way.

PMI®, *The Standard for Program Management*, 2013, 98

147. d. Risk avoidance

Benefits tend to be categorized as tangible and intangible. However risk avoidance should be considered as a further benefit as in many instances risk avoidance can be the main driver for a change.

PMI®, *Program Management Professional (PgMP)® Examination Content Outline*, 2011, 13

Williams and Parr, 2006, 179

148. c. Ways to ensure all stages of the program are managed in a way to satisfy the use of the program's outputs

The benefits realization plan defines each benefit, associated assumptions, and determines how each benefit will be achieved. Among other items, it should ensure all stages of the program are managed in a way to satisfy the utilization of the program's outputs, since the objective of managing by programs is to ensure there are more benefits than if projects were managed in a standalone way.

PMI®, *The Standard for Program Management*, 2013, 38–39

149. c. Aligning program objectives with strategic goals

Competencies can be personal ones or performance based. In the early stages, the program manager must ensure the program objectives are aligned with the strategic goals of the organization to best realize business value. Organizational and business strategies must be assessed to assist in this alignment.

PMI®, *The Standard for Program Management*, 2013, 26–27

PMI®, *Program Management Professional (PgMP)® Examination Content Outline*, 2011, 6

Levin and Ward, 2011, 11, 22, and 32

150. b. Develop a qualified seller list

The program manager negotiates and finalizes program-wide policies and agreements. Qualified seller lists can facilitate the procurement process, as procurement documents can be sent to these prospective sellers to gauge interest and to see whether they want to present a proposal or quotation.

PMI®, *The Standard for Program Management*, 2013, 91

151. d. Manage risk in accordance with the risk management plan

Using contractors is a way to transfer risks. All risks, however, need to be managed in accordance with the risk management plan in order to ensure benefit realization.

PMI®, *Program Management Professional (PgMP)® Examination Content Outline*, 2011, 11

152. d. You realize project stakeholders are also program stakeholders

The stakeholder register identifies stakeholders and their roles and responsibilities. Each component project also will have stakeholder engagement guidelines to be considered at the program level. The project stakeholders are also program stakeholders since dissatisfaction by project stakeholders can negatively impact stakeholder acceptance criteria of the whole program.

PMI®, *The Standard for Program Management*, 2013, 47, 49

153. a. Ensuring communications of closure to stakeholders

Approval by the Governance Board is typically required to close or transition a program component. As the Governance Board reviews recommendations for transition or closure a number of activities is performed. One is to ensure communications with program-level stakeholders that the component is ready to close in order that the stakeholders agree the component has met its requirements and delivered its benefits to the program.

PMI®, *The Standard for Program Management*, 2013, 61

154. d. Focus on management processes

Audis may be conducted by people internal or external to the organization. Program audits focus on program finances, management processes and practices, program quality, and program documentation.

PMI®, *The Standard for Program Management*, 2013, 65

155. b. A strong connection between execution output and strategic objectives

Organizational culture is an important part of the success of program management. If executives view development efforts as strategic and linked to the success of the business rather than as tactical, program management is recommended.

PMI®, *The Standard for Program Management*, 2013, 5, 14

PMI®, *Program Management Professional (PgMP)® Examination Content Outline*, 2011, 6

Milosevic et al., 2007, 430–431

156. d. Financial reports

The status report, financial report, and resource deviation report are examples of reports submitted to the Governance Board to assist the Board members in their ability to monitor program progress and strengthen the organization's ability to assess status and conformance with organizational controls.

PMI®, *The Standard for Program Management*, 2013, 57–58

157. c. Communications

Communications are the primary tool for engaging stakeholders; negotiation, conflict management, and influencing are also important, but communications are the most important competency for program managers.

PMI®, *The Standard for Program Management*, 2013, 15, 45

158. b. Propose a solution to these risks escalated by the project managers

As the program manager, you must resolve risks raised by your project managers. When risks remain unresolved, the program manager ensures that they are escalated progressively higher in the organization until they are resolved. The escalation approach can be part of the risk management plan as part of authority levels for decision making.

PMI®, *The Standard for Program Management*, 2013, 96–97

159. b. Program B

Programs should have a strategic fit with the organization's long-term goals. In this example, Program B fully supports four of the five goals.

PMI®, *The Standard for Program Management*, 2008, 23

Milosevic et al., 2007, 286

160. b. Document the relevant parties' responsibilities regarding risk.

At the program level, responsibility in Program Procurement it is necessary to negotiate and finalize various agreements and award contracts that will support the project components and other ongoing work of the program. If these agreements involve insurance or services to protect the program, the relative parties' responsibilities regarding potential risks must be documented and incorporated into contracts and program files.

PMI®, *The Standard for Program Management*, 2013, 90–91

161. c. Set up a program management information system

Project governance provides support to program management. The Governance Board may support the program management capabilities by establishing a program management information system that enables collecting, accessing, reporting, and analysis of information relevant to program management.

PMI®, *The Standard for Program Management*, 2013, 65

162. c. Determine how the program will help the organization meet its business and strategic goals

There are many reasons why a business case should be prepared, and its primary reason is to answer the following critical question: "How will this program help our company meet its business and strategic goals?" With a business case, all crucial information for the program is included. It then is used to assess the feasibility of investing in the program based on cost, benefit, and business risk and once prepared can provide the vision to guide program planning and execution.

PMI®. *The Standard for Program Management*, 201, 23

Milosevic et al., 2007, 284

163. a. PWBS

In Program Procurement Planning, techniques such as make-or-buy decisions and the PWBS aid the program manager in developing the procurement management plan, determining procurement standards, and determining whether updates are needed to the program's financial plan or to the budget.

PMI®, *The Standard for Program Management*, 2013, 90

164. d. Review the benefits realization plan

The benefits realization plan, among other items, should ensure the program delivers its expected benefits. This plan is reviewed in Benefit Delivery before the benefits are transitioned by the Governance Board. The actual benefits delivered should be regularly evaluated against the expected benefits in the plan.

PMI®, *The Standard for Program Management*, 2013, 39–41

165. a. Market needs and expectations

Market knowledge is required to understand customer and end-user expectations. Such knowledge is helpful in making the business case for a program, because it provides information—such as market size, market segmentation, and sales potential—that will increase the probability of program and organizational success.

Milosevic et al., 2007, 368

PMI®, *Program Management Professional (PgMP)® Examination Content Outline*, 2011, 6

166. a. Address commonalities and differences across components

Early and intensive planning is critical to success in planning program procurements. The program manager looks across all components to develop the procurement management plan to optimize objectives and for benefit delivery. By addressing commonalities and differences across components, then the best type of procurement approaches for the program can be determined.

PMI®, *The Standard for Program Management*, 2013, 90

167. c. Using mentoring

Mentoring can be used effectively in this scenario to model the appropriate behavior these two project managers should follow especially as they learn the various standard processes to use. As they gain confidence, the mentoring relationship then can change from one that is less formal and is more consultative as they will not need your active involvement as often.

PMI®, *Program Management Professional (PgMP)® Examination Content Outline*, 2011, 10

Levin and Ward, 2011, 90–93

168. c. Quality

Changes on programs should be managed in accordance with the change management plan in order to control scope, quality, schedule, cost, contacts, risks, and rewards.

PMI®, *Program Management Professional (PgMP)® Examination Content Outline*, 2011, 11

169. b. Describe the business opportunity and product, service, or result that you are proposing

Before going into detail in the business case, first define the business opportunity. Then, relate it to the organization's strategic goals and show the benefits associated with this program. Later, describe the cost/benefit analysis and other financial benefits, intangible benefits, and the risk and complexity.

PMI®, *The Standard for Program Management*, 2008, 28

PMI®, *Program Management Professional (PgMP)® Examination Content Outline*, 2011, 6

Milosevic et al., 2007, 285

170. d. Provide training in program management

Program governance is responsible for a number of supporting functions. It can support program management by providing organizational training in it, especially in program management roles and responsibilities, skills, capabilities, and competencies. This sponsorship by governance enables focused training on specific practices and needs of the organization to ensure those responsible for important programs are prepared to fulfill their roles.

PMI®, *The Standard for Program Management*, 2013, 66

Appendix: Study Matrix

Study Matrix—Practice Test 1

Practice Test Question Number	*Performance Domain*	*Study Notes*	*Level of Difficulty*
1	Strategic Program Management		
2	Executing		
3	Stakeholder Management		
4	Initiating		
5	Governance		
6	Strategic Program Management		
7	Benefits Management		
8	Benefits Management		
9	Planning		
10	Stakeholder Management		
11	Strategic Program Management		
12	Controlling		
13	Planning		
14	Planning		
15	Executing		
16	Benefits Management		
17	Governance		
18	Strategic Program Management		
19	Initiating		
20	Executing		
21	Planning		
22	Planning		
23	Controlling		
24	Executing		
25	Stakeholder Management		
26	Strategic Program Management		
27	Benefits Management		
28	Initiating		
29	Executing		

continued

Practice Test Question Number	*Performance Domain*	*Study Notes*	*Level of Difficulty*
30	Controlling		
31	Closing		
32	Executing		
33	Controlling		
34	Strategic Program Management		
35	Strategic Program Management		
36	Stakeholder Management		
37	Stakeholder Management		
38	Executing		
39	Governance		
40	Benefits Management		
41	Controlling		
42	Stakeholder Management		
43	Strategic Program Management		
44	Governance		
45	Executing		
46	Closing		
47	Planning		
48	Stakeholder Management		
49	Strategic Program Management		
50	Planning		
51	Benefits Management		
52	Stakeholder Management		
53	Controlling		
54	Initiating		
55	Strategic Program Management		
56	Planning		
57	Stakeholder Management		
58	Stakeholder Management		
59	Governance		
60	Executing		

Practice Test Question Number	Performance Domain	Study Notes	Level of Difficulty
61	Benefits Management		
62	Strategic Program Management		
63	Executing		
64	Stakeholder Management		
65	Initiating		
66	Governance		
67	Benefits Management		
68	Strategic Program Management		
69	Executing		
70	Stakeholder Management		
71	Governance		
72	Initiating		
73	Closing		
74	Governance		
75	Executing		
76	Stakeholder Management		
77	Controlling		
78	Stakeholder Management		
79	Governance		
80	Strategic Program Management		
81	Controlling		
82	Benefits Management		
83	Executing		
84	Governance		
85	Planning		
86	Stakeholder Management		
87	Governance		
88	Strategic Program Management		
89	Planning		
90	Executing		

continued

Practice Test Question Number	*Performance Domain*	*Study Notes*	*Level of Difficulty*
91	Governance		
92	Controlling		
93	Governance		
94	Strategic Program Management		
95	Planning		
96	Stakeholder Management		
97	Executing		
98	Controlling		
99	Strategic Program Management		
100	Initiating		
101	Planning		
102	Benefits Management		
103	Controlling		
104	Stakeholder Management		
105	Planning		
106	Controlling		
107	Strategic Program Management		
108	Executing		
109	Closing		
110	Benefits Management		
111	Initiating		
112	Executing		
113	Controlling		
114	Controlling		
115	Strategic Program Management		
116	Planning		
117	Benefits Management		
118	Benefits Management		
119	Executing		
120	Executing		
121	Governance		

Practice Test Question Number	Performance Domain	Study Notes	Level of Difficulty
122	Strategic Program Management		
123	Benefits Management		
124	Benefits Management		
125	Planning		
126	Governance		
127	Executing		
128	Executing		
129	Stakeholder Management		
130	Stakeholder Management		
131	Strategic Program Management		
132	Governance		
133	Stakeholder Management		
134	Controlling		
135	Governance		
136	Initiating		
137	Planning		
138	Executing		
139	Governance		
140	Stakeholder Management		
141	Governance		
142	Strategic Program Management		
143	Executing		
144	Benefits Management		
145	Planning		
146	Stakeholder Management		
147	Planning		
148	Controlling		
149	Governance		
150	Stakeholder Management		
151	Strategic Program Management		

continued

Practice Test Question Number	*Performance Domain*	*Study Notes*	*Level of Difficulty*
152	Governance		
153	Benefits Management		
154	Governance		
155	Stakeholder Management		
156	Strategic Program Management		
157	Closing		
158	Stakeholder Management		
159	Governance		
160	Benefits Management		
161	Strategic Program Management		
162	Initiating		
163	Planning		
164	Executing		
165	Controlling		
166	Stakeholder Management		
167	Strategic Program Management		
168	Governance		
169	Stakeholder Management		
170	Benefits Management		

Study Matrix—Practice Test 2

Practice Test Question Number	Performance Domain	Study Notes
1	Benefits Management	
2	Strategic Program Management	
3	Executing	
4	Initiating	
5	Executing	
6	Controlling	
7	Strategic Program Management	
8	Planning	
9	Closing	
10	Executing	
11	Stakeholder Management	
12	Benefits Management	
13	Controlling	
14	Governance	
15	Initiating	
16	Strategic Program Management	
17	Executing	
18	Governance	
19	Planning	
20	Controlling	
21	Governance	
22	Benefits Management	
23	Strategic Program Management	
24	Strategic Program Management	
25	Executing	
26	Governance	
27	Planning	
28	Controlling	
29	Closing	
30	Initiating	

continued

Practice Test Question Number	*Performance Domain*	*Study Notes*
31	Planning	
32	Benefits Management	
33	Strategic Program Management	
34	Executing	
35	Stakeholder Management	
36	Controlling	
37	Governance	
38	Planning	
39	Planning	
40	Controlling	
41	Strategic Program Management	
42	Initiating	
43	Executing	
44	Benefits Management	
45	Stakeholder Management	
46	Stakeholder Management	
47	Executing	
48	Strategic Program Management	
49	Benefits Management	
50	Stakeholder Management	
51	Governance	
52	Controlling	
53	Benefits Management	
54	Benefits Management	
55	Strategic Program Management	
56	Governance	
57	Stakeholder Management	
58	Benefits Management	
59	Stakeholder Management	
60	Planning	
61	Executing	
62	Controlling	

Practice Test Question Number	Performance Domain	Study Notes
63	Stakeholder Management	
64	Stakeholder Management	
65	Benefits Management	
66	Governance	
67	Stakeholder Management	
68	Initiating	
69	Strategic Program Management	
70	Benefits Management	
71	Benefits Management	
72	Planning	
73	Controlling	
74	Executing	
75	Executing	
76	Executing	
77	Stakeholder Management	
78	Strategic Program Management	
79	Stakeholder Management	
80	Governance	
81	Stakeholder Management	
82	Stakeholder Management	
83	Executing	
84	Controlling	
85	Governance	
86	Stakeholder Management	
87	Strategic Program Management	
88	Initiating	
89	Governance	
90	Stakeholder Management	
91	Planning	
92	Controlling	
93	Stakeholder Management	

continued

Practice Test Question Number	Performance Domain	Study Notes
94	Stakeholder Management	
95	Stakeholder Management	
96	Governance	
97	Benefits Management	
98	Strategic Program Management	
99	Executing	
100	Governance	
101	Initiating	
102	Initiating	
103	Planning	
104	Governance	
105	Strategic Program Management	
106	Executing	
107	Governance	
108	Closing	
109	Benefits Management	
110	Stakeholder Management	
111	Stakeholder Management	
112	Governance	
113	Stakeholder Management	
114	Strategic Program Management	
115	Planning	
116	Planning	
117	Executing	
118	Executing	
119	Controlling	
120	Closing	
121	Strategic Program Management	
122	Governance	
123	Executing	
124	Controlling	
125	Initiating	

Practice Test Question Number	Performance Domain	Study Notes
126	Planning	
127	Benefits Management	
128	Benefits Management	
129	Governance	
130	Strategic Program Management	
131	Planning	
132	Governance	
133	Executing	
134	Controlling	
135	Stakeholder Management	
136	Stakeholder Management	
137	Strategic Program Management	
138	Controlling	
139	Initiating	
140	Closing	
141	Executing	
142	Stakeholder Management	
143	Strategic Program Management	
144	Planning	
145	Planning	
146	Executing	
147	Benefits Management	
148	Benefits Management	
149	Strategic Program Management	
150	Executing	
151	Controlling	
152	Stakeholder Management	
153	Governance	
154	Governance	
155	Strategic Program Management	
156	Governance	

continued

Practice Test Question Number	Performance Domain	Study Notes
158	Planning	
159	Strategic Program Management	
160	Executing	
161	Governance	
162	Strategic Program Management	
163	Planning	
164	Benefits Management	
165	Strategic Program Management	
166	Planning	
167	Executing	
168	Controlling	
169	Strategic Program Management	
170	Governance	

References

Levin, Ginger and Allen R. Green. *Implementing Program Management. Templates and Forms Aligned with The Standard for Program Management*—Third Edition (2013). Boca Raton, FL: CRC Press. 2013.

Levin, Ginger. *Program Management A Life Cycle Approach*. Boca Raton, FL: CRC Press, 2012.

Levin, Ginger and J. LeRoy Ward. *Program Management Complexity: A Competency Model*. Boca Raton, FL: CRC Press, 2011.

Milosevic, Dragan Z. *Project Management Toolbox: Tools and Techniques for the Practicing Project Manager*. Hoboken, NJ: John Wiley & Sons, Inc., 2003.

Milosevic, Dragan Z., Russ J. Martinelli, and James M. Waddell. *Program Management for Improved Business Results*. Hoboken, NJ: John Wiley & Sons, Inc., 2007.

Pritchard, Carl L. *The Project Management Drill Book: A Self-Study Guide*. Arlington, VA: ESI International, 2003.

Project Management Institute. *A Guide to the Project Management Body of Knowledge (PMBOK® Guide), Fifth Edition*. Newtown Square, PA: Project Management Institute, 2013.

Project Management Institute. *Project Manager Competency Development Framework*—Second Edition. Newtown Square, PA: Project Management Institute, 2007.

Project Management Institute. *PMI Code of Ethics and Professional Conduct*. Available from http://www.pmi.org/codeofethicsPDF.

Project Management Institute. *PMI Lexicon of Project Management Terms*. 2012. Available from http://www.pmi.org/lexiconterms.

Project Management Institute. *Program Management Professional (PgMP®) Examination Content Outline*. Newtown Square, PA: Project Management Institute, 2011.

Project Management Institute. *The Standard for Program Management*—Third Edition (2013). Newtown Square, PA: Project Management Institute, 2013.

Shimizu, Motoh. *Fundamentals of Program Management Strategic Program Bootstrapping for Business Innovation and Change*. Newtown, Square, PA: Project Management Institute, 2012.

Thiry, Michel. *Program Management*. Surrey, England: Gower Publishing Limited, 2010.

Williams, David, and Tim Parr. *Enterprise Programme Management Delivering Value*. Hampshire, England: Palgrave MacMillan, 2006.